DIVINITY III

STALINVERSE

MATT KINDT | TREVOR HAIRSINE | RYAN WINN | DAVID BARON

CONTENTS

Collection Cover Art: Jelena Kevic-Djurdjevic

Associate Editor: Danny Khazem
Editor: Warren Simons

VALIANT

Peter Cuneo
Chairman

Dinesh Shamdasani
CEO & Chief Creative Officer

Gavin Cuneo
Chief Operating Officer & CFO

Fred Pierce
Publisher

Warren Simons
Editor-in-Chief

Walter Black
VP Operations

Hunter Gorinson
VP Marketing & Communications

Atom! Freeman
Director of Sales

Andy Liegl
Alex Rae
Sales Managers

Annie Rosa
Sales Coordinator

Josh Johns
Director of Digital Media and Development

Travis Escarfullery
Jeff Walker
Production & Design Managers

Kyle Andrukiewicz
Editor and Creative Executive

Robert Meyers
Managing Editor

Peter Stern
Publishing & Operations Manager

Andrew Steinbeiser
Marketing & Communications Manager

Danny Khazem
Charlotte Greenbaum
Associate Editors

Lauren Hitzhusen
Assistant Editor

Benjamin Peterson
Editorial Assistant

Shanyce Lora
Digital Media Coordinator

Ivan Cohen
Collection Editor

Steve Blackwell
Collection Designer

Rian Hughes/Device
Original Trade Dress & Book Design

Russell Brown
President, Consumer Products,
Promotions and Ad Sales

Caritza Berlioz
Licensing Coodinator

Divinity™ III: Stalinverse. Published by Valiant Entertainment LLC. Office of Publication: 350 Seventh Avenue, New York, NY 10001. Printed in the U.S.A. First Printing. ISBN: 9781682152072.

VALIANT
STALINVERSE #1
DIVINITY III
CCCP
ATT KINDT
REVOR HAIRSINE
YAN WINN
AVID BARON

Year	Event
1922	JOSEPH STALIN ASSASSINATES VLADIMIR LENIN AND BECOMES LEADER OF THE SOVIET UNION.
1934	RUSSIA FORMS THE SOVIET UNION BY ANNEXING THE BALTIC STATES AS WELL AS POLAND, HUNGARY, GERMANY AND FRANCE.
1939	GREAT PATRIOTIC WAR OF EUROPE BEGINS.
1945	SOVIET UNION EMERGES TRIUMPHANT AFTER THE GREAT PATRIOTIC WAR.
1946	SOVIET UNION ENVELOPES ALL OF EUROPE EXCEPT FOR GREAT BRITAIN.
1947	BATTLE OF BRITAIN. ENGLAND, SCOTLAND, AND IRELAND FALL UNDER SOVIET RULE.
1948	WAR FOR ASIA BEGINS.
1949	SOVIET UNION DROPS ATOM BOMB ON TOKYO, ENDING THE WAR FOR ASIA.
1951	USSR INSTALLS JOSEPH McCARTHY AS PUPPET PRESIDENT OF THE UNITED STATES.
1960	SOVIET UNION ACCELERATES DEEP SPACE EXPLORATION.
1963	SINO-SOVIET PACT SIGNED.
1968	AMERICAN CIVIL WAR II BEGINS.
1969	THE FIRST BATTLE OF LOS ANGELES.
1972	SOVIET UNION ANNEXES SOUTH AMERICA AND NORTH AMERICAN WEST COAST.
1973	AMERICAN REBEL LEADER, JOHN KENNEDY, IS ASSASSINATED OFF THE COAST OF CUBA.
1987	COSMONAUTS BEGIN MAPPING NEIGHBORING GALAXIES.
1993	THE SECOND BATTLE OF LOS ANGELES.
1994	SEATTLE PEACE ACCORDS ARE SIGNED.
1995	THE AMERICAS OFFICIALLY BECOME SOVIET COLONIES. MASS INSURGENCIES CONTINUE.
2012	ARIC, SON OF THE REVOLUTION, APPEARS IN ROMANIA.
2016	THE RED BRIGADE IS FORMALLY ANNOUNCED AS WORLD SECURITY FORCE.

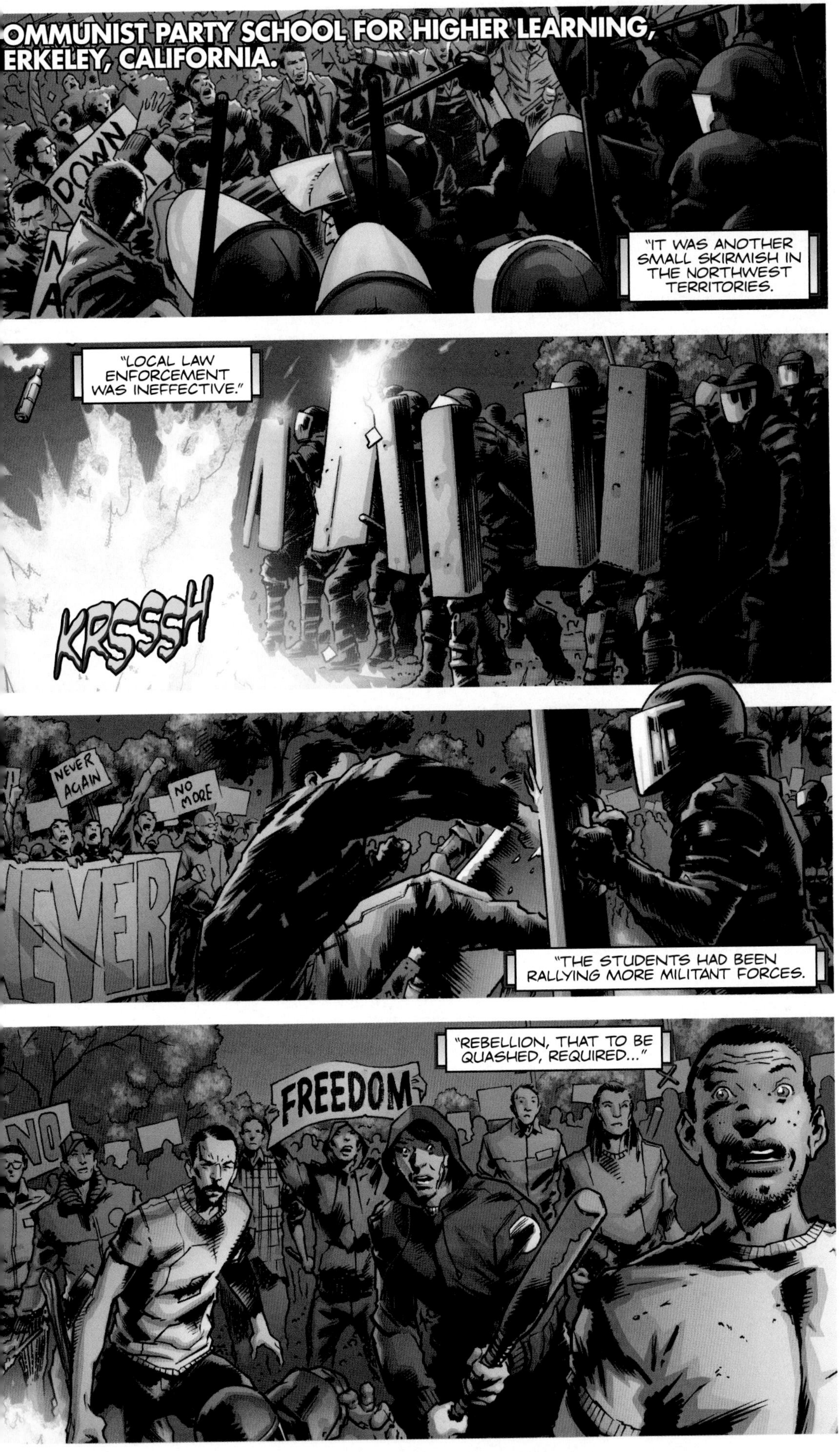
OMMUNIST PARTY SCHOOL FOR HIGHER LEARNING,
ERKELEY, CALIFORNIA.
DOWN
"IT WAS ANOTHER SMALL SKIRMISH IN THE NORTHWEST TERRITORIES.
"LOCAL LAW ENFORCEMENT WAS INEFFECTIVE."
KRSSSH
NEVER AGAIN
NO MORE
EVER
"THE STUDENTS HAD BEEN RALLYING MORE MILITANT FORCES.
"REBELLION, THAT TO BE QUASHED, REQUIRED..."
FREEDOM
NO

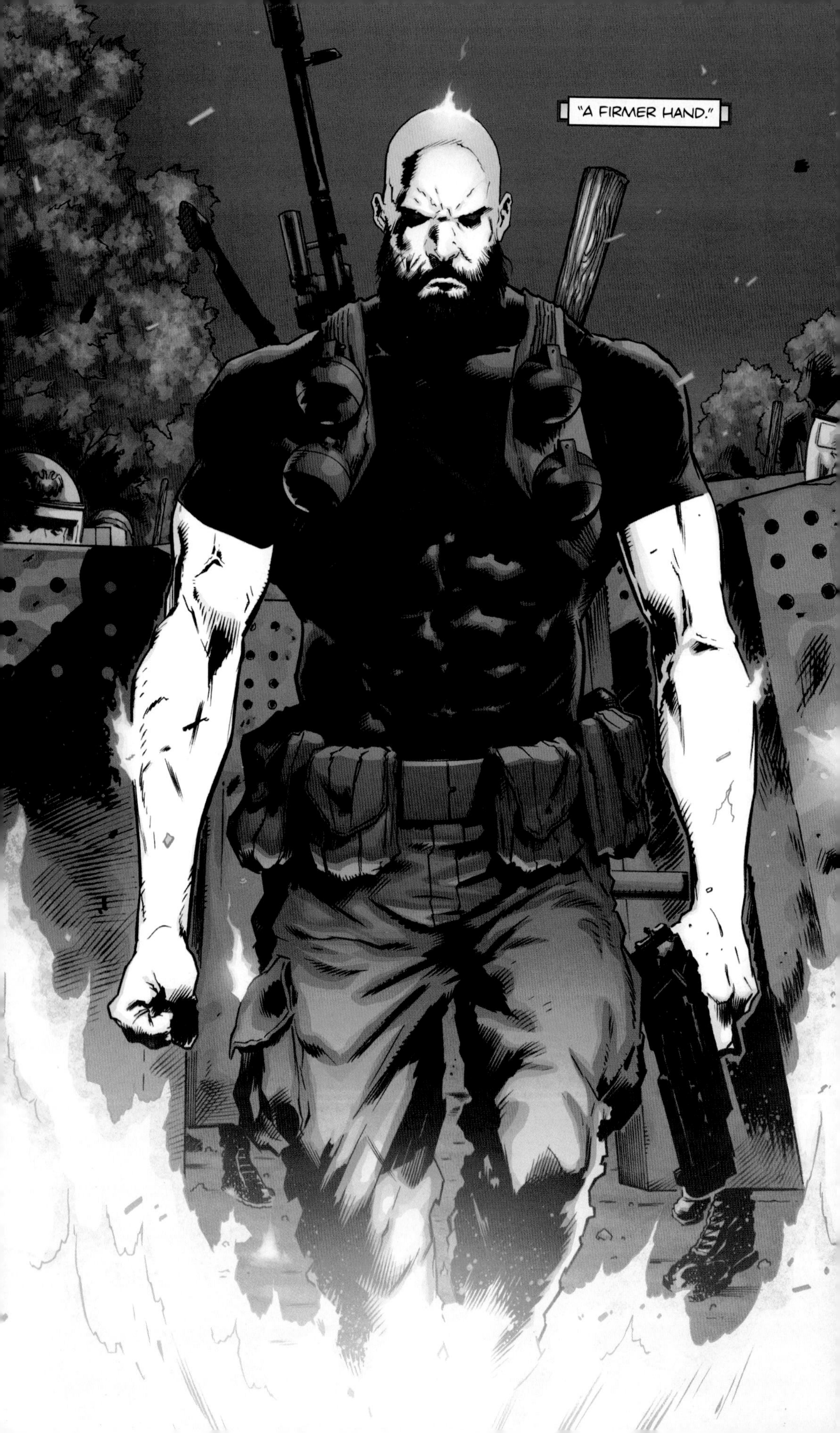
"A FIRMER HAND."

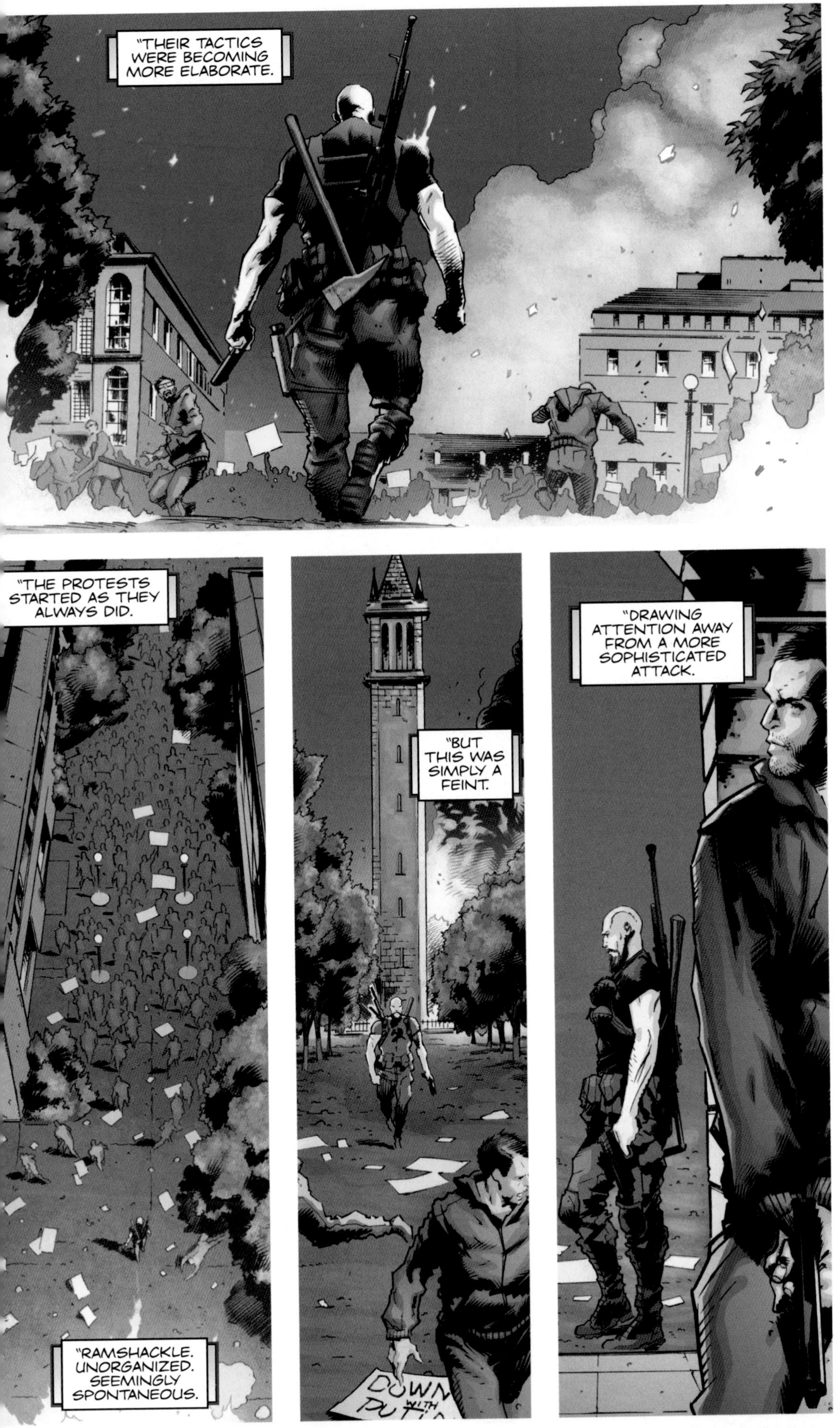
"THEIR TACTICS WERE BECOMING MORE ELABORATE.
"THE PROTESTS STARTED AS THEY ALWAYS DID.
"RAMSHACKLE. UNORGANIZED. SEEMINGLY SPONTANEOUS.
"BUT THIS WAS SIMPLY A FEINT.
DOWN
WITH
"DRAWING ATTENTION AWAY FROM A MORE SOPHISTICATED ATTACK.

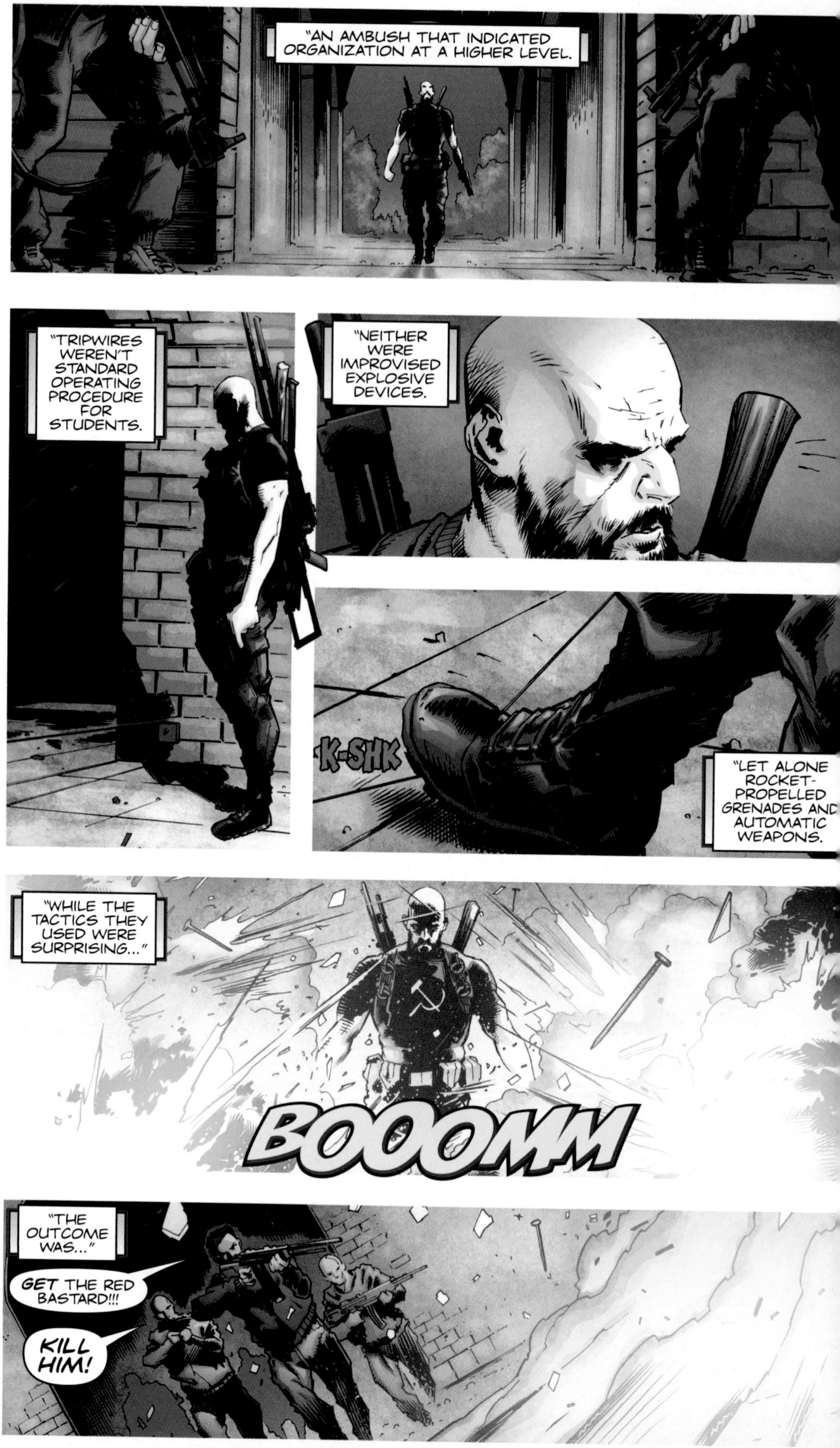
"AN AMBUSH THAT INDICATED ORGANIZATION AT A HIGHER LEVEL.
"TRIPWIRES WEREN'T STANDARD OPERATING PROCEDURE FOR STUDENTS.
"NEITHER WERE IMPROVISED EXPLOSIVE DEVICES.
K-SHK
"LET ALONE ROCKET-PROPELLED GRENADES AND AUTOMATIC WEAPONS.
"WHILE THE TACTICS THEY USED WERE SURPRISING..."
BOOOMM
"THE OUTCOME WAS..."
GET THE RED BASTARD!!!
KILL HIM!

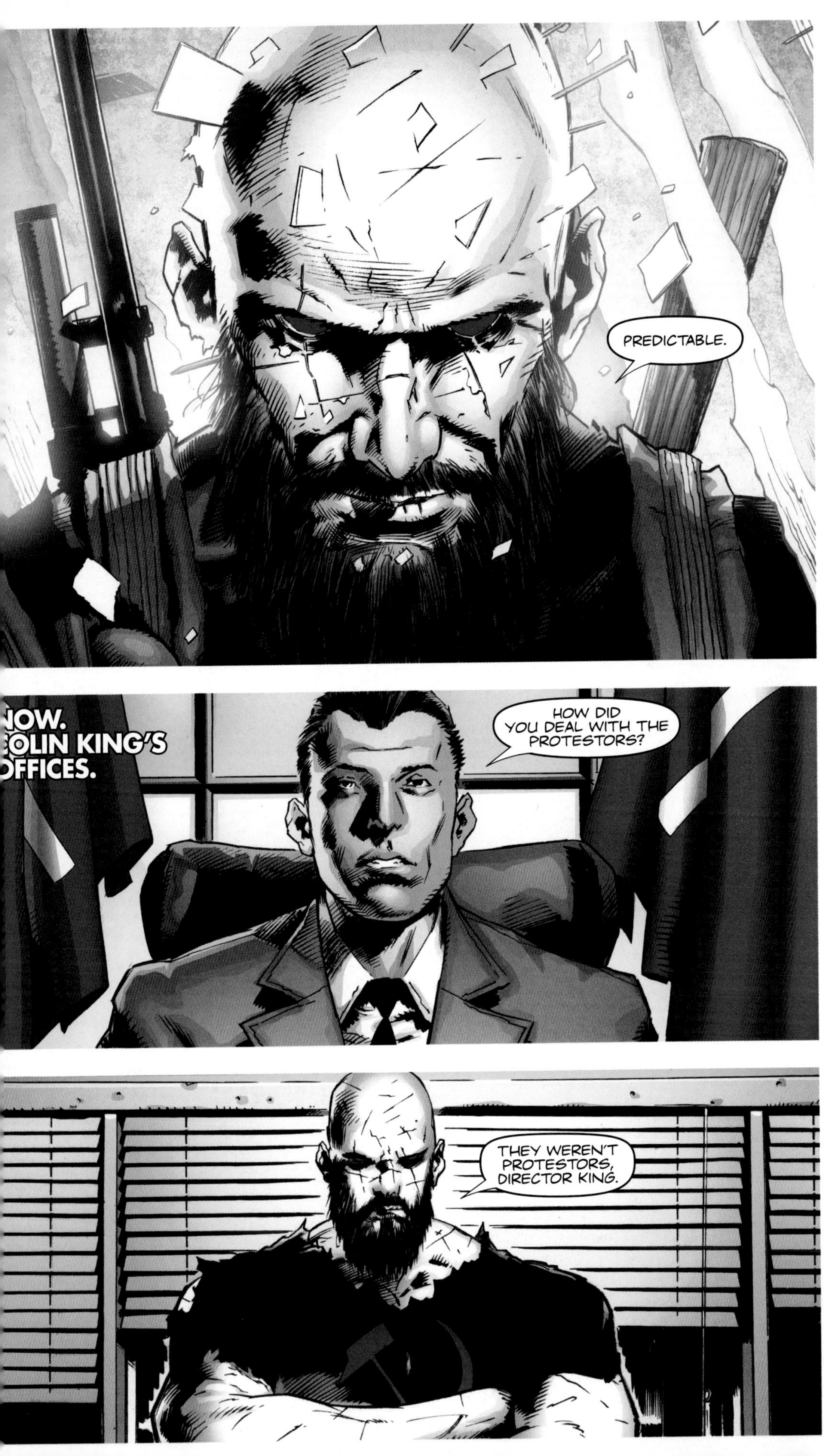
PREDICTABLE.
NOW.
OLIN KING'S
OFFICES.
HOW DID YOU DEAL WITH THE PROTESTORS?
THEY WEREN'T PROTESTORS, DIRECTOR KING.

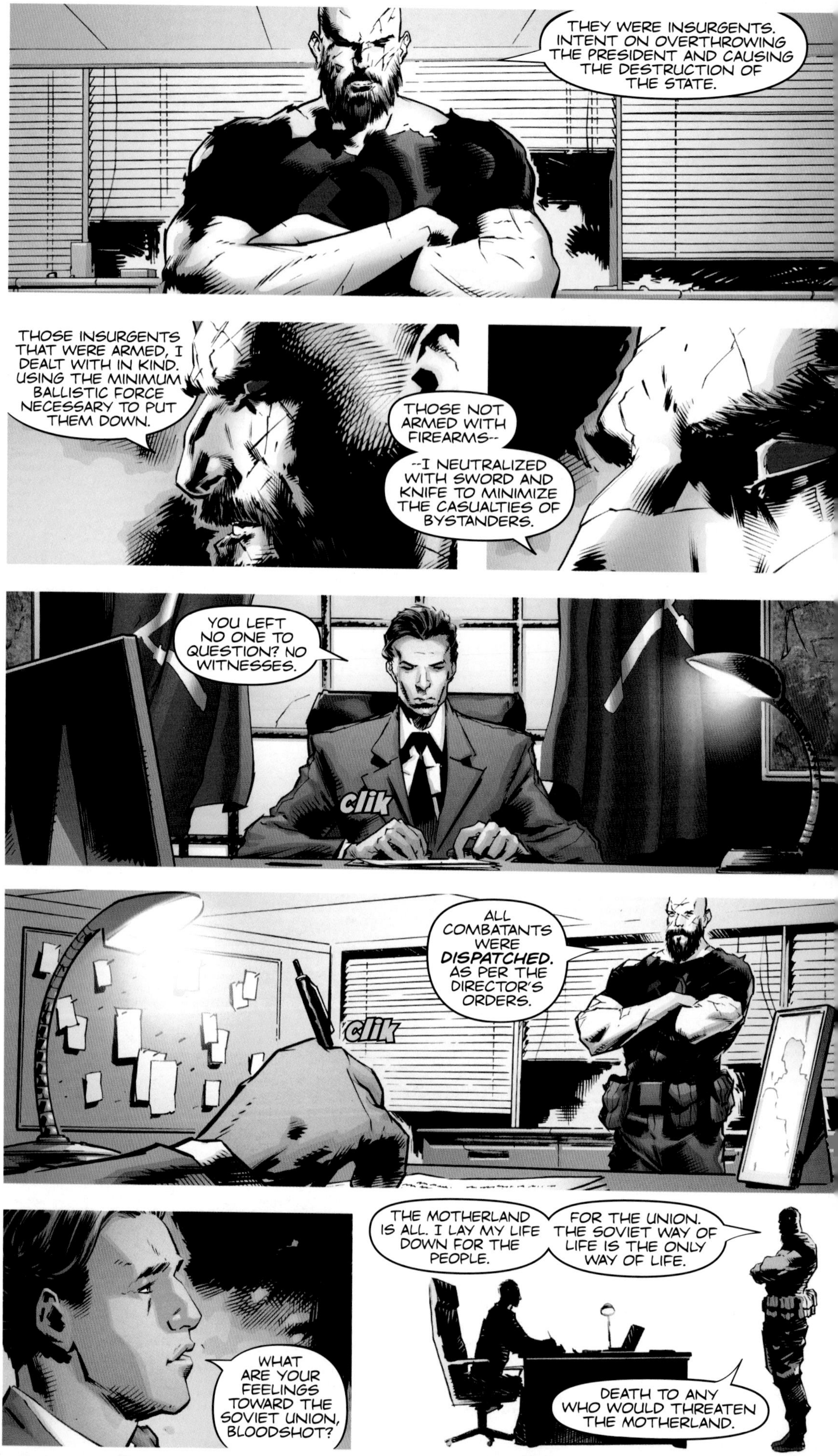
THEY WERE INSURGENTS. INTENT ON OVERTHROWING THE PRESIDENT AND CAUSING THE DESTRUCTION OF THE STATE.
THOSE INSURGENTS THAT WERE ARMED, I DEALT WITH IN KIND. USING THE MINIMUM BALLISTIC FORCE NECESSARY TO PUT THEM DOWN.
THOSE NOT ARMED WITH FIREARMS--
--I NEUTRALIZED WITH SWORD AND KNIFE TO MINIMIZE THE CASUALTIES OF BYSTANDERS.
YOU LEFT NO ONE TO QUESTION? NO WITNESSES.
clik
clik
ALL COMBATANTS WERE **DISPATCHED.** AS PER THE DIRECTOR'S ORDERS.
WHAT ARE YOUR FEELINGS TOWARD THE SOVIET UNION, BLOODSHOT?
THE MOTHERLAND IS ALL. I LAY MY LIFE DOWN FOR THE PEOPLE.
FOR THE UNION. THE SOVIET WAY OF LIFE IS THE ONLY WAY OF LIFE.
DEATH TO ANY WHO WOULD THREATEN THE MOTHERLAND.

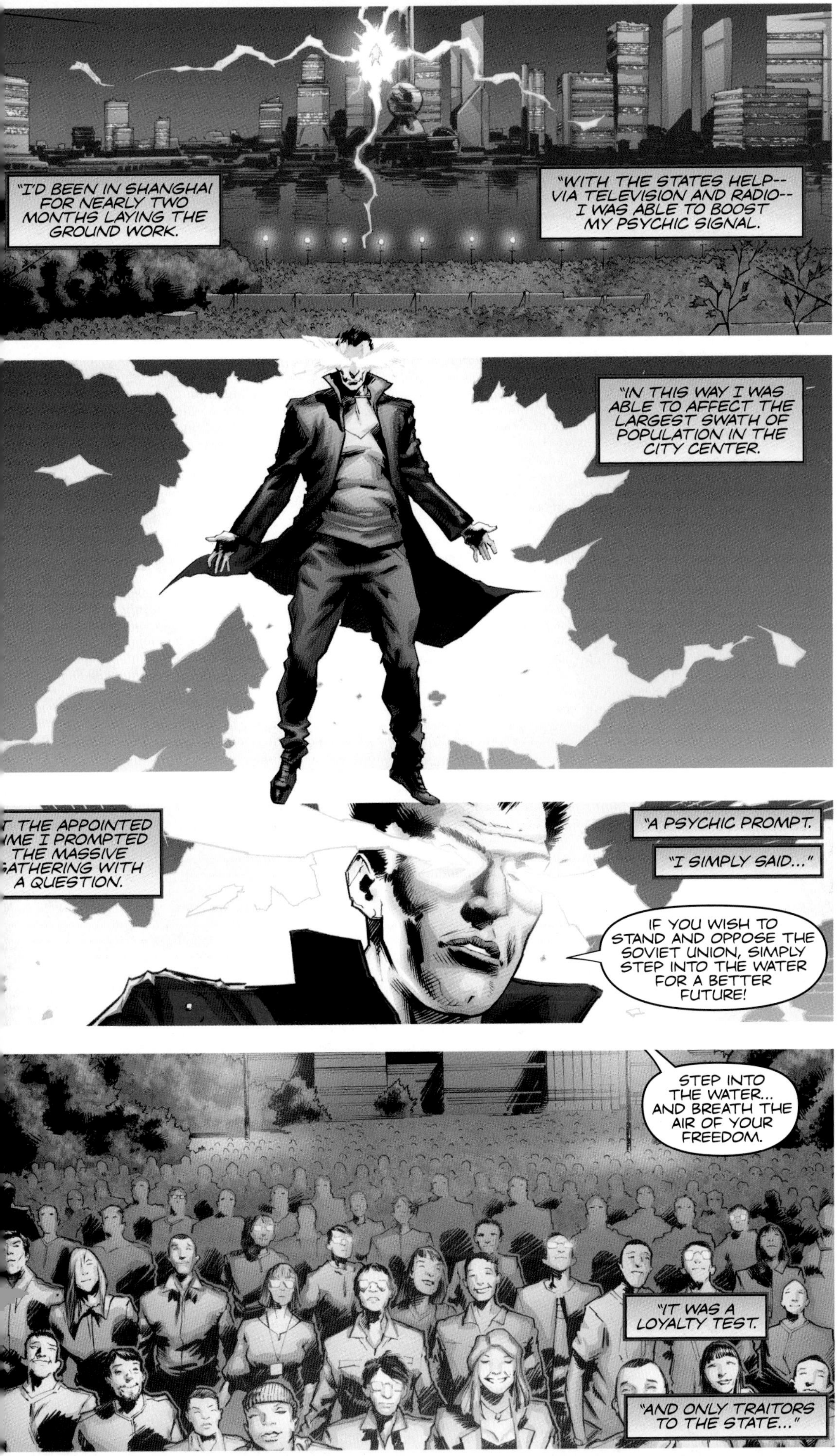
"I'D BEEN IN SHANGHAI FOR NEARLY TWO MONTHS LAYING THE GROUND WORK.
"WITH THE STATES HELP-- VIA TELEVISION AND RADIO-- I WAS ABLE TO BOOST MY PSYCHIC SIGNAL.
"IN THIS WAY I WAS ABLE TO AFFECT THE LARGEST SWATH OF POPULATION IN THE CITY CENTER.
T THE APPOINTED IME I PROMPTED THE MASSIVE GATHERING WITH A QUESTION.
"A PSYCHIC PROMPT.
"I SIMPLY SAID..."
IF YOU WISH TO STAND AND OPPOSE THE SOVIET UNION, SIMPLY STEP INTO THE WATER FOR A BETTER FUTURE!
STEP INTO THE WATER... AND BREATH THE AIR OF YOUR FREEDOM.
"IT WAS A LOYALTY TEST.
"AND ONLY TRAITORS TO THE STATE..."

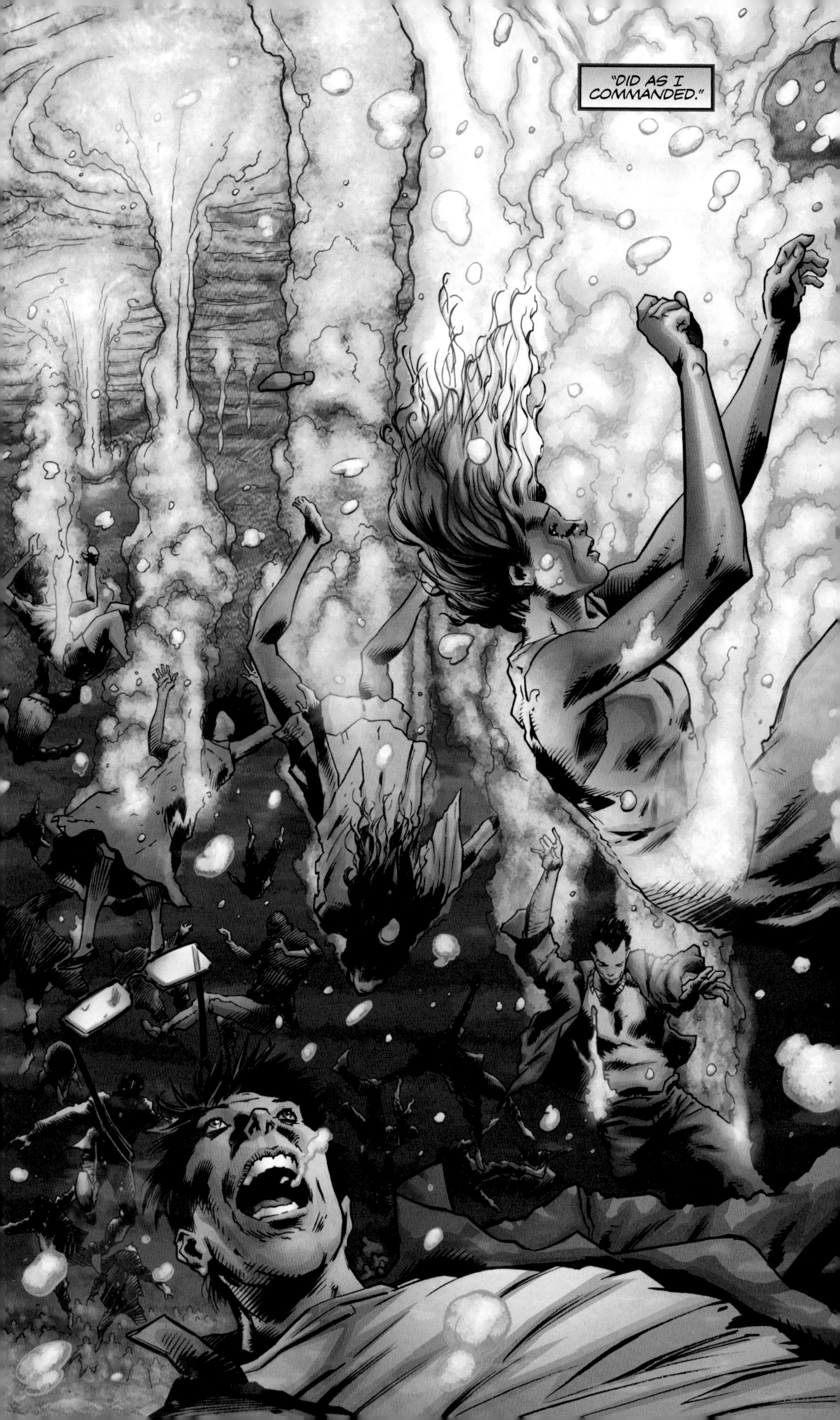
"DID AS I COMMANDED."

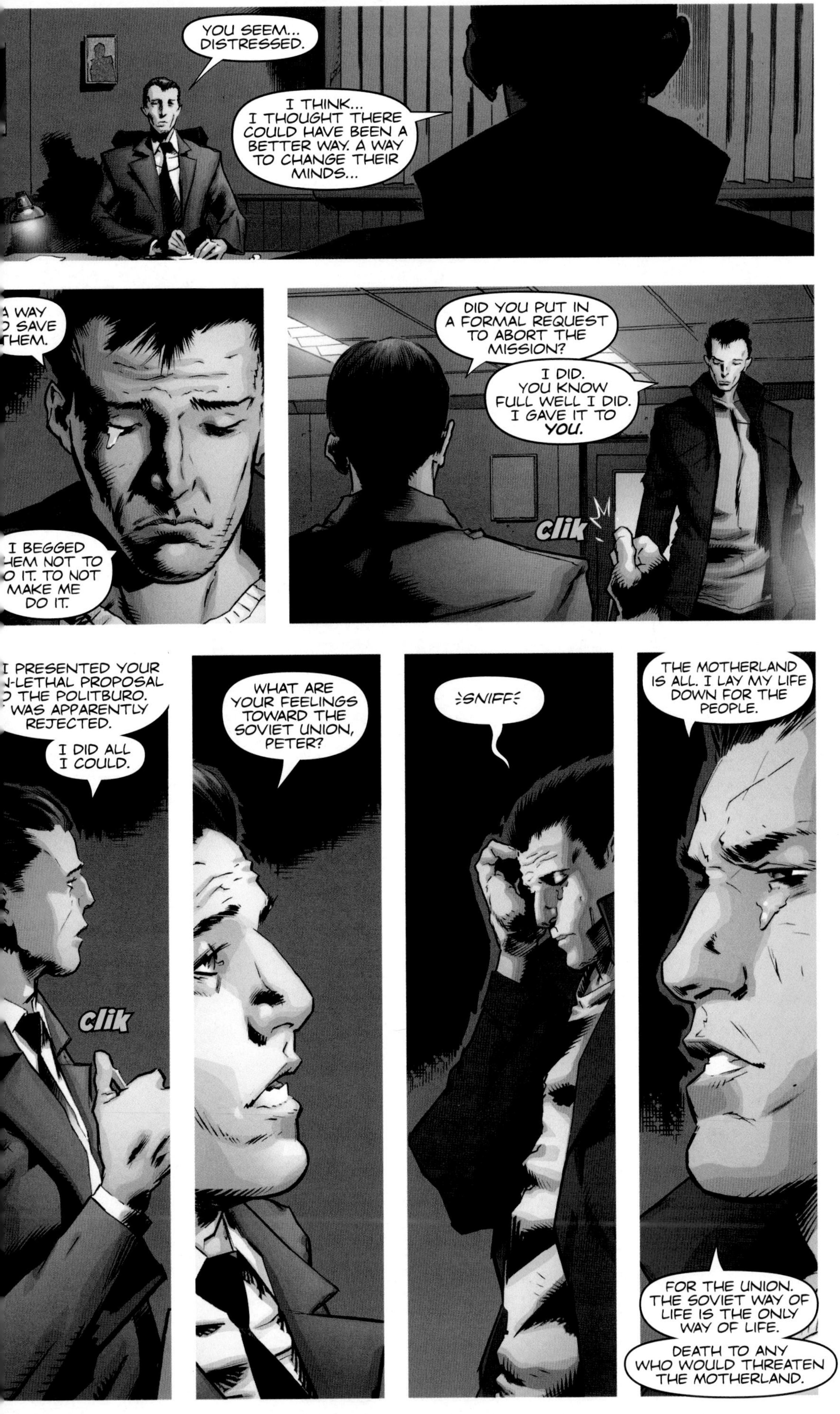
YOU SEEM... DISTRESSED.
I THINK... I THOUGHT THERE COULD HAVE BEEN A BETTER WAY. A WAY TO CHANGE THEIR MINDS...
A WAY O SAVE THEM.
I BEGGED HEM NOT TO O IT. TO NOT MAKE ME DO IT.
DID YOU PUT IN A FORMAL REQUEST TO ABORT THE MISSION?
I DID. YOU KNOW FULL WELL I DID. I GAVE IT TO YOU.
clik
I PRESENTED YOUR -LETHAL PROPOSAL O THE POLITBURO. WAS APPARENTLY REJECTED.
I DID ALL I COULD.
clik
WHAT ARE YOUR FEELINGS TOWARD THE SOVIET UNION, PETER?
SNIFF
THE MOTHERLAND IS ALL. I LAY MY LIFE DOWN FOR THE PEOPLE.
FOR THE UNION. THE SOVIET WAY OF LIFE IS THE ONLY WAY OF LIFE.
DEATH TO ANY WHO WOULD THREATEN THE MOTHERLAND.

"I WAS IN THE NEW DEADSIDE OIL FIELDS OUTSIDE OF KABUL, AFGHANISTAN."

WHAT IS THIS?

NOT A TRADITIONAL *IED*... NO EXPLOSIVES. LET'S SEE WHAT IT DOES--

SH-WHOOM

"EVER SINCE MYSHK. TAPPED INTO THE DEADSIDE TO TRIPLE THE OIL OUTPUT... DEADSIDE INSURGENT HAVE BEEN BREACHIN OUR WORLD WITH TH HELP OF EARTH-BOUN COLLABORATORS."

FZZT

"THE EARTH-BOUND AGENTS HAVE BEEN DEPLOYING IMD'S (IMPROVISED MAGICAL DEVICES) TO OPEN UP OUR WORLD TO THE DEADSIDE.

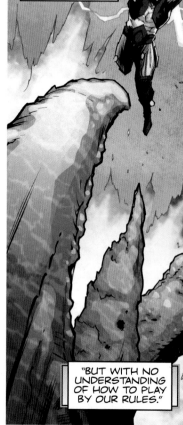

"THE DEADSIDE WANTING WHAT WE HAVE.

"BUT WITH NO UNDERSTANDING OF HOW TO PLAY BY OUR RULES."

WHAM

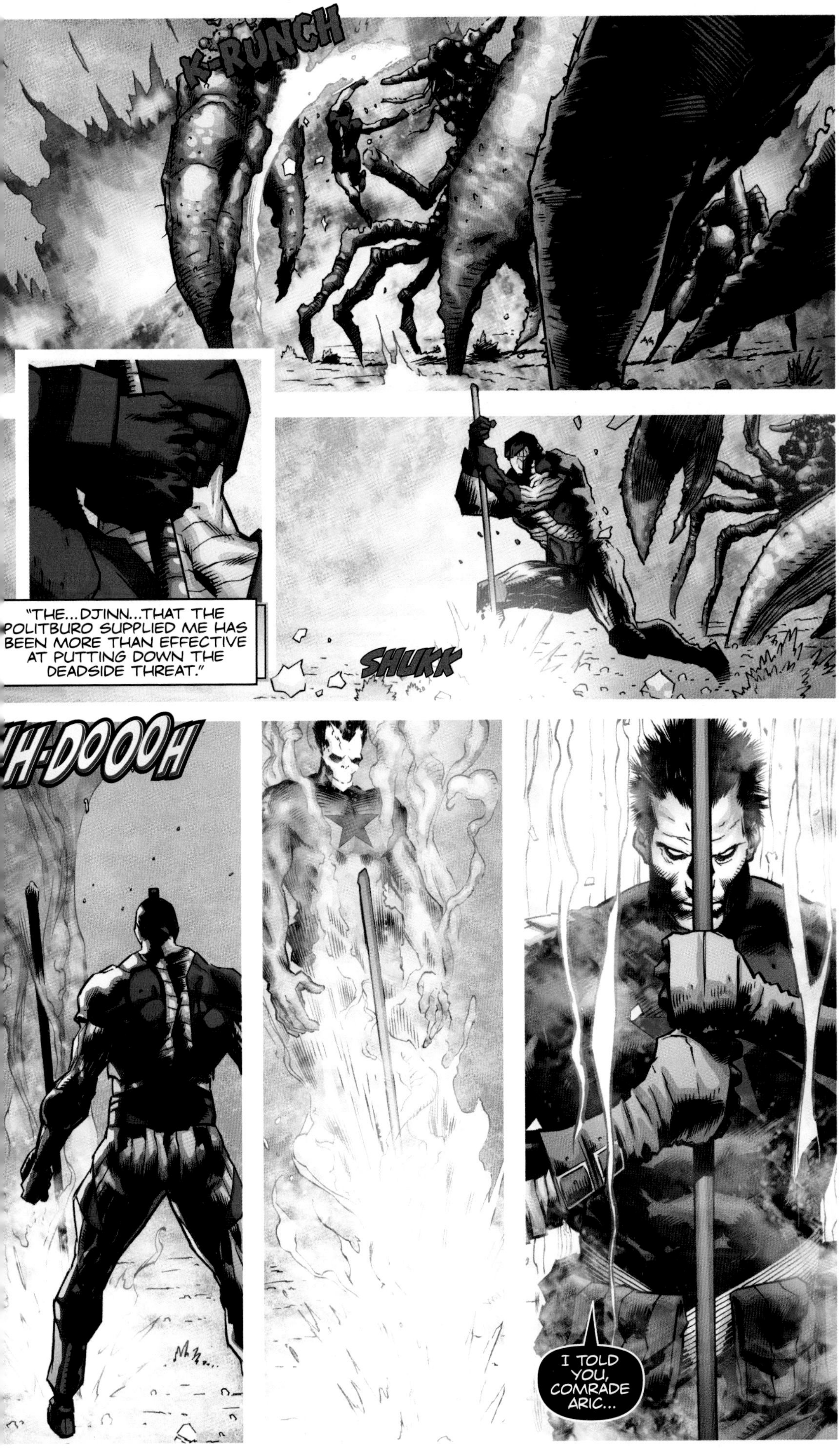
K-RUNCH
"THE...DJINN...THAT THE POLITBURO SUPPLIED ME HAS BEEN MORE THAN EFFECTIVE AT PUTTING DOWN THE DEADSIDE THREAT."
SHUKK
H-DOOOH
I TOLD YOU, COMRADE ARIC...

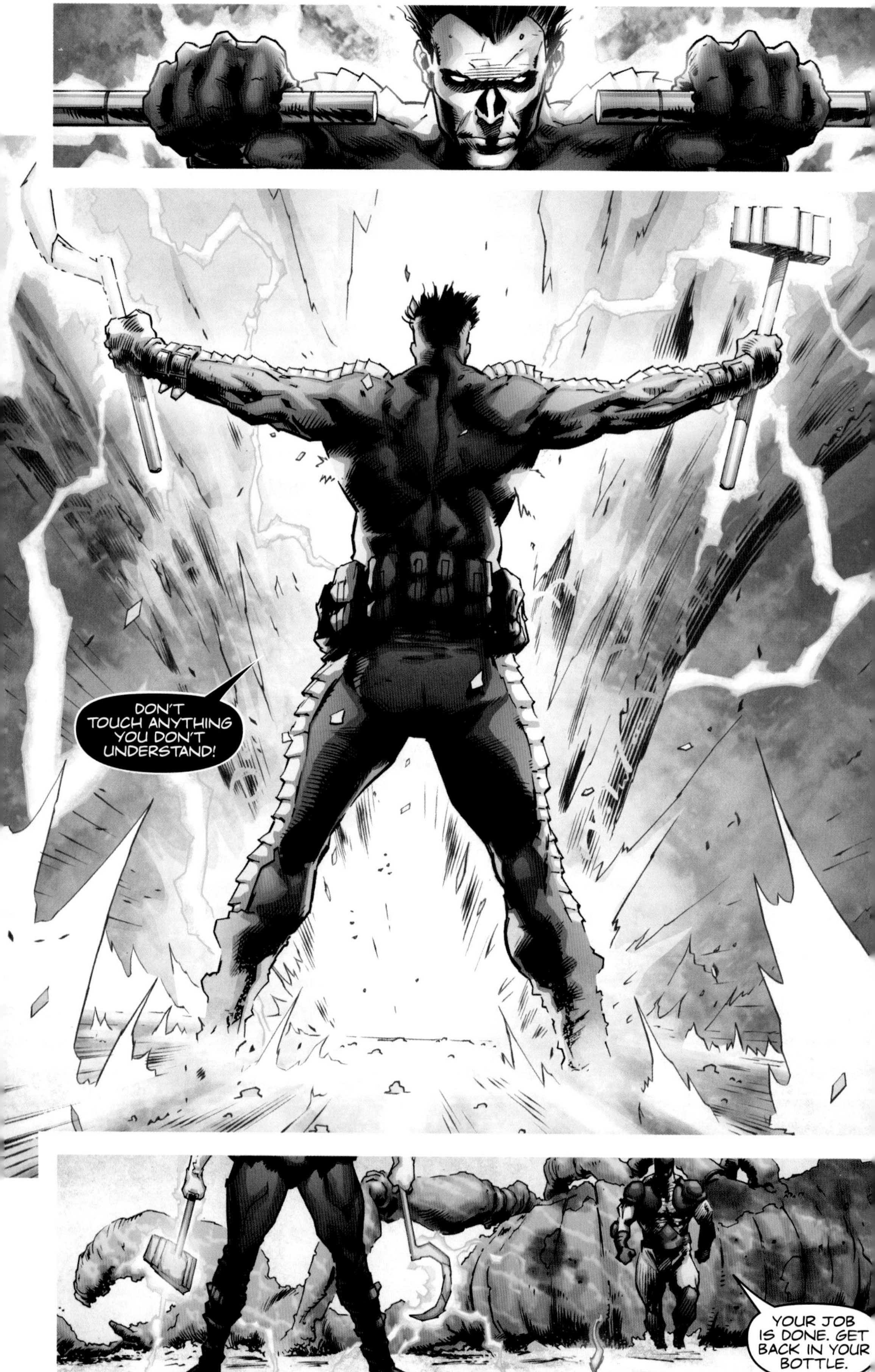
DON'T TOUCH ANYTHING YOU DON'T UNDERSTAND!
YOUR JOB IS DONE. GET BACK IN YOUR BOTTLE.

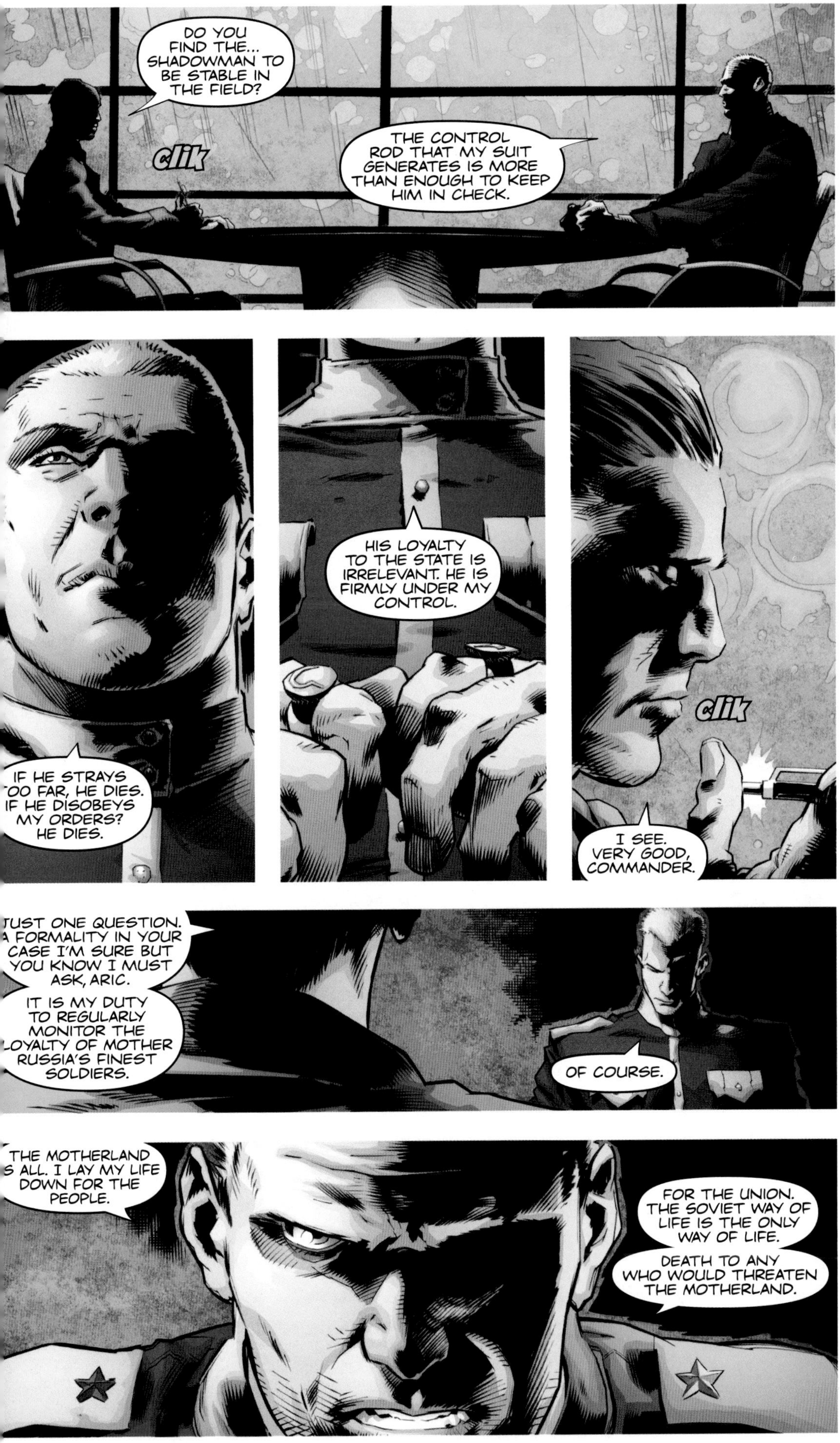
DO YOU FIND THE... SHADOWMAN TO BE STABLE IN THE FIELD?
CLIK
THE CONTROL ROD THAT MY SUIT GENERATES IS MORE THAN ENOUGH TO KEEP HIM IN CHECK.
IF HE STRAYS TOO FAR, HE DIES. IF HE DISOBEYS MY ORDERS? HE DIES.
HIS LOYALTY TO THE STATE IS IRRELEVANT. HE IS FIRMLY UNDER MY CONTROL.
CLIK
I SEE. VERY GOOD, COMMANDER.
JUST ONE QUESTION. A FORMALITY IN YOUR CASE I'M SURE BUT YOU KNOW I MUST ASK, ARIC.
IT IS MY DUTY TO REGULARLY MONITOR THE LOYALTY OF MOTHER RUSSIA'S FINEST SOLDIERS.
OF COURSE.
THE MOTHERLAND IS ALL. I LAY MY LIFE DOWN FOR THE PEOPLE.
FOR THE UNION. THE SOVIET WAY OF LIFE IS THE ONLY WAY OF LIFE.
DEATH TO ANY WHO WOULD THREATEN THE MOTHERLAND.

COLIN KING FIELD REPORT: THE SCHEDULED SOLDIER MAINTENANCE AND TESTING WENT AS EXPECTED.

ALL AGENTS ARE EXTREMELY LOYAL AND DEDICATED.

THEY ALL ARE SUPREMELY EFFECTIVE IN THE FIELD, HAVING EFFICIENTLY PUT DOWN NUMEROUS INSURRECTIONS AND UPRISINGS ACROSS THE GLOBE WITH EASE.

IT IS MY PROFESSIONAL OPINION AS FIELD ADVISOR AND POLITBURO COUNSELOR, THAT OUR FIELD OPERATIONS COULD NOT BE MORE EFFECTIVE.

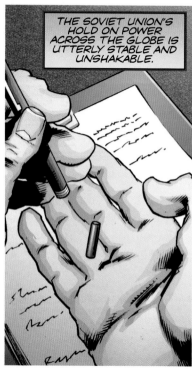

THE SOVIET UNION'S HOLD ON POWER ACROSS THE GLOBE IS UTTERLY STABLE AND UNSHAKABLE.

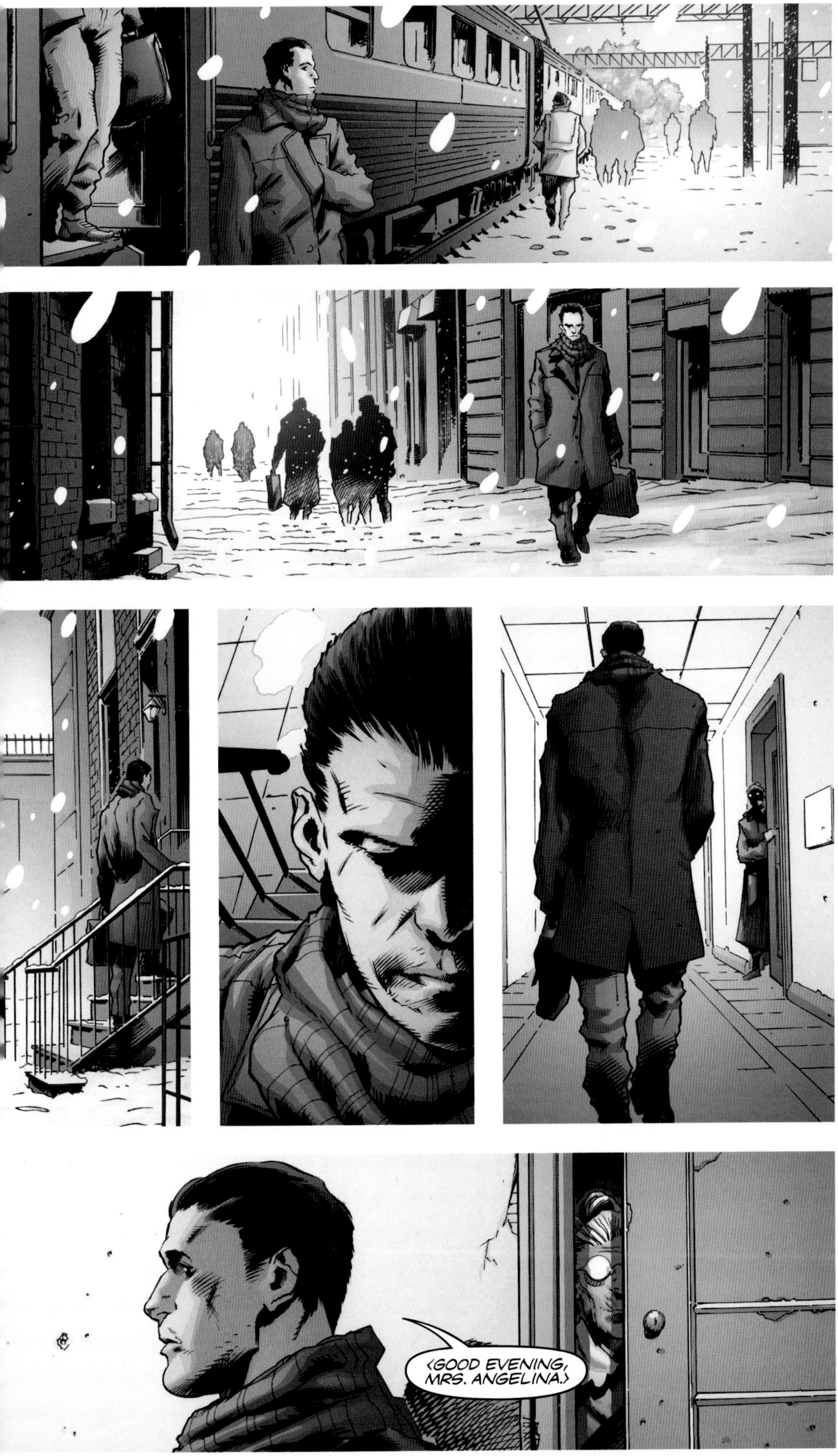
‹GOOD EVENING, MRS. ANGELINA.›

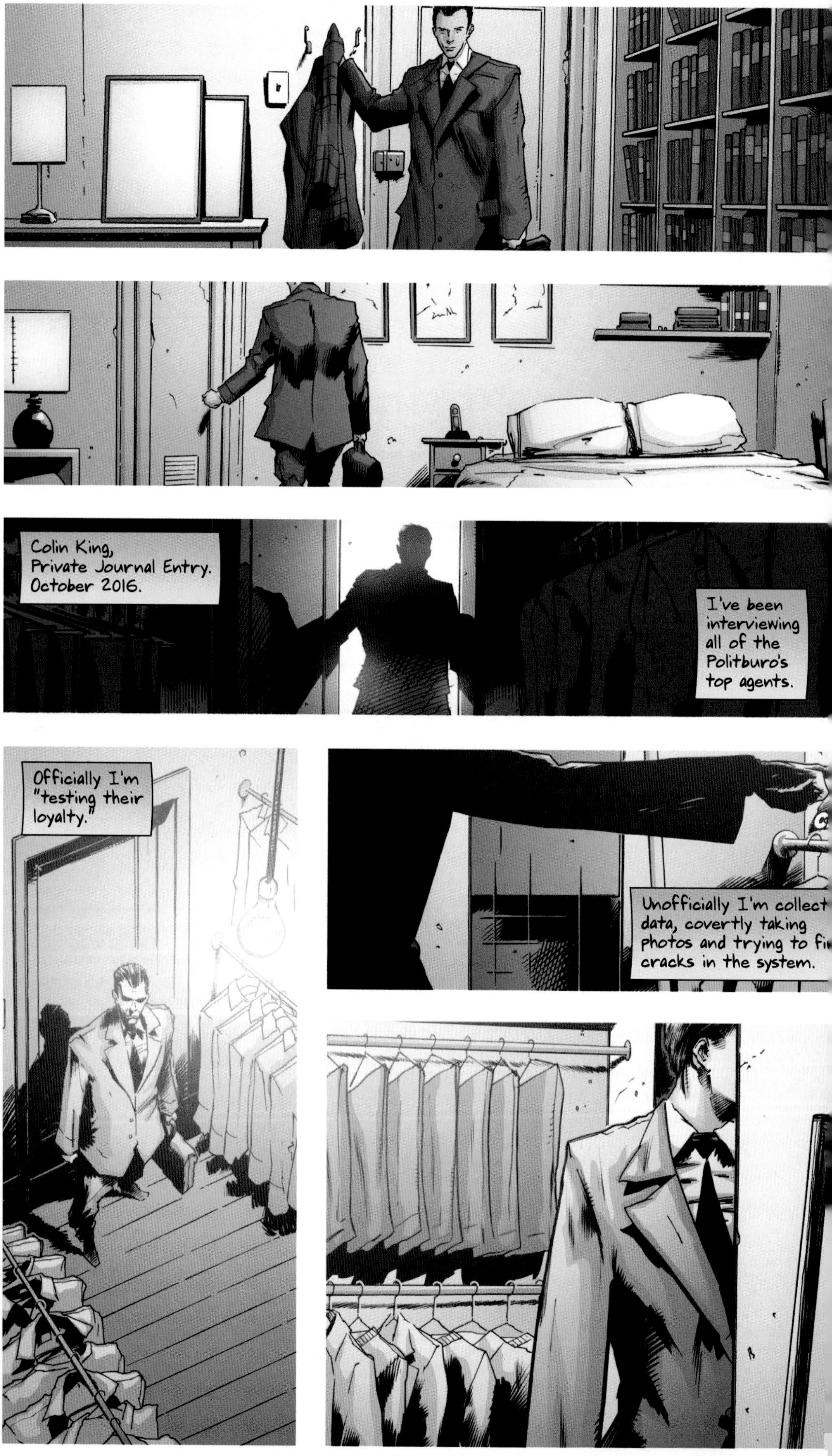
Colin King, Private Journal Entry. October 2016.
I've been interviewing all of the Politburo's top agents.
Officially I'm "testing their loyalty."
Unofficially I'm collect data, covertly taking photos and trying to fi cracks in the system.

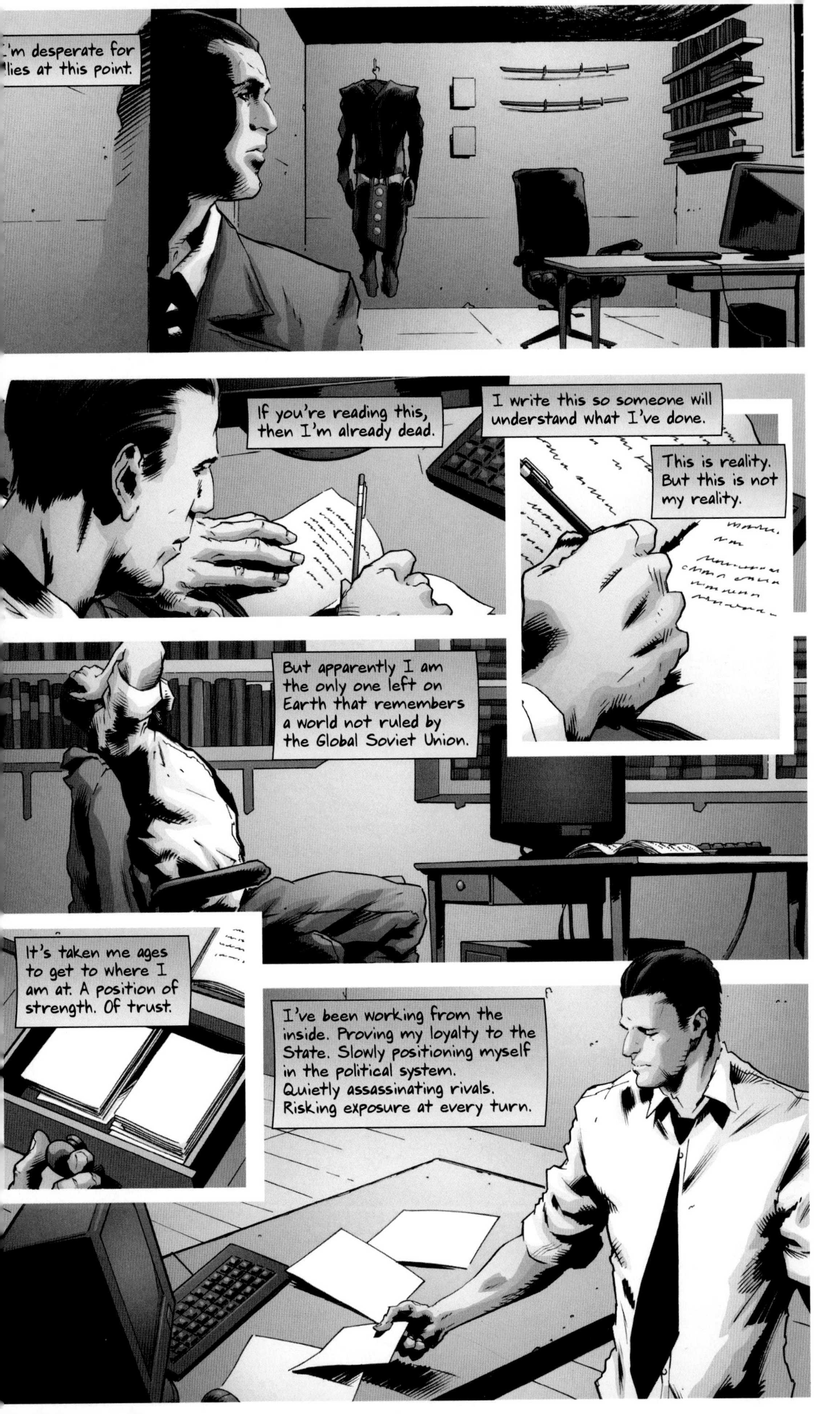
'm desperate for lies at this point.
If you're reading this, then I'm already dead.
I write this so someone will understand what I've done.
This is reality. But this is not my reality.
But apparently I am the only one left on Earth that remembers a world not ruled by the Global Soviet Union.
It's taken me ages to get to where I am at. A position of strength. Of trust.
I've been working from the inside. Proving my loyalty to the State. Slowly positioning myself in the political system. Quietly assassinating rivals. Risking exposure at every turn.

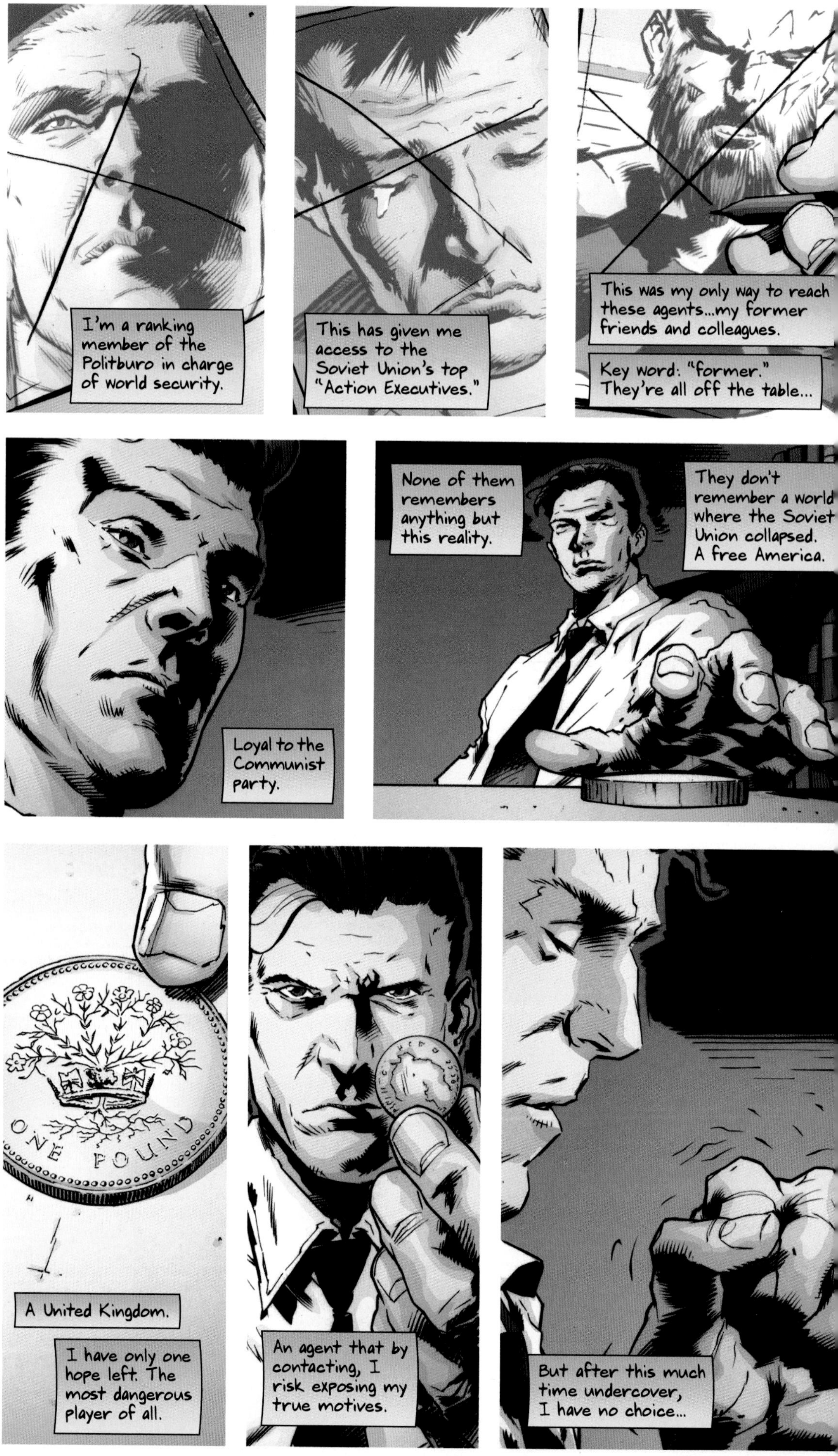

I'm a ranking member of the Politburo in charge of world security.
This has given me access to the Soviet Union's top "Action Executives."
This was my only way to reach these agents...my former friends and colleagues.
Key word: "former." They're all off the table...
Loyal to the Communist party.
None of them remembers anything but this reality.
They don't remember a world where the Soviet Union collapsed. A free America.
ONE POUND
A United Kingdom.
I have only one hope left. The most dangerous player of all.
An agent that by contacting, I risk exposing my true motives.
But after this much time undercover, I have no choice...

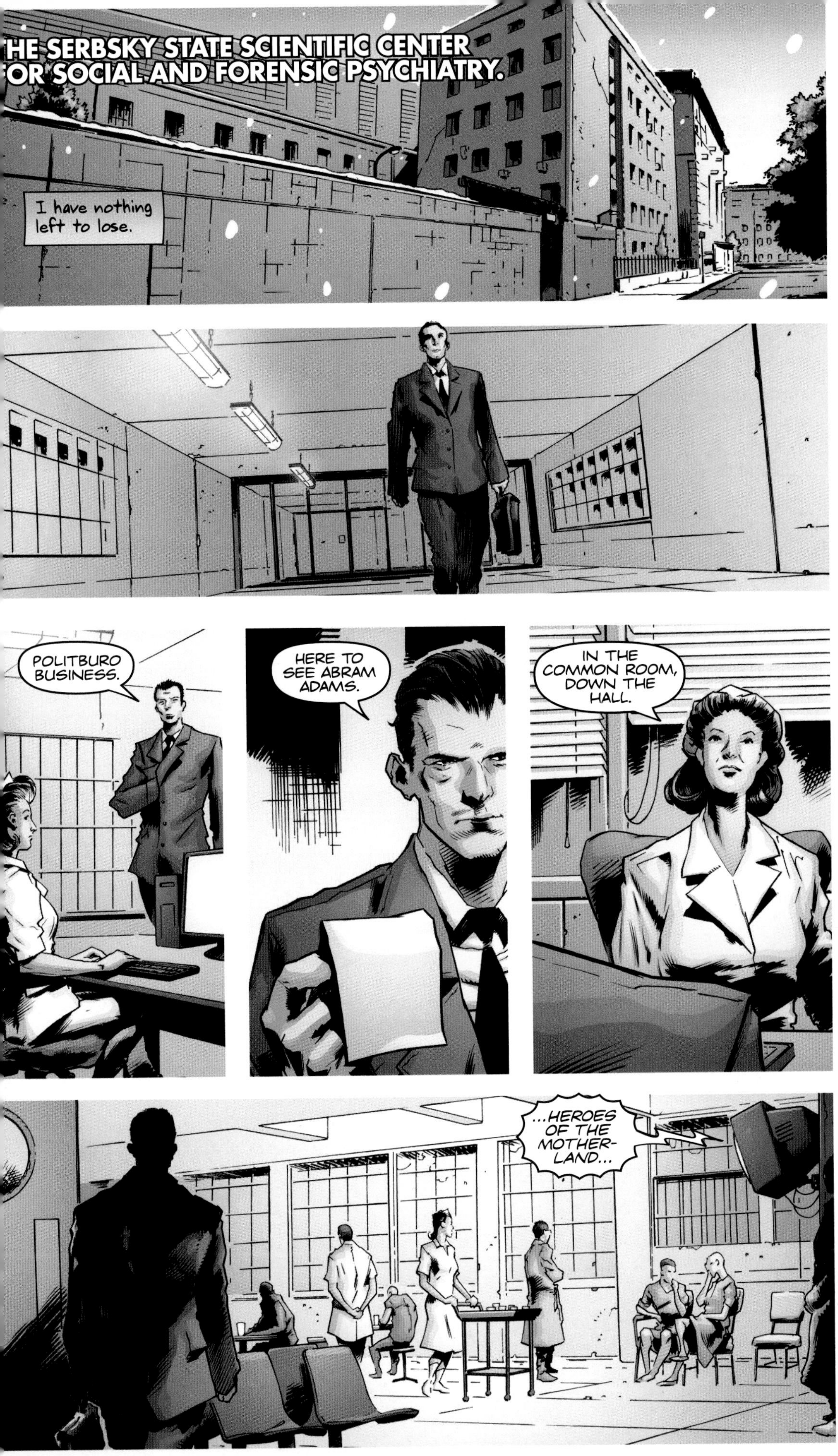
THE SERBSKY STATE SCIENTIFIC CENTER FOR SOCIAL AND FORENSIC PSYCHIATRY.
I have nothing left to lose.
POLITBURO BUSINESS.
HERE TO SEE ABRAM ADAMS.
IN THE COMMON ROOM, DOWN THE HALL.
...HEROES OF THE MOTHER-LAND...

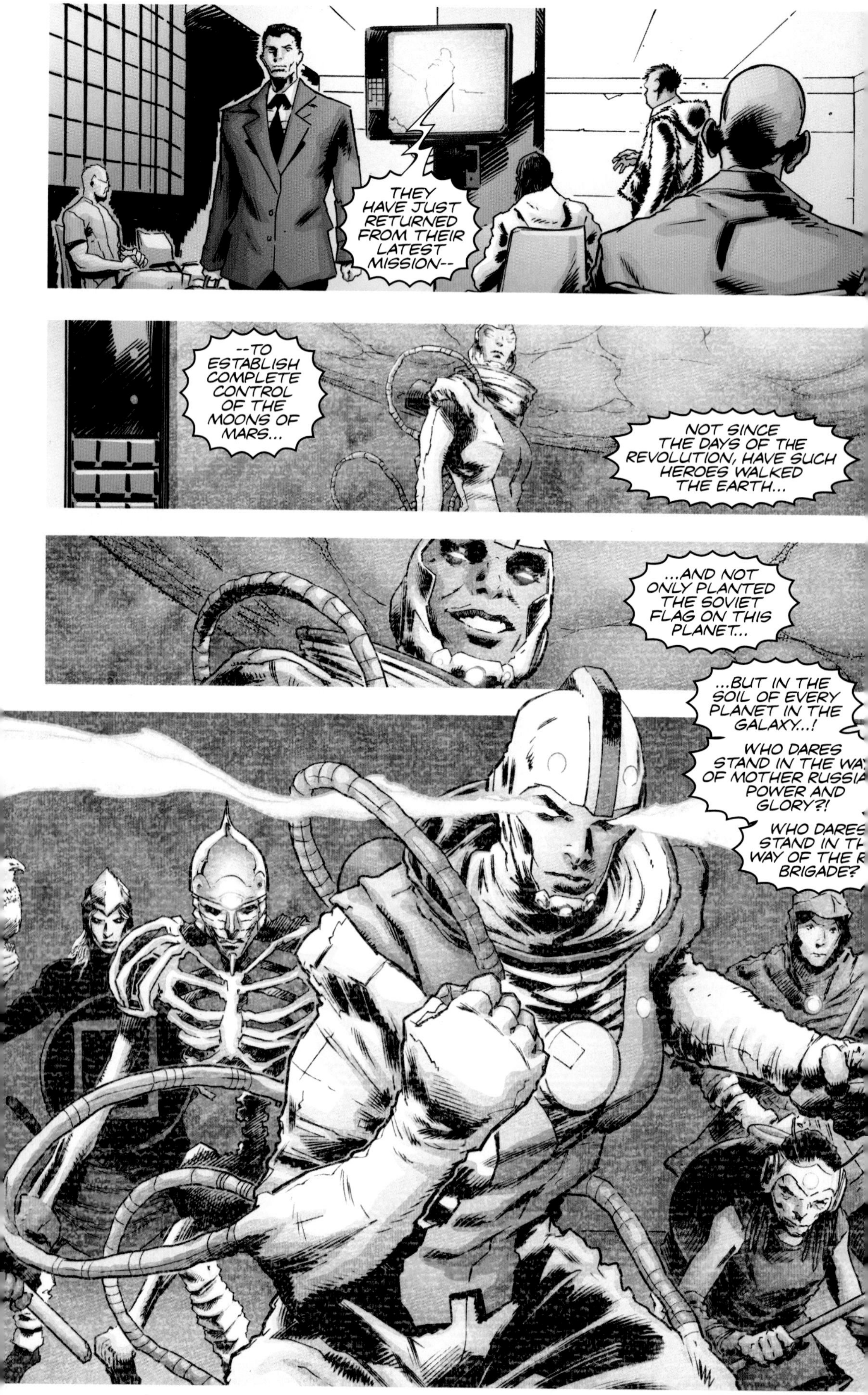
THEY HAVE JUST RETURNED FROM THEIR LATEST MISSION--
--TO ESTABLISH COMPLETE CONTROL OF THE MOONS OF MARS...
NOT SINCE THE DAYS OF THE REVOLUTION, HAVE SUCH HEROES WALKED THE EARTH...
...AND NOT ONLY PLANTED THE SOVIET FLAG ON THIS PLANET...
...BUT IN THE SOIL OF EVERY PLANET IN THE GALAXY...!
WHO DARES STAND IN THE WA OF MOTHER RUSSIA POWER AND GLORY?!
WHO DARES STAND IN TH WAY OF THE BRIGADE?

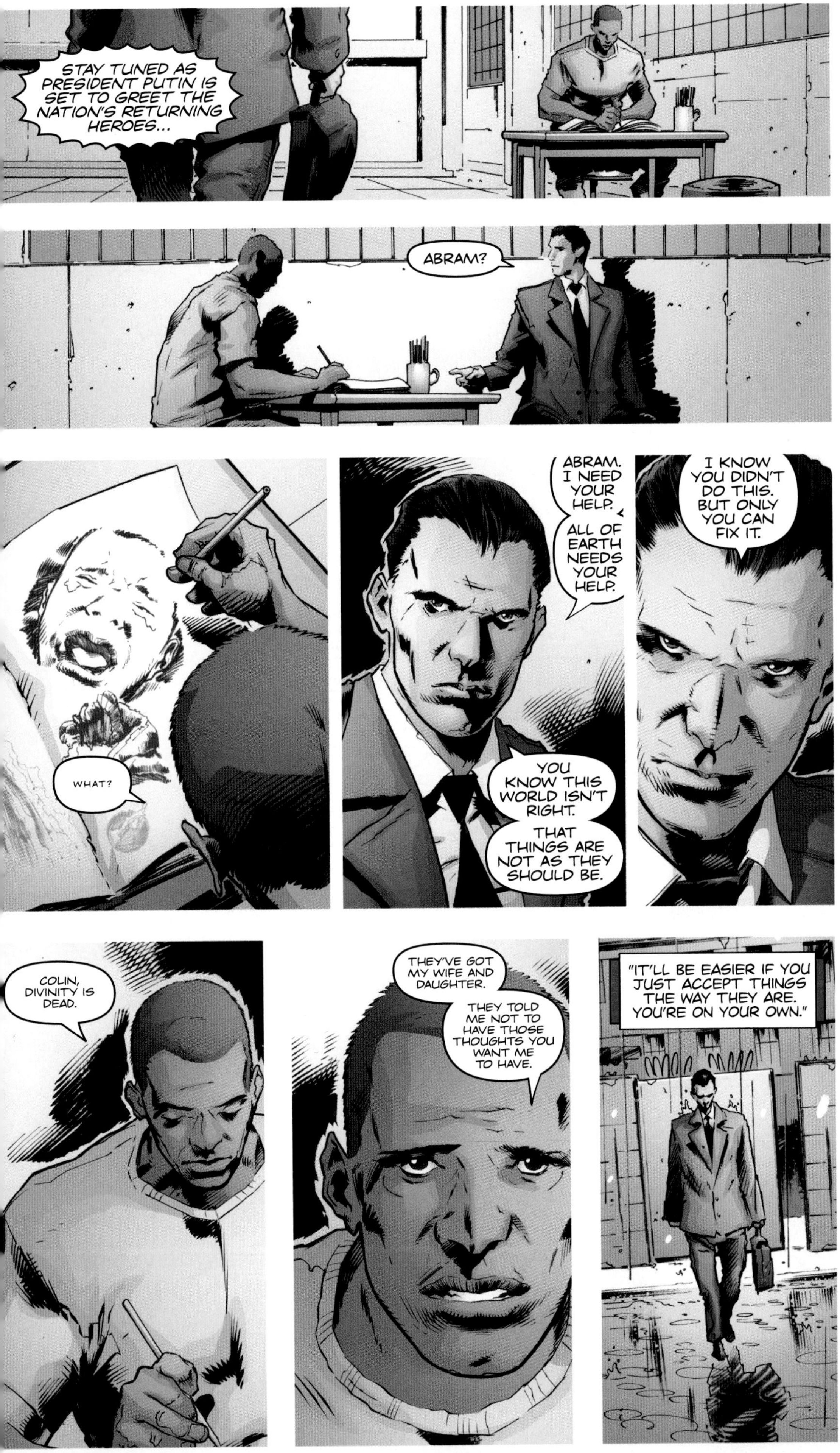
STAY TUNED AS PRESIDENT PUTIN IS SET TO GREET THE NATION'S RETURNING HEROES...
ABRAM?
WHAT?
ABRAM. I NEED YOUR HELP.
ALL OF EARTH NEEDS YOUR HELP.
YOU KNOW THIS WORLD ISN'T RIGHT.
THAT THINGS ARE NOT AS THEY SHOULD BE.
I KNOW YOU DIDN'T DO THIS. BUT ONLY YOU CAN FIX IT.
COLIN, DIVINITY IS DEAD.
THEY'VE GOT MY WIFE AND DAUGHTER.
THEY TOLD ME NOT TO HAVE THOSE THOUGHTS YOU WANT ME TO HAVE.
"IT'LL BE EASIER IF YOU JUST ACCEPT THINGS THE WAY THEY ARE. YOU'RE ON YOUR OWN."

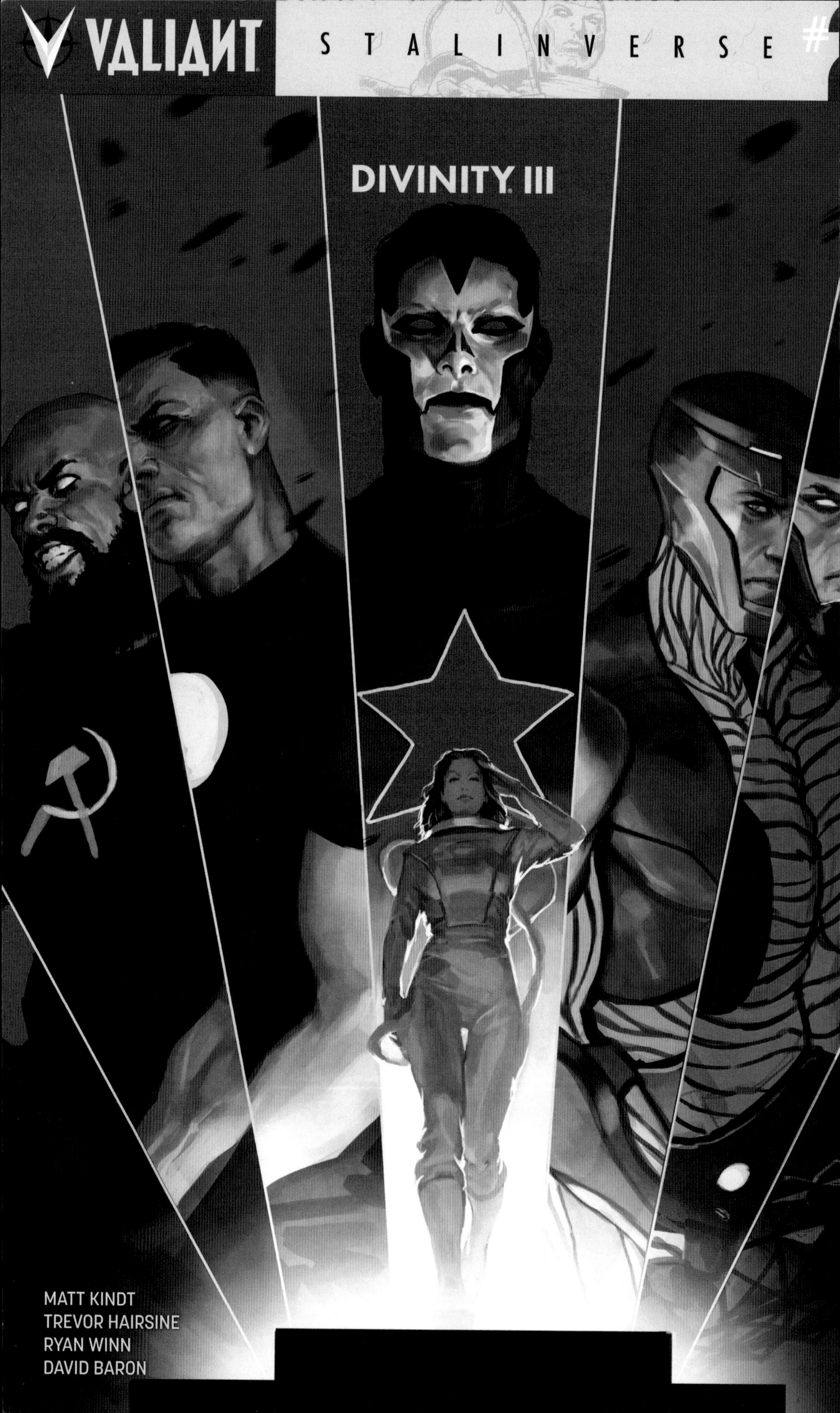
VALIANT
STALINVERSE #
DIVINITY III
MATT KINDT
TREVOR HAIRSINE
RYAN WINN
DAVID BARON

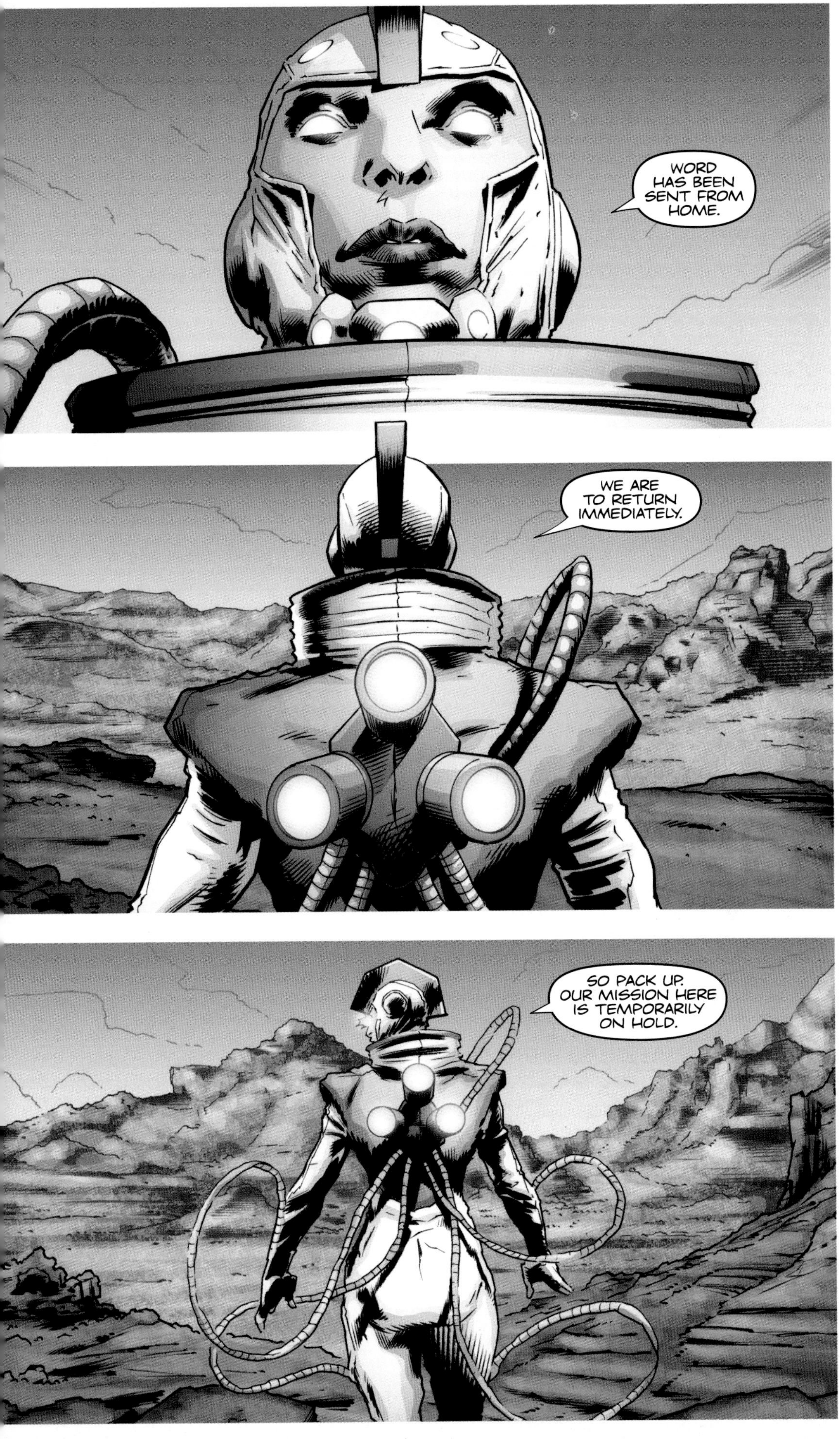
WORD HAS BEEN SENT FROM HOME.
WE ARE TO RETURN IMMEDIATELY.
SO PACK UP. OUR MISSION HERE IS TEMPORARILY ON HOLD.

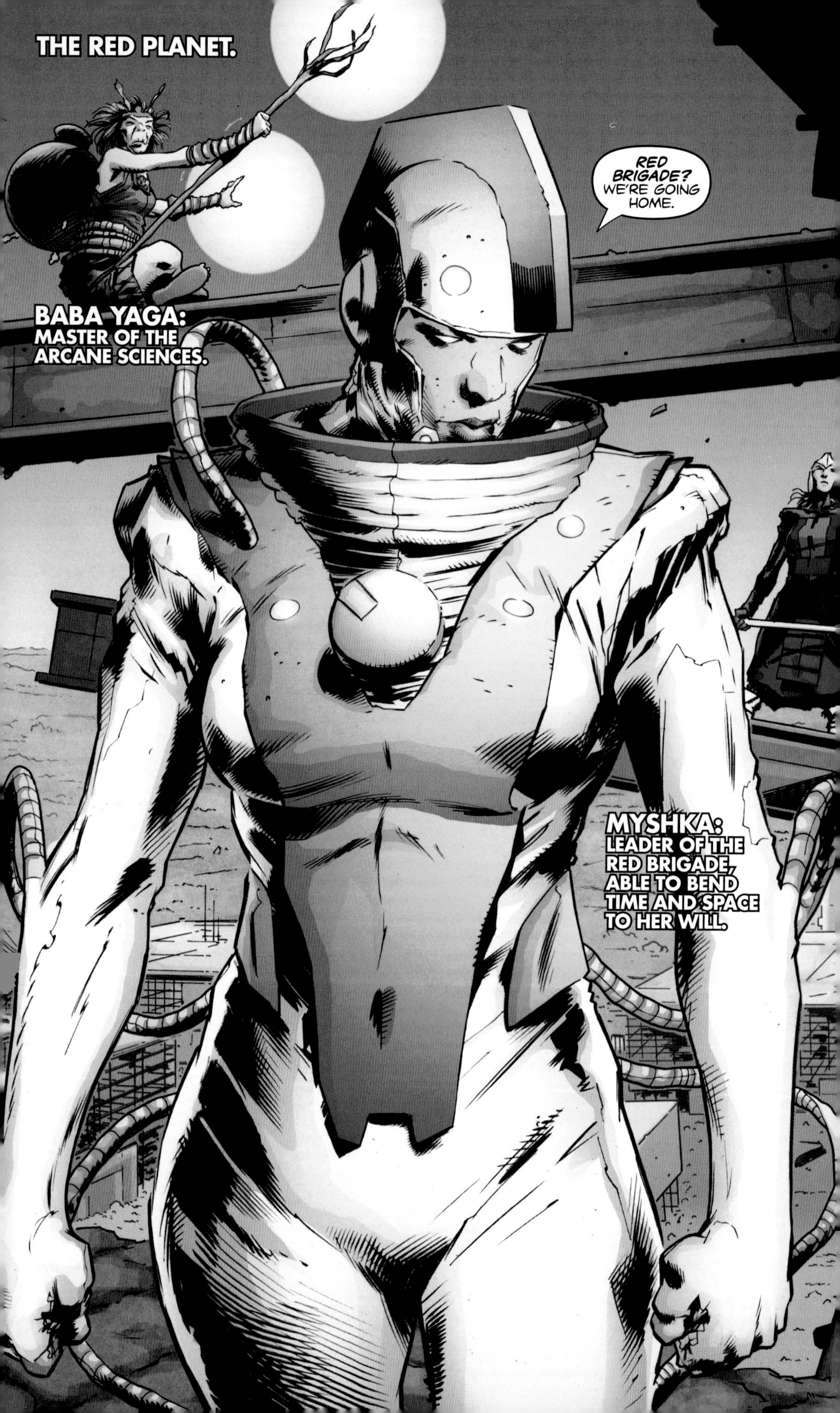
THE RED PLANET.
RED BRIGADE? WE'RE GOING HOME.
BABA YAGA: MASTER OF THE ARCANE SCIENCES.
MYSHKA: LEADER OF THE RED BRIGADE, ABLE TO BEND TIME AND SPACE TO HER WILL.

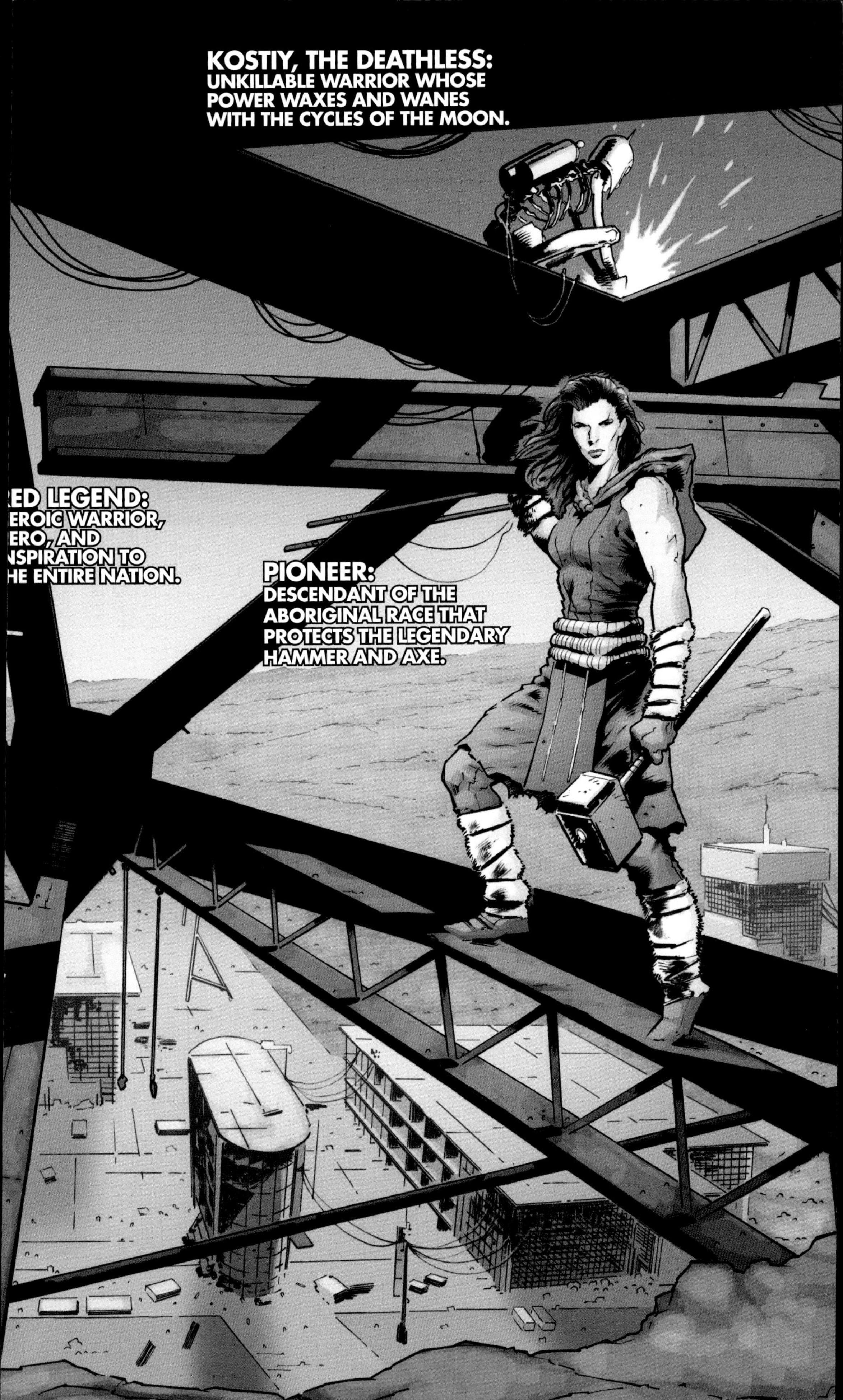
KOSTIY, THE DEATHLESS:
UNKILLABLE WARRIOR WHOSE POWER WAXES AND WANES WITH THE CYCLES OF THE MOON.
RED LEGEND:
EROIC WARRIOR, ERO, AND NSPIRATION TO HE ENTIRE NATION.
PIONEER:
DESCENDANT OF THE ABORIGINAL RACE THAT PROTECTS THE LEGENDARY HAMMER AND AXE.

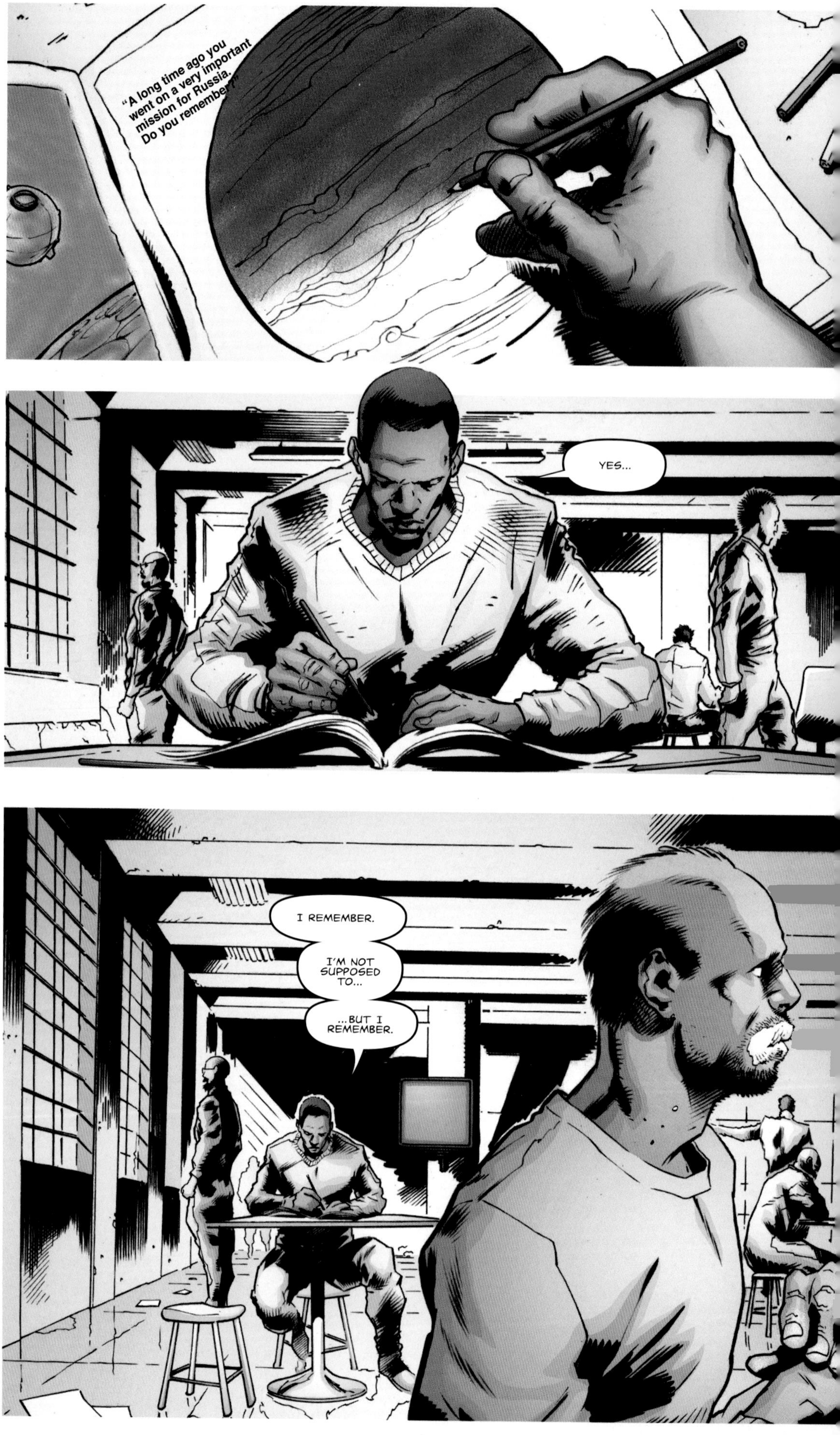
"A long time ago you went on a very important mission for Russia. Do you remember?"
YES...
I REMEMBER.
I'M NOT SUPPOSED TO...
...BUT I REMEMBER.

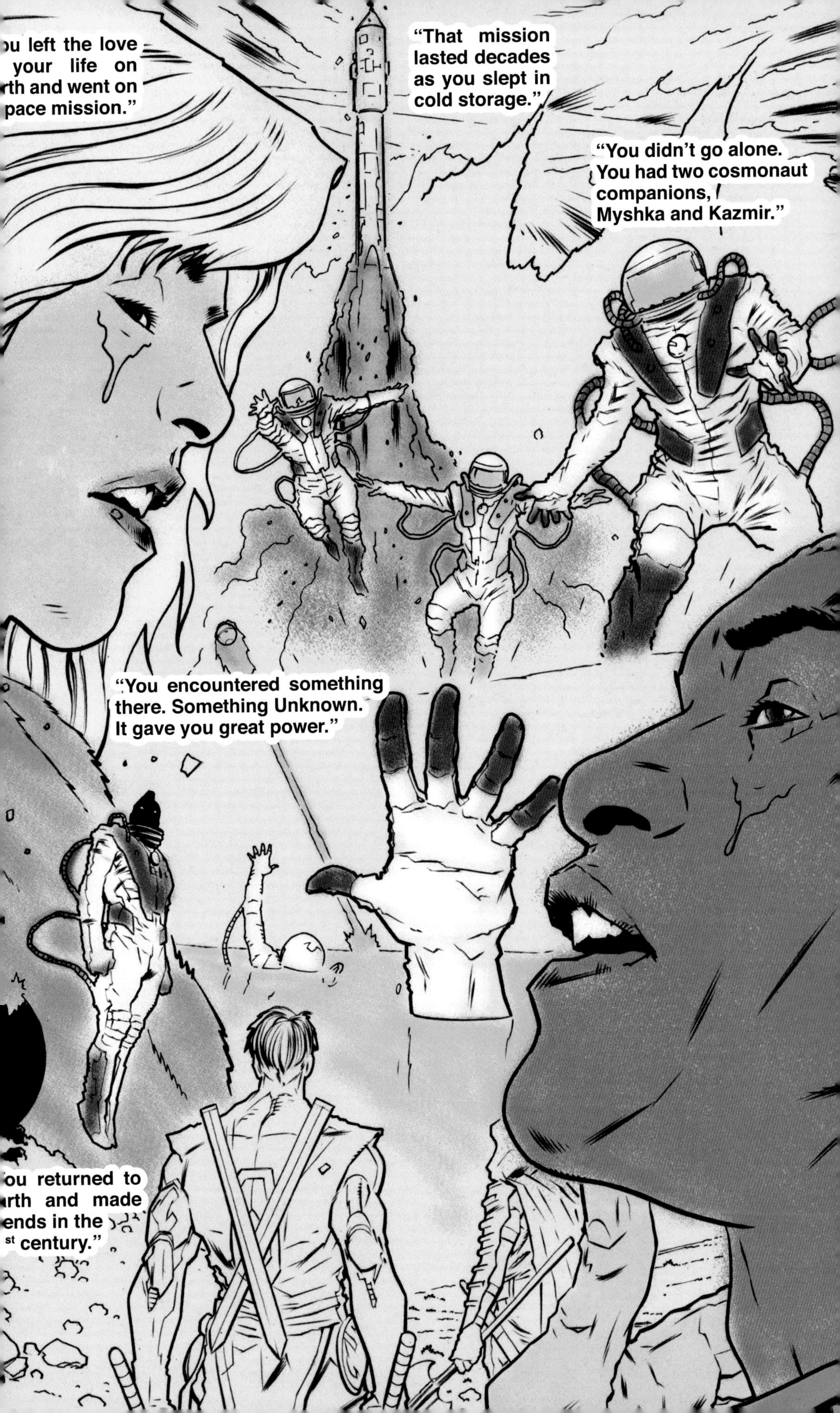
ou left the love your life on rth and went on pace mission."
"That mission lasted decades as you slept in cold storage."
"You didn't go alone. You had two cosmonaut companions, Myshka and Kazmir."
"You encountered something there. Something Unknown. It gave you great power."
ou returned to rth and made ends in the st century."

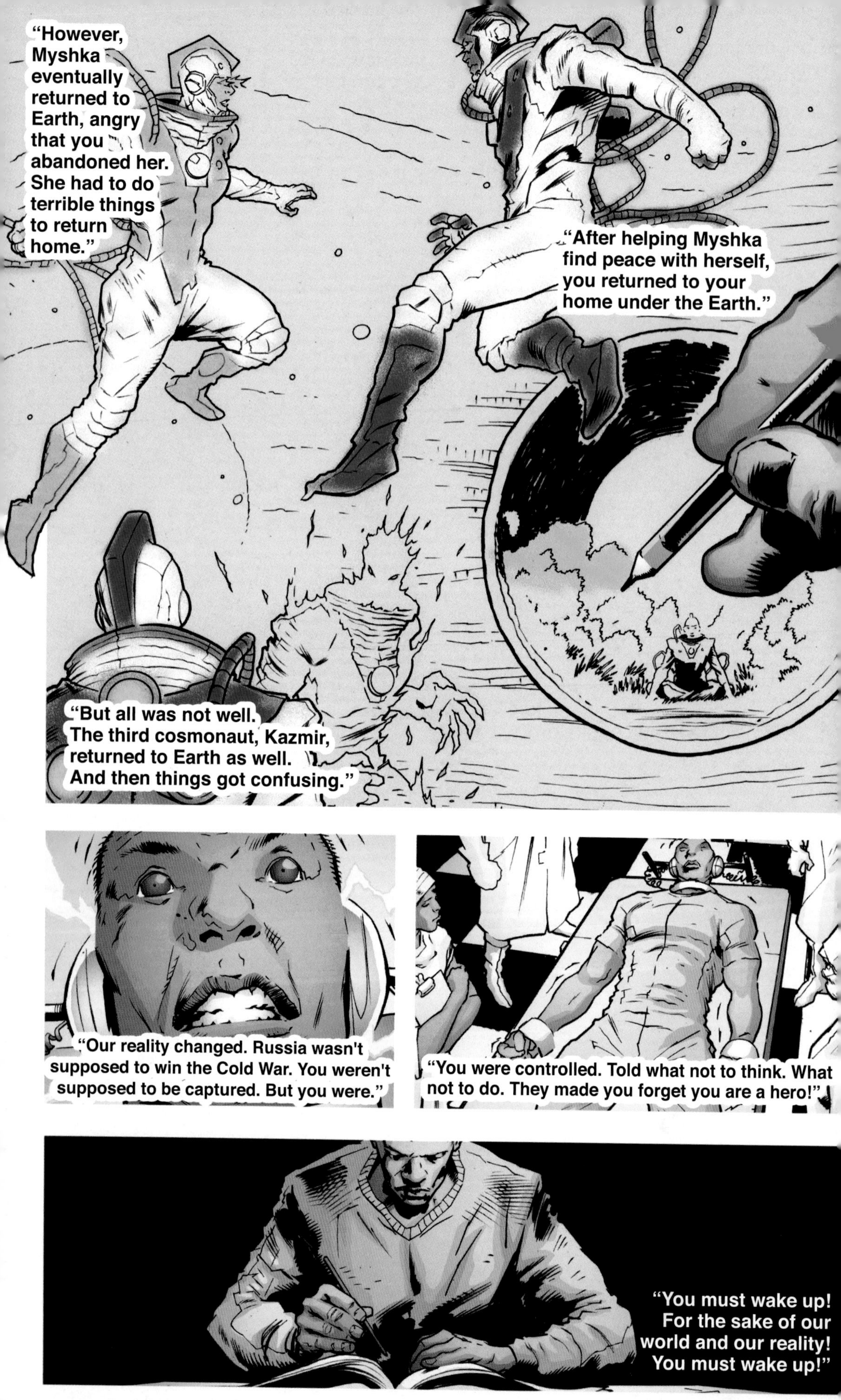
"However, Myshka eventually returned to Earth, angry that you abandoned her. She had to do terrible things to return home."
"After helping Myshka find peace with herself, you returned to your home under the Earth."
"But all was not well. The third cosmonaut, Kazmir, returned to Earth as well. And then things got confusing."
"Our reality changed. Russia wasn't supposed to win the Cold War. You weren't supposed to be captured. But you were."
"You were controlled. Told what not to think. What not to do. They made you forget you are a hero!"
"You must wake up! For the sake of our world and our reality! You must wake up!"

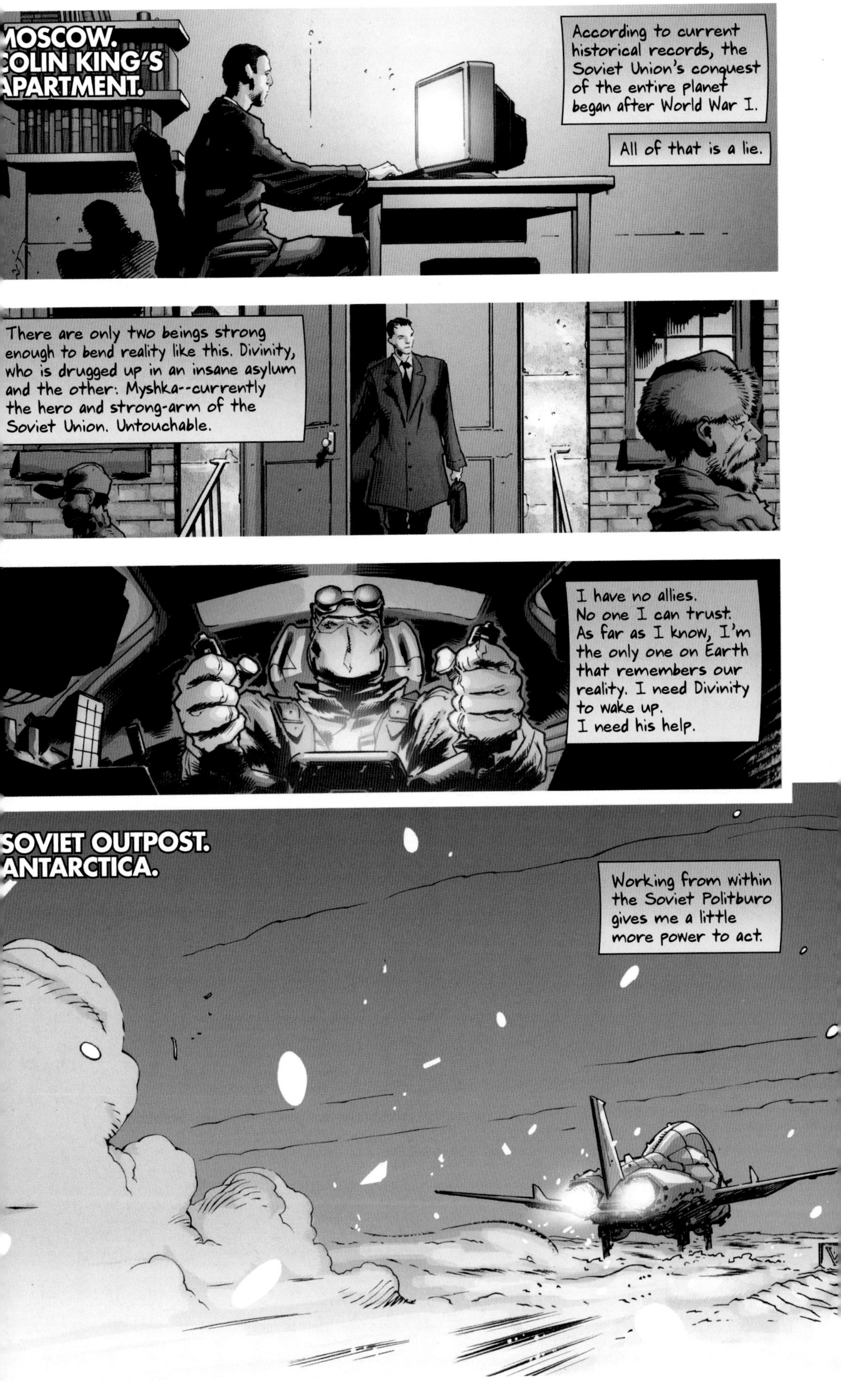
MOSCOW. COLIN KING'S APARTMENT.
According to current historical records, the Soviet Union's conquest of the entire planet began after World War I.
All of that is a lie.
There are only two beings strong enough to bend reality like this. Divinity, who is drugged up in an insane asylum and the other: Myshka--currently the hero and strong-arm of the Soviet Union. Untouchable.
I have no allies. No one I can trust. As far as I know, I'm the only one on Earth that remembers our reality. I need Divinity to wake up. I need his help.
SOVIET OUTPOST. ANTARCTICA.
Working from within the Soviet Politburo gives me a little more power to act.

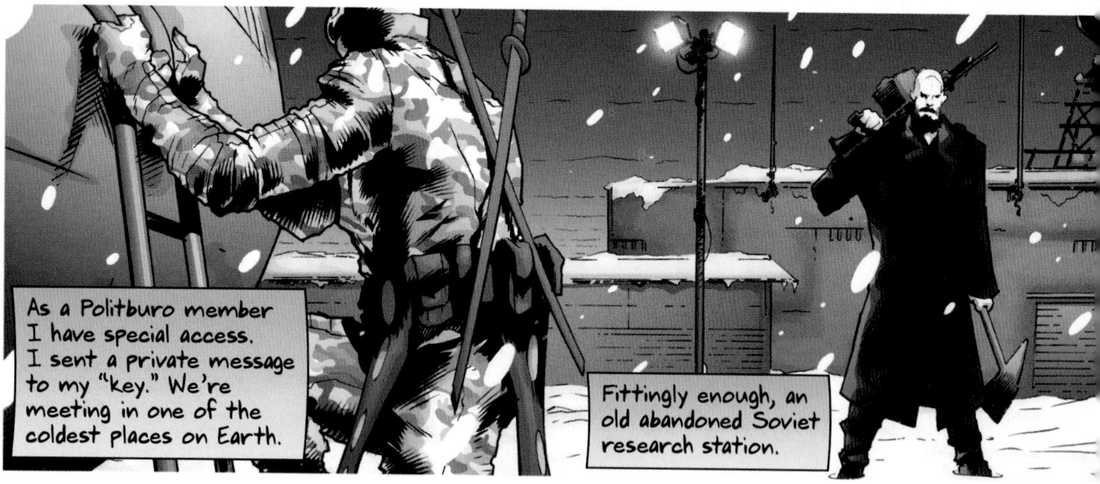
As a Politburo member I have special access. I sent a private message to my "key." We're meeting in one of the coldest places on Earth.
Fittingly enough, an old abandoned Soviet research station.

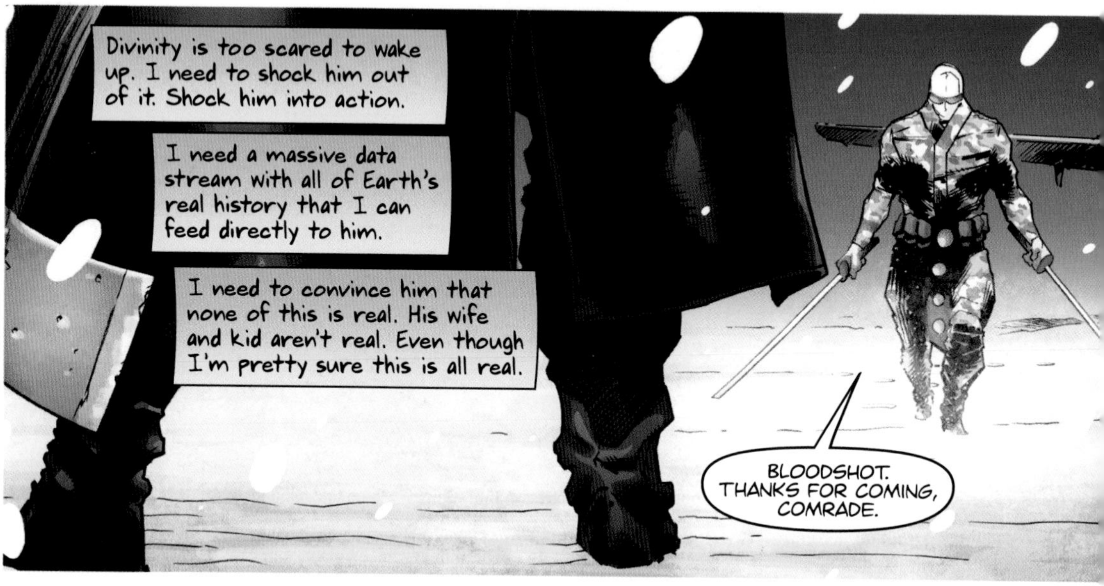
Divinity is too scared to wake up. I need to shock him out of it. Shock him into action.
I need a massive data stream with all of Earth's real history that I can feed directly to him.
I need to convince him that none of this is real. His wife and kid aren't real. Even though I'm pretty sure this is all real.
BLOODSHOT. THANKS FOR COMING, COMRADE.

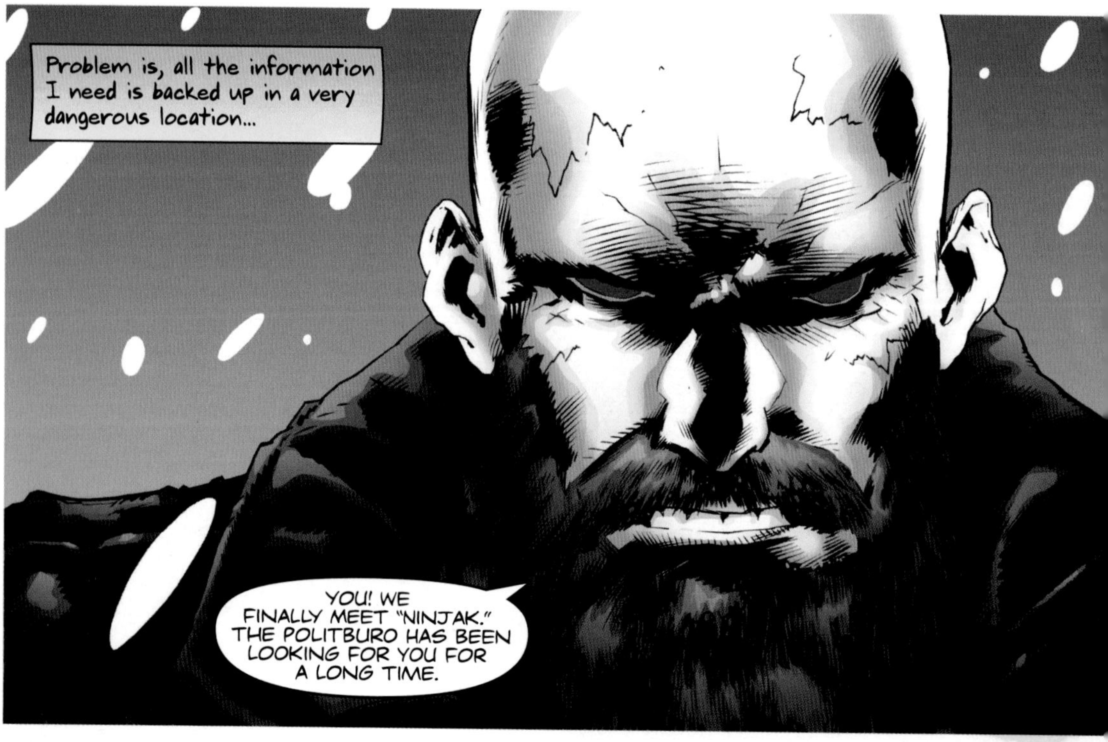
Problem is, all the information I need is backed up in a very dangerous location...
YOU! WE FINALLY MEET "NINJAK." THE POLITBURO HAS BEEN LOOKING FOR YOU FOR A LONG TIME.

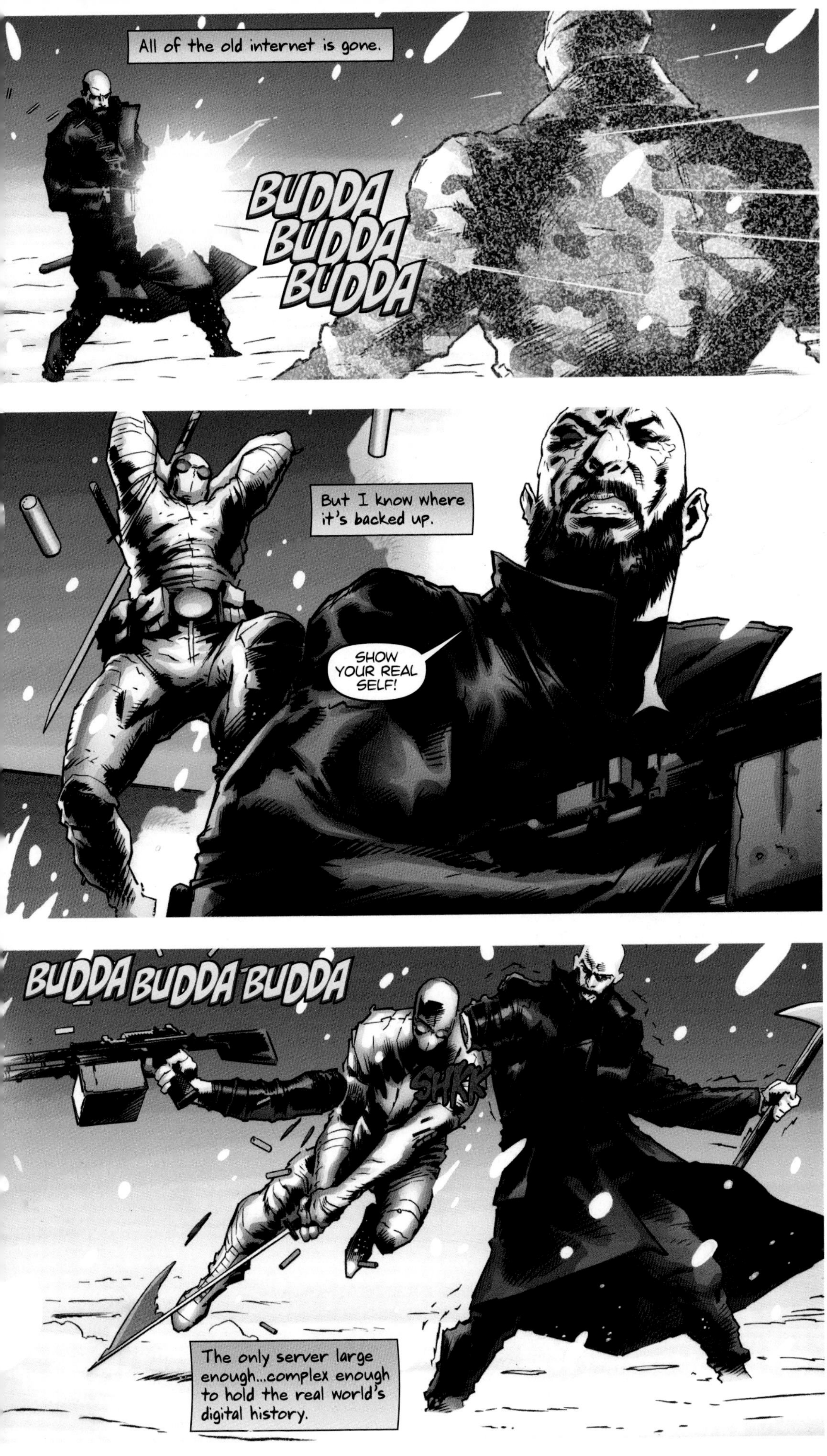
All of the old internet is gone.
BUDDA BUDDA BUDDA
But I know where it's backed up.
SHOW YOUR REAL SELF!
BUDDA BUDDA BUDDA
SHKK
The only server large enough...complex enough to hold the real world's digital history.

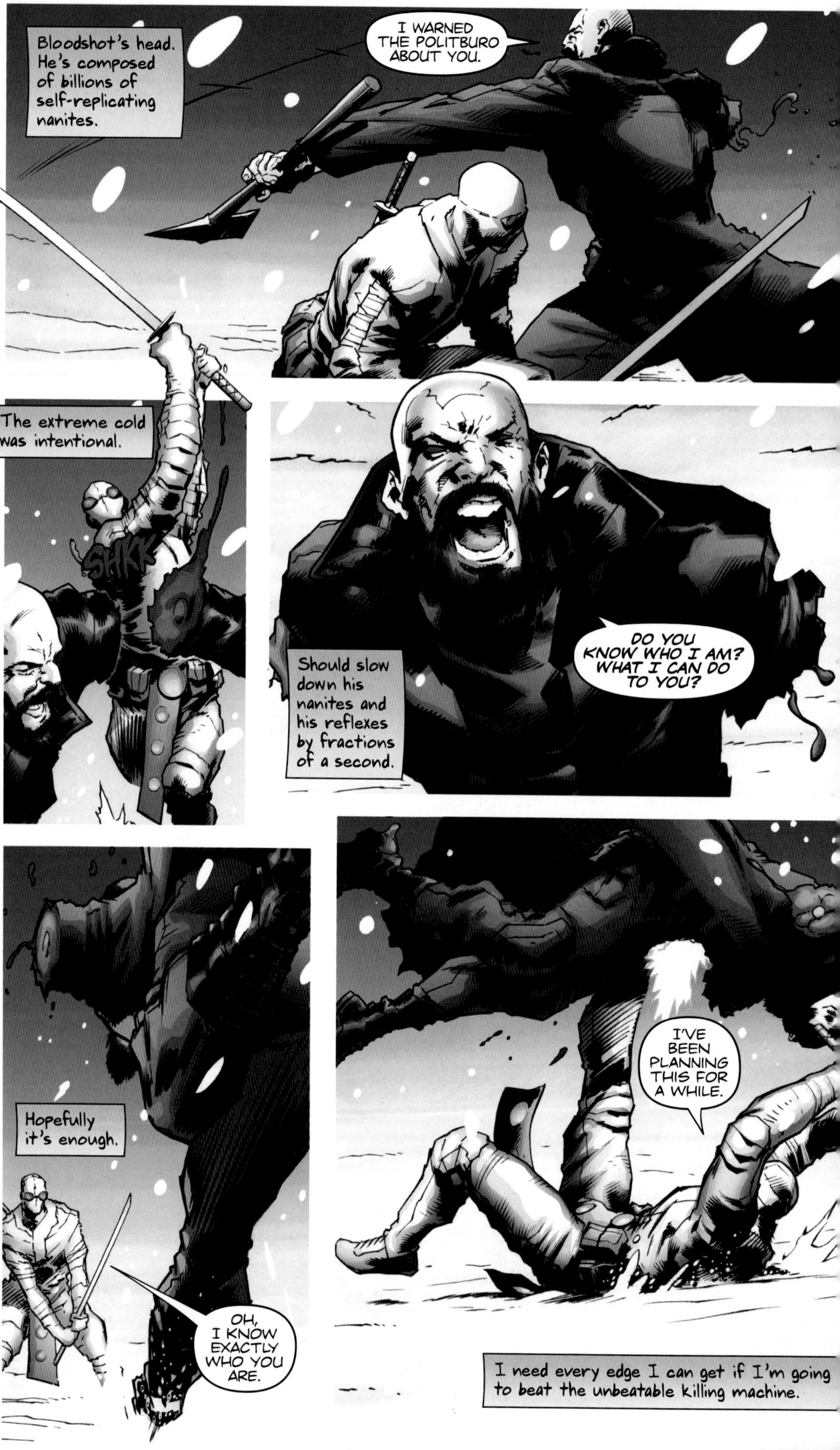
Bloodshot's head. He's composed of billions of self-replicating nanites.
I WARNED THE POLITBURO ABOUT YOU.
The extreme cold was intentional.
SHKK
Should slow down his nanites and his reflexes by fractions of a second.
DO YOU KNOW WHO I AM? WHAT I CAN DO TO YOU?
Hopefully it's enough.
OH, I KNOW EXACTLY WHO YOU ARE.
I'VE BEEN PLANNING THIS FOR A WHILE.
I need every edge I can get if I'm going to beat the unbeatable killing machine.

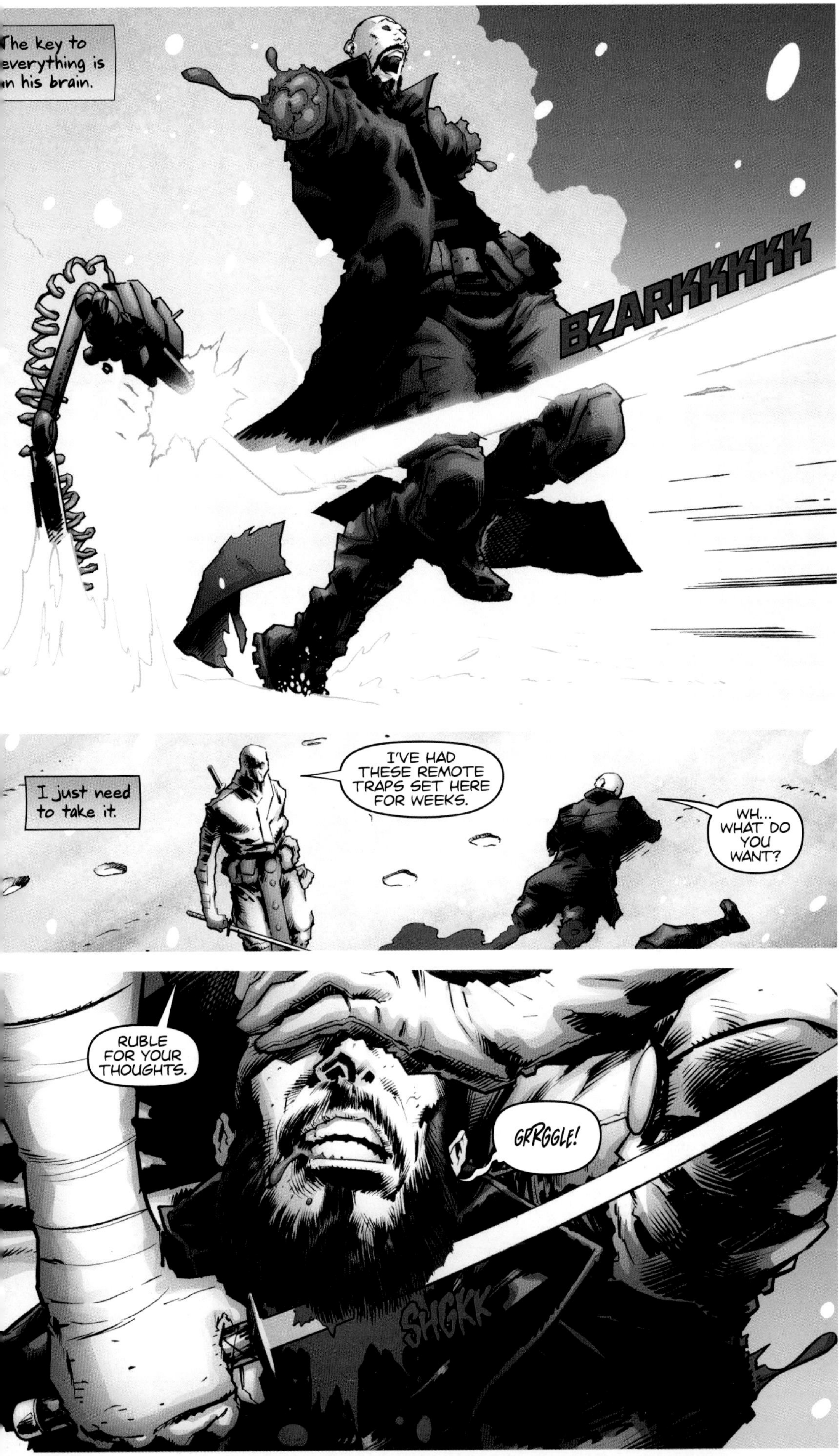
The key to everything is in his brain.
BZARKKKKK
I just need to take it.
I'VE HAD THESE REMOTE TRAPS SET HERE FOR WEEKS.
WH... WHAT DO YOU WANT?
RUBLE FOR YOUR THOUGHTS.
GRRGGLE!
SHGKK

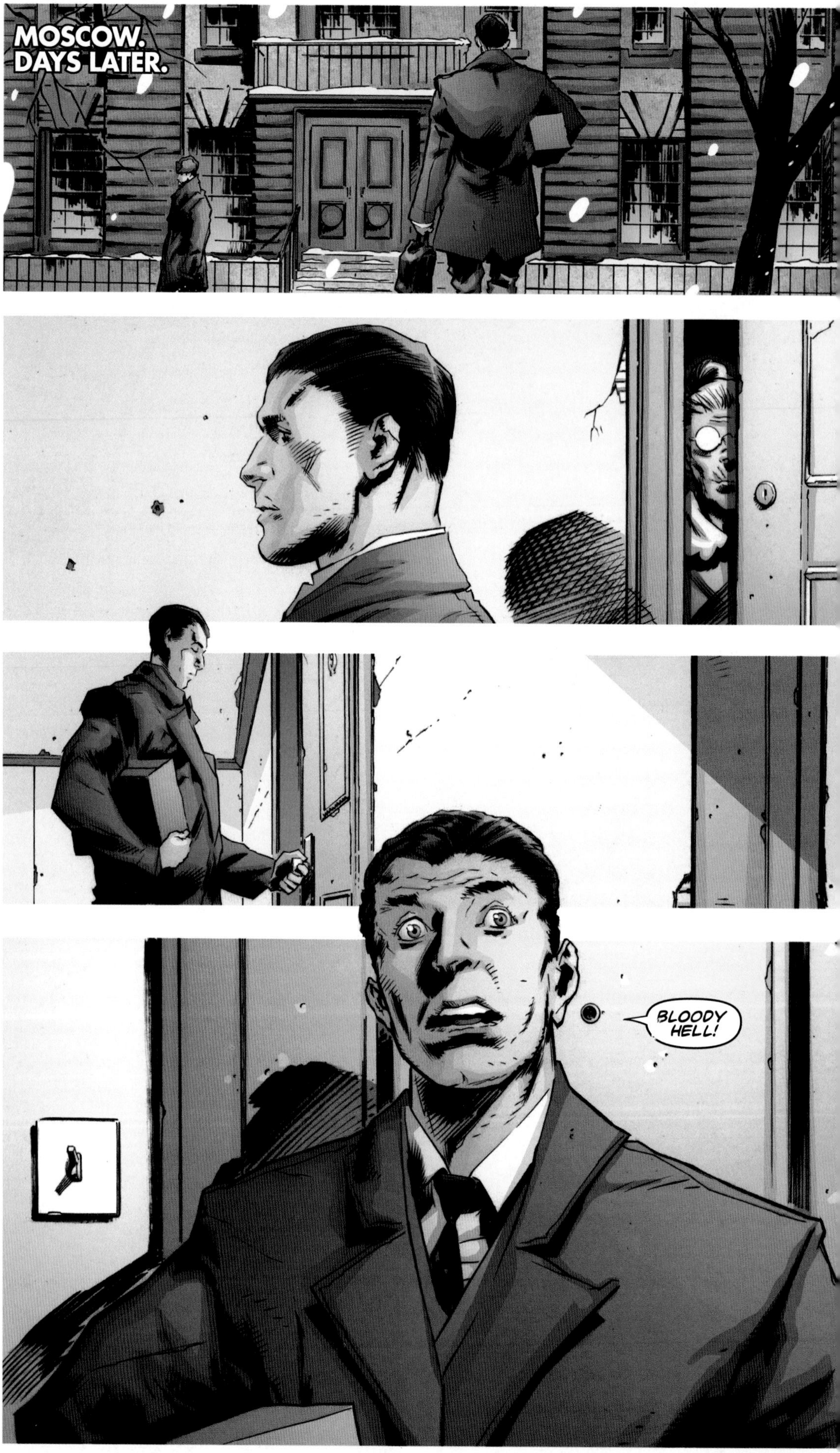
MOSCOW.
DAYS LATER.
BLOODY HELL!

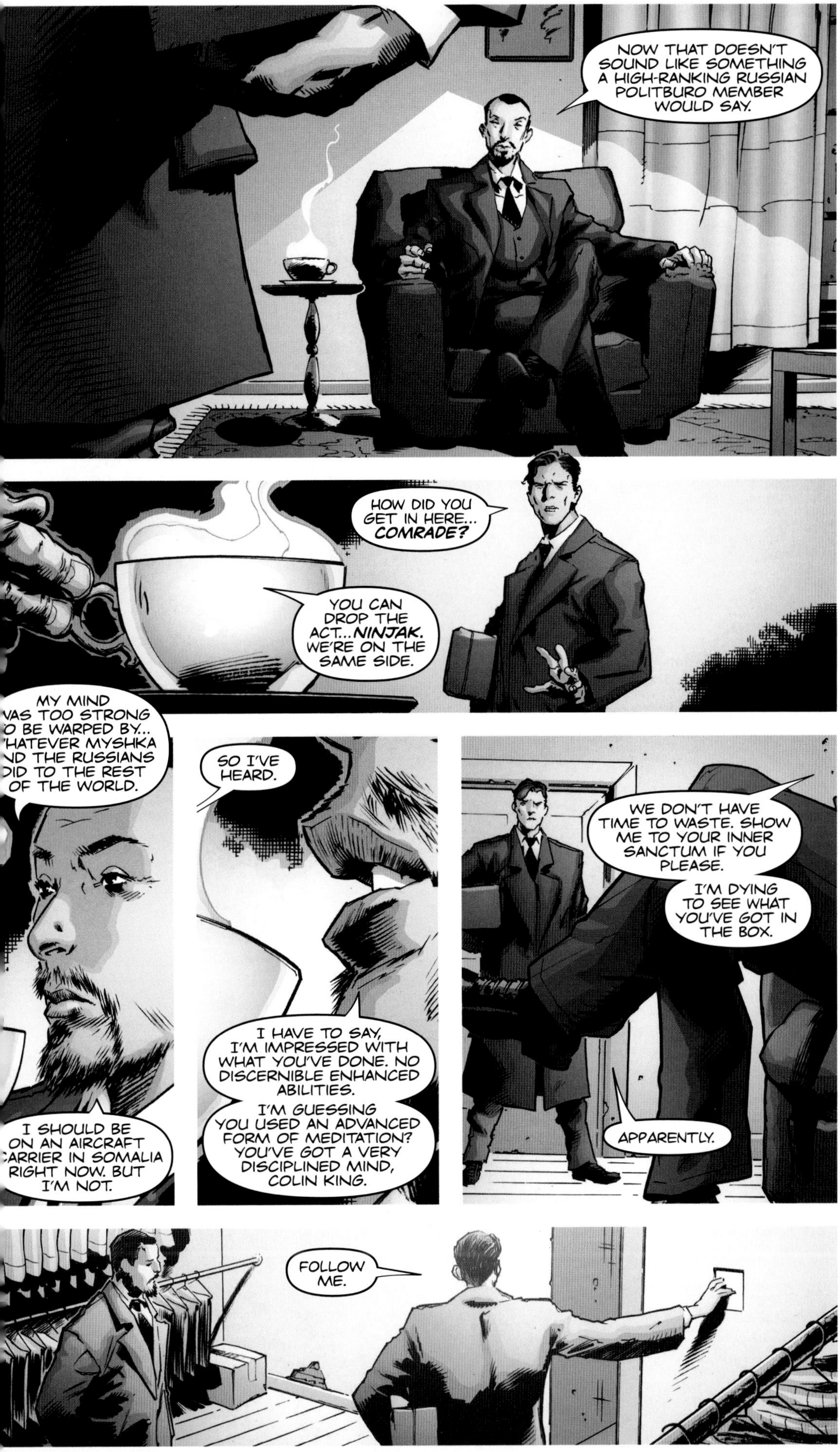
NOW THAT DOESN'T SOUND LIKE SOMETHING A HIGH-RANKING RUSSIAN POLITBURO MEMBER WOULD SAY.
HOW DID YOU GET IN HERE... COMRADE?
YOU CAN DROP THE ACT... NINJAK. WE'RE ON THE SAME SIDE.
MY MIND WAS TOO STRONG TO BE WARPED BY... WHATEVER MYSHKA AND THE RUSSIANS DID TO THE REST OF THE WORLD.
I SHOULD BE ON AN AIRCRAFT CARRIER IN SOMALIA RIGHT NOW. BUT I'M NOT.
SO I'VE HEARD.
I HAVE TO SAY, I'M IMPRESSED WITH WHAT YOU'VE DONE. NO DISCERNIBLE ENHANCED ABILITIES.
I'M GUESSING YOU USED AN ADVANCED FORM OF MEDITATION? YOU'VE GOT A VERY DISCIPLINED MIND, COLIN KING.
WE DON'T HAVE TIME TO WASTE. SHOW ME TO YOUR INNER SANCTUM IF YOU PLEASE.
I'M DYING TO SEE WHAT YOU'VE GOT IN THE BOX.
APPARENTLY.
FOLLOW ME.

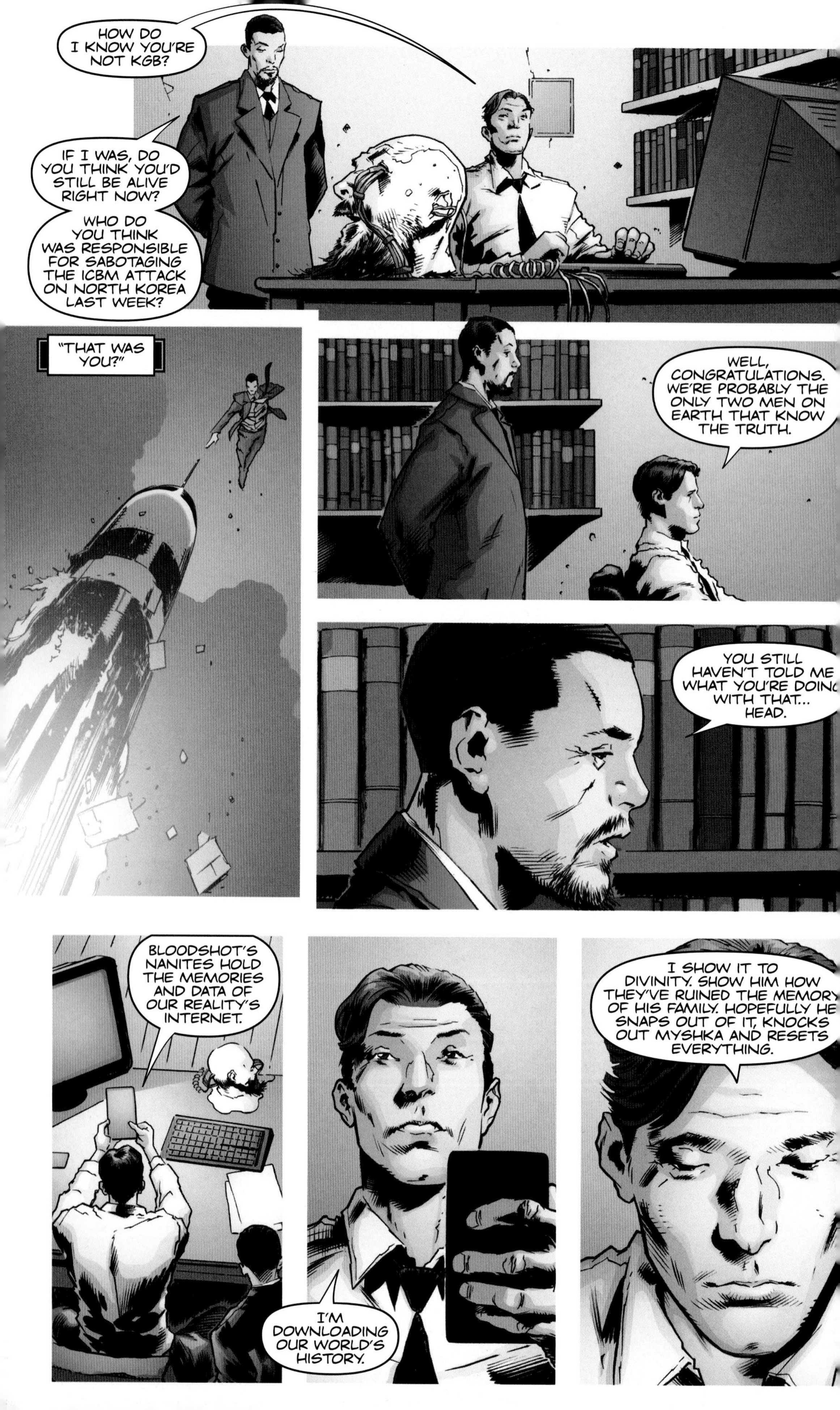
HOW DO I KNOW YOU'RE NOT KGB?
IF I WAS, DO YOU THINK YOU'D STILL BE ALIVE RIGHT NOW?
WHO DO YOU THINK WAS RESPONSIBLE FOR SABOTAGING THE ICBM ATTACK ON NORTH KOREA LAST WEEK?
"THAT WAS YOU?"
WELL, CONGRATULATIONS. WE'RE PROBABLY THE ONLY TWO MEN ON EARTH THAT KNOW THE TRUTH.
YOU STILL HAVEN'T TOLD ME WHAT YOU'RE DOIN WITH THAT... HEAD.
BLOODSHOT'S NANITES HOLD THE MEMORIES AND DATA OF OUR REALITY'S INTERNET.
I'M DOWNLOADING OUR WORLD'S HISTORY.
I SHOW IT TO DIVINITY. SHOW HIM HOW THEY'VE RUINED THE MEMORY OF HIS FAMILY. HOPEFULLY HE SNAPS OUT OF IT, KNOCKS OUT MYSHKA AND RESETS EVERYTHING.

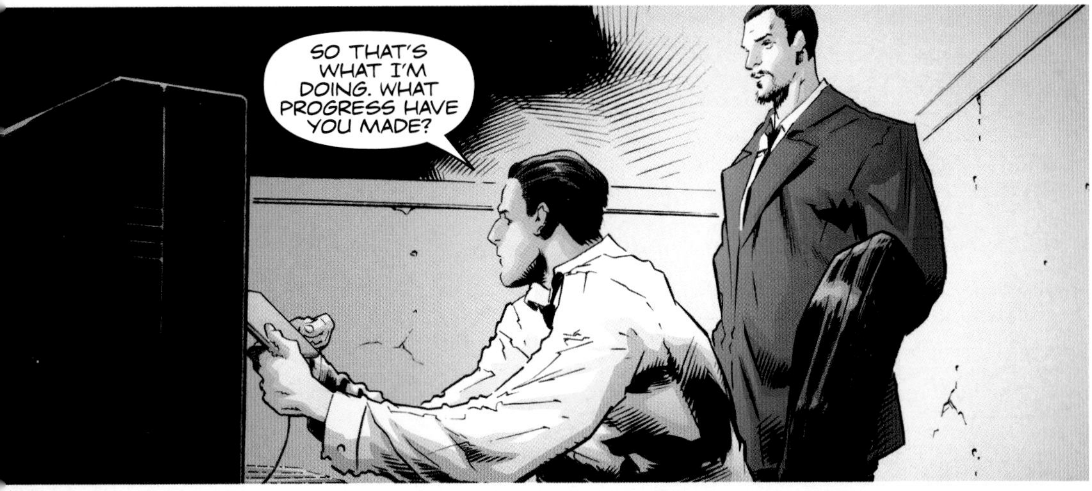
SO THAT'S WHAT I'M DOING. WHAT PROGRESS HAVE YOU MADE?

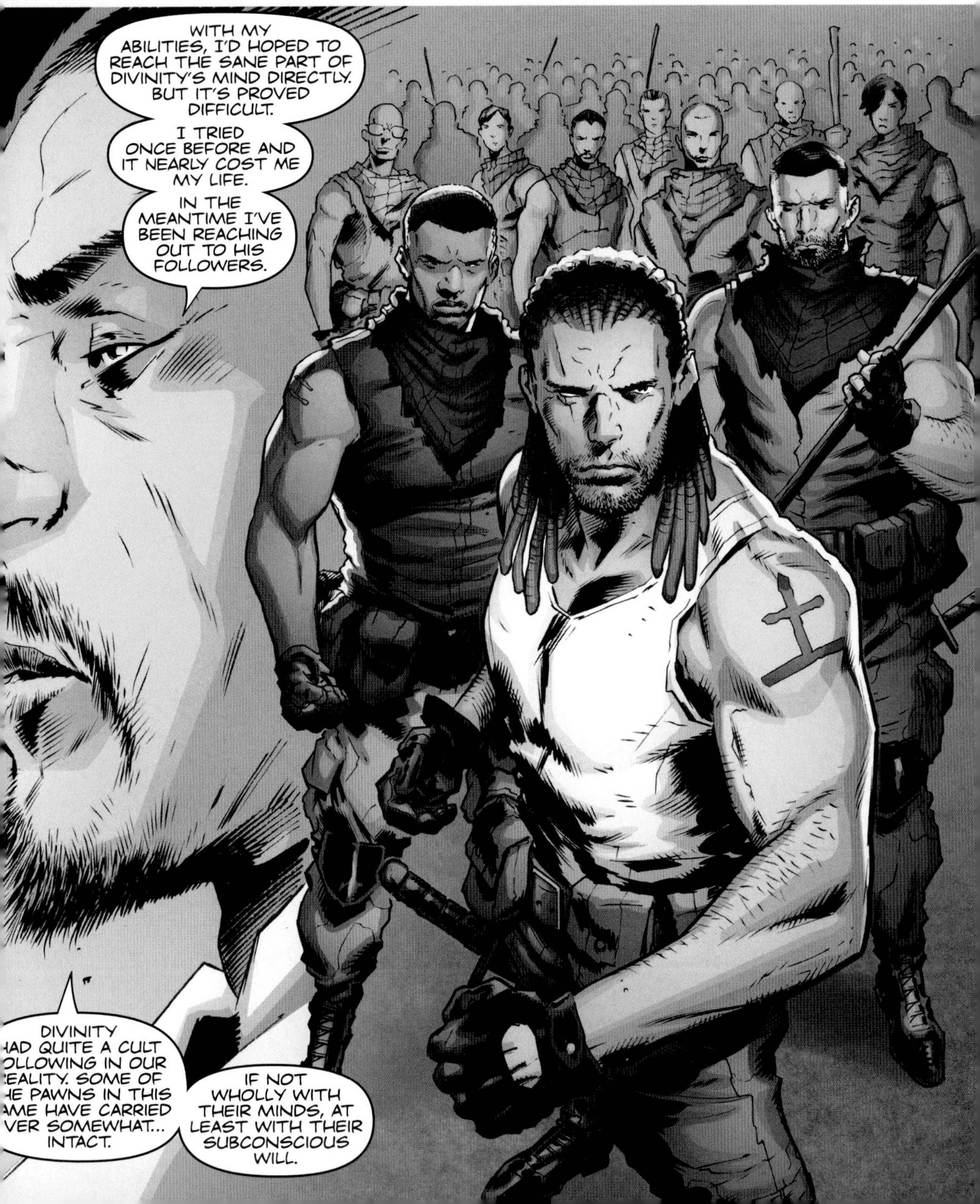
WITH MY ABILITIES, I'D HOPED TO REACH THE SANE PART OF DIVINITY'S MIND DIRECTLY. BUT IT'S PROVED DIFFICULT.
I TRIED ONCE BEFORE AND IT NEARLY COST ME MY LIFE.
IN THE MEANTIME I'VE BEEN REACHING OUT TO HIS FOLLOWERS.
DIVINITY HAD QUITE A CULT FOLLOWING IN OUR REALITY. SOME OF THE PAWNS IN THIS GAME HAVE CARRIED OVER SOMEWHAT... INTACT.
IF NOT WHOLLY WITH THEIR MINDS, AT LEAST WITH THEIR SUBCONSCIOUS WILL.

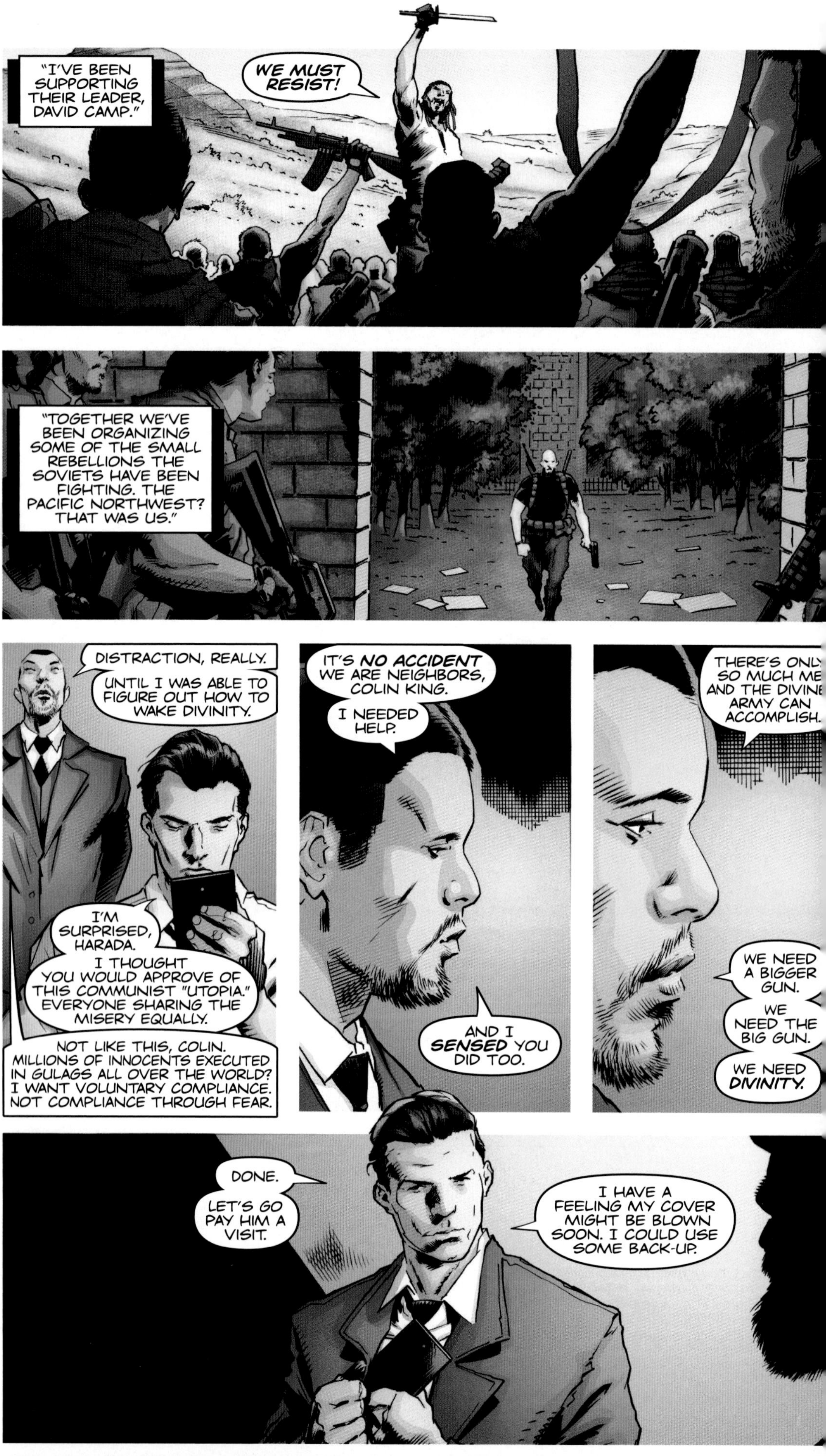
"I'VE BEEN SUPPORTING THEIR LEADER, DAVID CAMP."
WE MUST RESIST!
"TOGETHER WE'VE BEEN ORGANIZING SOME OF THE SMALL REBELLIONS THE SOVIETS HAVE BEEN FIGHTING. THE PACIFIC NORTHWEST? THAT WAS US."
DISTRACTION, REALLY.
UNTIL I WAS ABLE TO FIGURE OUT HOW TO WAKE DIVINITY.
I'M SURPRISED, HARADA.
I THOUGHT YOU WOULD APPROVE OF THIS COMMUNIST "UTOPIA." EVERYONE SHARING THE MISERY EQUALLY.
NOT LIKE THIS, COLIN. MILLIONS OF INNOCENTS EXECUTED IN GULAGS ALL OVER THE WORLD? I WANT VOLUNTARY COMPLIANCE. NOT COMPLIANCE THROUGH FEAR.
IT'S NO ACCIDENT WE ARE NEIGHBORS, COLIN KING.
I NEEDED HELP.
AND I SENSED YOU DID TOO.
THERE'S ONLY SO MUCH ME AND THE DIVINE ARMY CAN ACCOMPLISH.
WE NEED A BIGGER GUN.
WE NEED THE BIG GUN.
WE NEED DIVINITY.
DONE.
LET'S GO PAY HIM A VISIT.
I HAVE A FEELING MY COVER MIGHT BE BLOWN SOON. I COULD USE SOME BACK-UP.

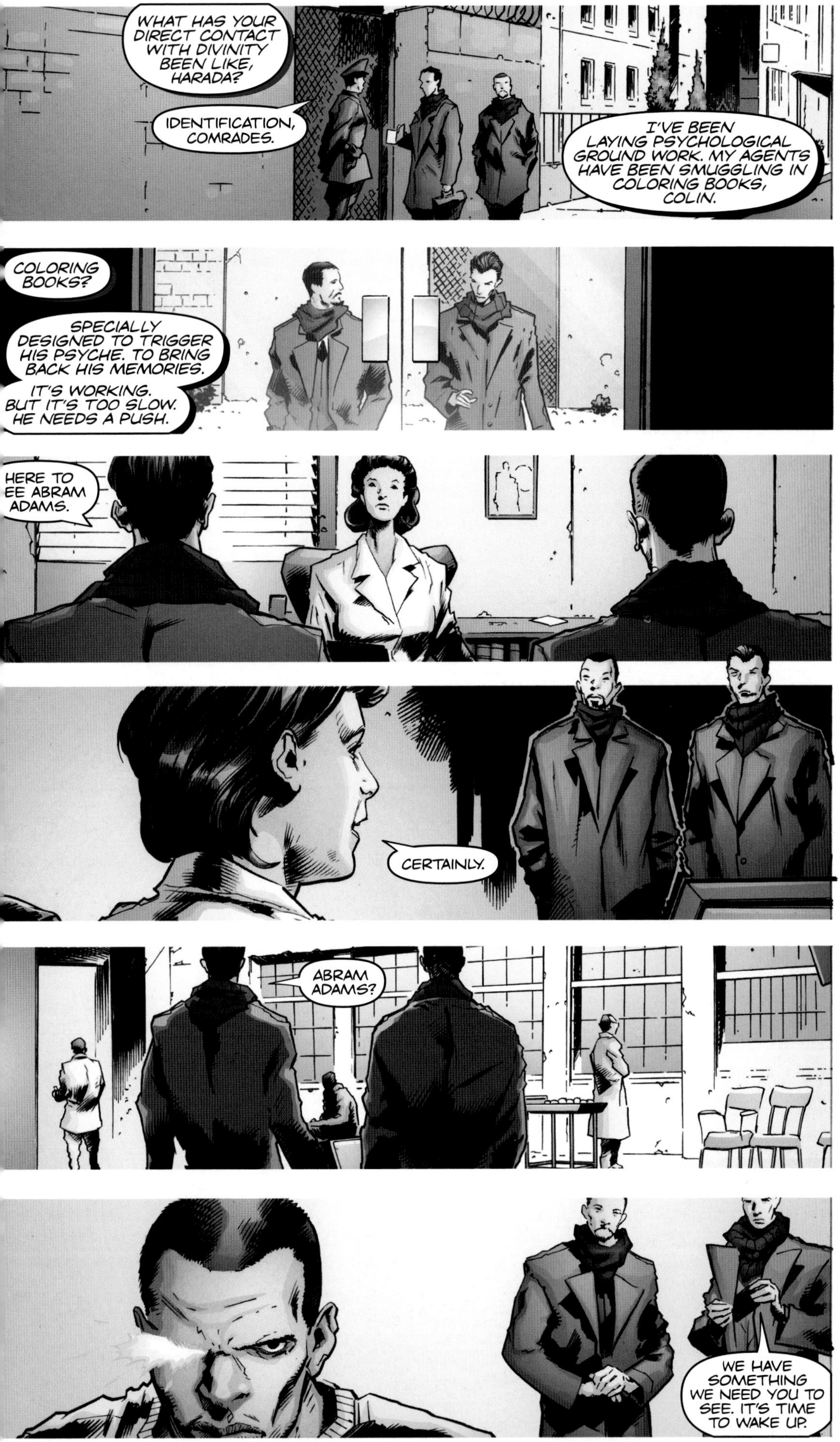
WHAT HAS YOUR DIRECT CONTACT WITH DIVINITY BEEN LIKE, HARADA?
IDENTIFICATION, COMRADES.
I'VE BEEN LAYING PSYCHOLOGICAL GROUND WORK. MY AGENTS HAVE BEEN SMUGGLING IN COLORING BOOKS, COLIN.
COLORING BOOKS?
SPECIALLY DESIGNED TO TRIGGER HIS PSYCHE. TO BRING BACK HIS MEMORIES.
IT'S WORKING. BUT IT'S TOO SLOW. HE NEEDS A PUSH.
HERE TO EE ABRAM ADAMS.
CERTAINLY.
ABRAM ADAMS?
WE HAVE SOMETHING WE NEED YOU TO SEE. IT'S TIME TO WAKE UP.

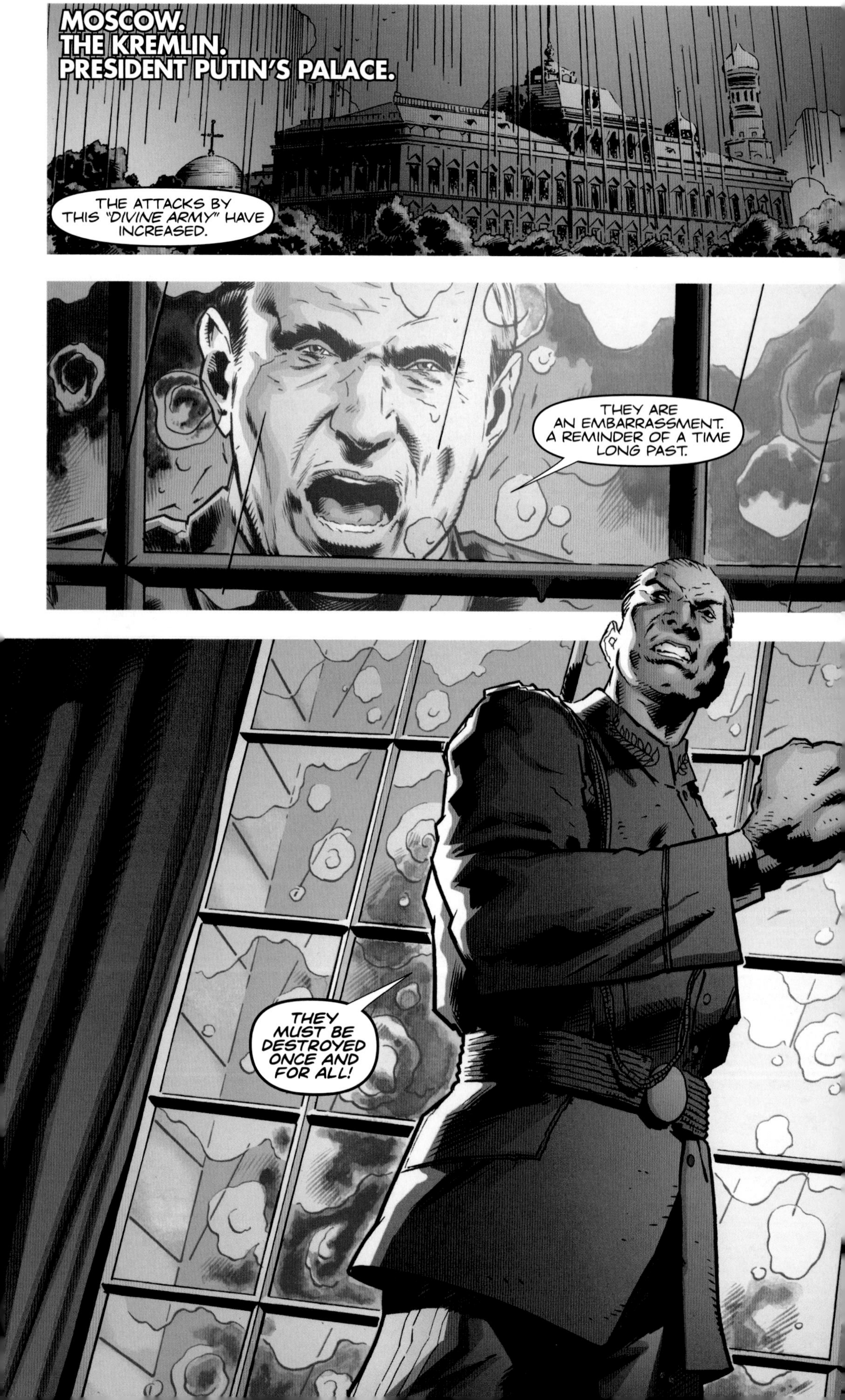
MOSCOW.
THE KREMLIN.
PRESIDENT PUTIN'S PALACE.
THE ATTACKS BY THIS "DIVINE ARMY" HAVE INCREASED.
THEY ARE AN EMBARRASSMENT. A REMINDER OF A TIME LONG PAST.
THEY MUST BE DESTROYED ONCE AND FOR ALL!

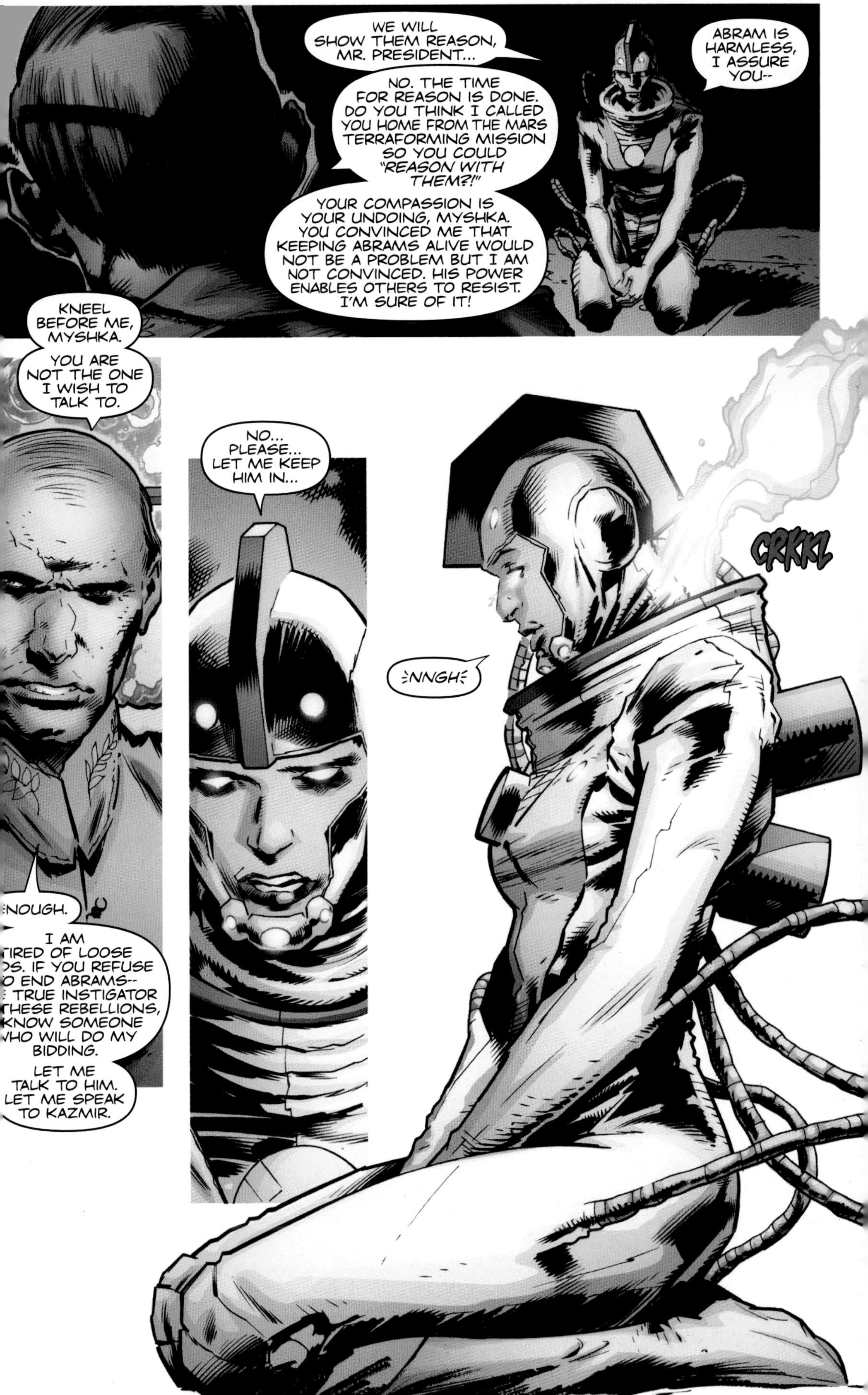

WE WILL SHOW THEM REASON, MR. PRESIDENT...
ABRAM IS HARMLESS, I ASSURE YOU--
NO. THE TIME FOR REASON IS DONE. DO YOU THINK I CALLED YOU HOME FROM THE MARS TERRAFORMING MISSION SO YOU COULD "REASON WITH THEM?!"
YOUR COMPASSION IS YOUR UNDOING, MYSHKA. YOU CONVINCED ME THAT KEEPING ABRAMS ALIVE WOULD NOT BE A PROBLEM BUT I AM NOT CONVINCED. HIS POWER ENABLES OTHERS TO RESIST. I'M SURE OF IT!
KNEEL BEFORE ME, MYSHKA.
YOU ARE NOT THE ONE I WISH TO TALK TO.
NO... PLEASE... LET ME KEEP HIM IN...
CRKKL
NNGH
ENOUGH.
I AM TIRED OF LOOSE DS. IF YOU REFUSE O END ABRAMS-- TRUE INSTIGATOR THESE REBELLIONS, KNOW SOMEONE WHO WILL DO MY BIDDING.
LET ME TALK TO HIM. LET ME SPEAK TO KAZMIR.

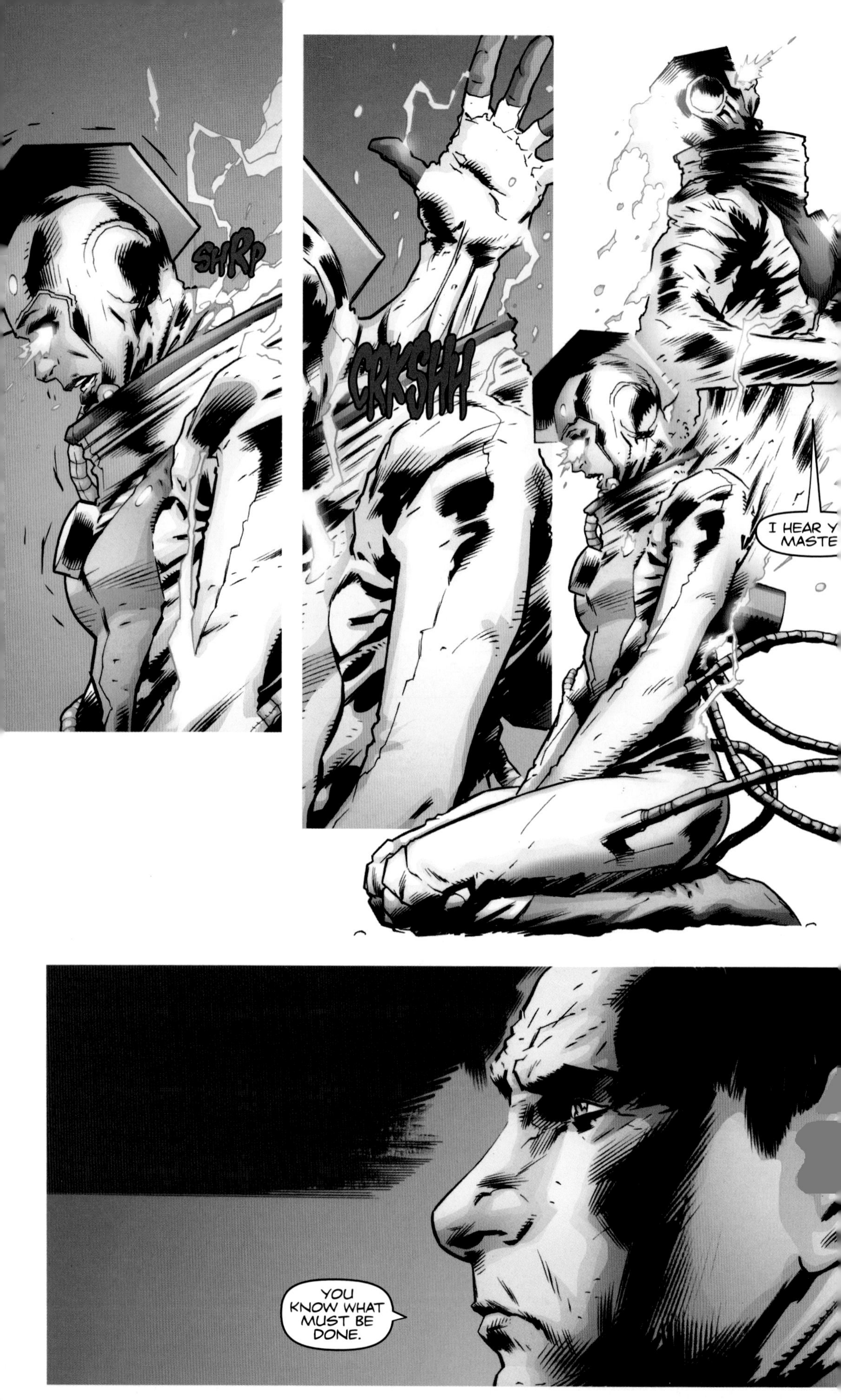
SHRP
CRKSHH
I HEAR Y
MASTE
YOU KNOW WHAT MUST BE DONE.

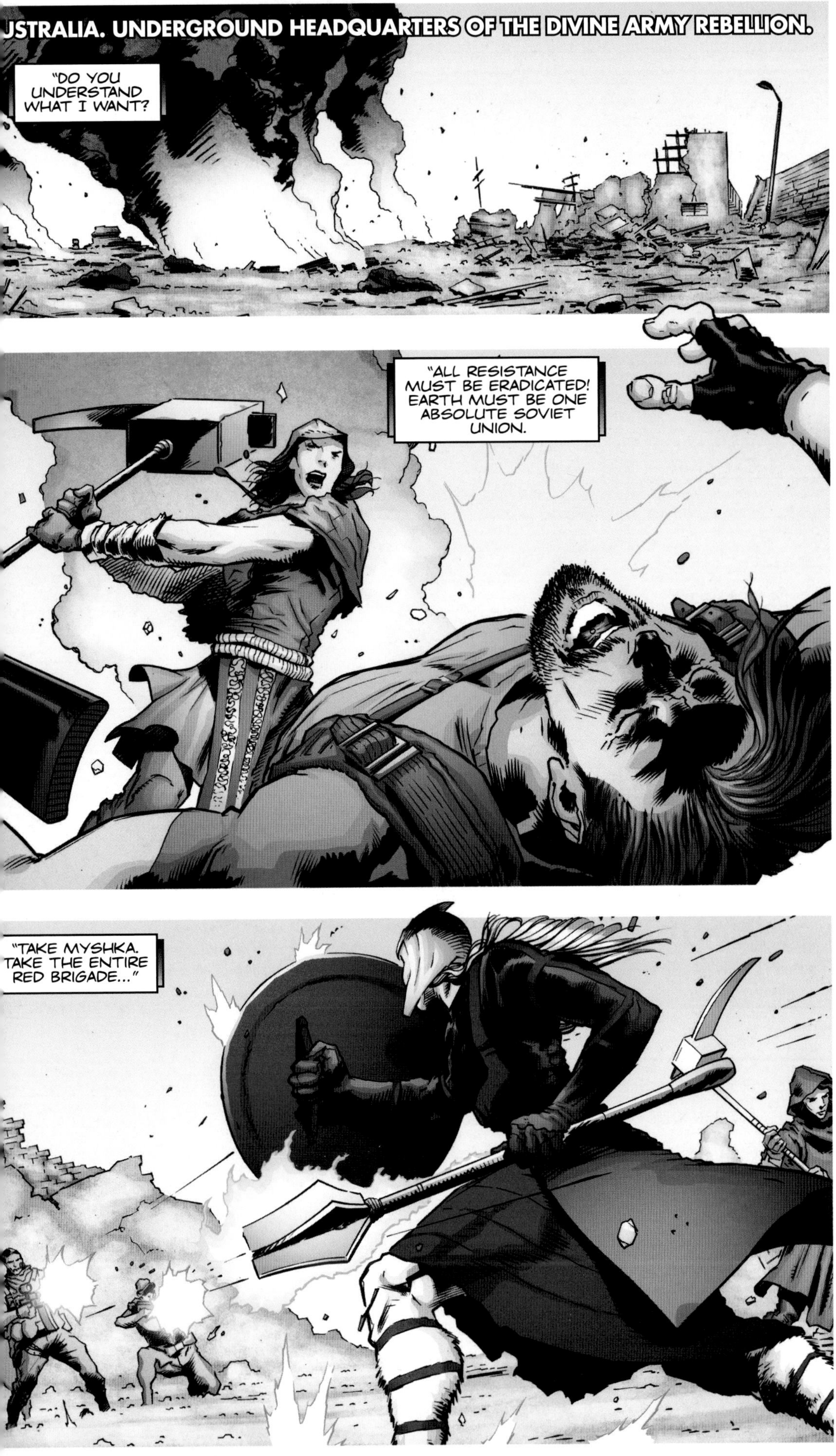
USTRALIA. UNDERGROUND HEADQUARTERS OF THE DIVINE ARMY REBELLION.
"DO YOU UNDERSTAND WHAT I WANT?
"ALL RESISTANCE MUST BE ERADICATED! EARTH MUST BE ONE ABSOLUTE SOVIET UNION.
"TAKE MYSHKA. TAKE THE ENTIRE RED BRIGADE..."

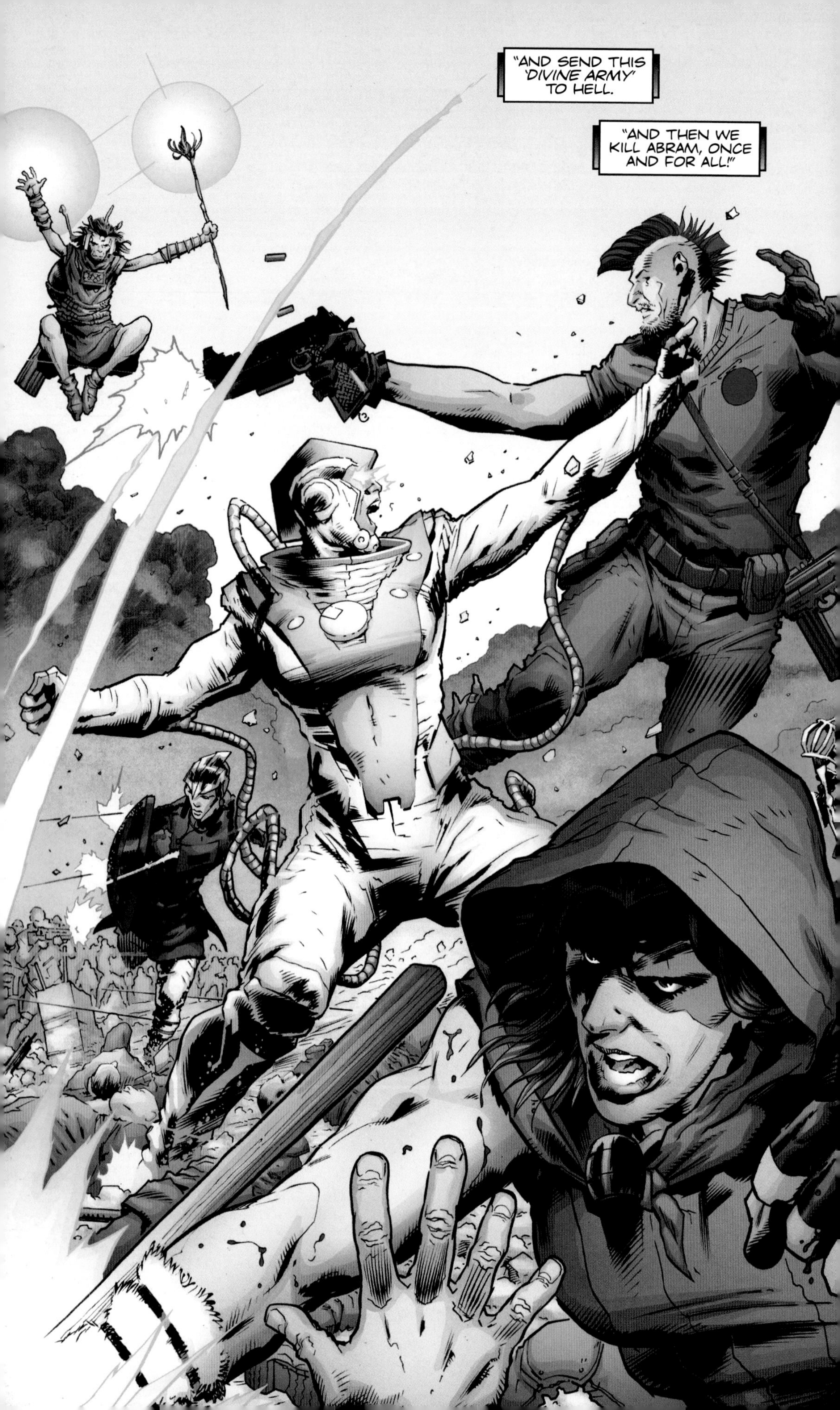
"AND SEND THIS 'DIVINE ARMY' TO HELL.
"AND THEN WE KILL ABRAM, ONCE AND FOR ALL!"

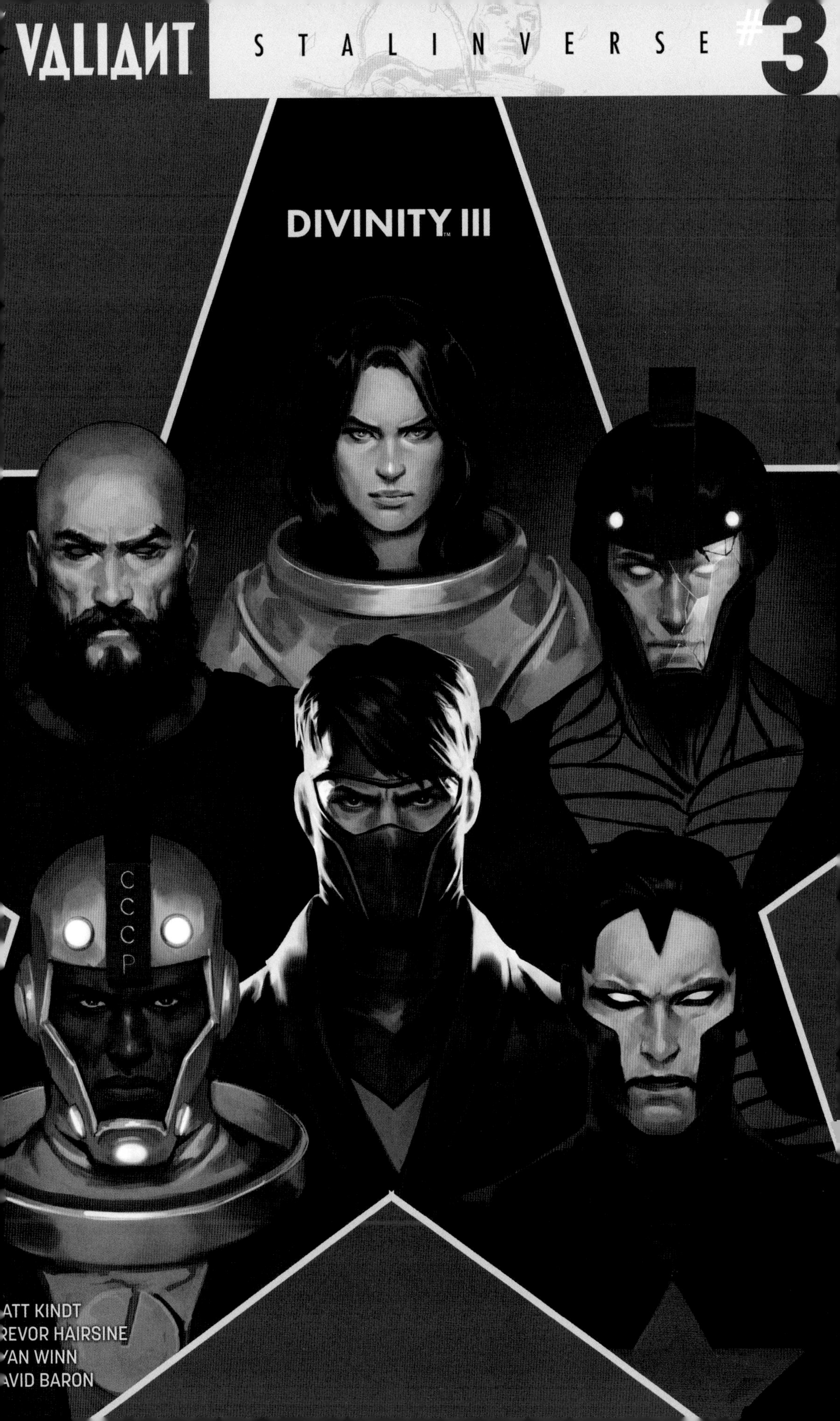
VALIANT
STALINVERSE #3
DIVINITY III
CCCP
ATT KINDT
REVOR HAIRSINE
YAN WINN
AVID BARON

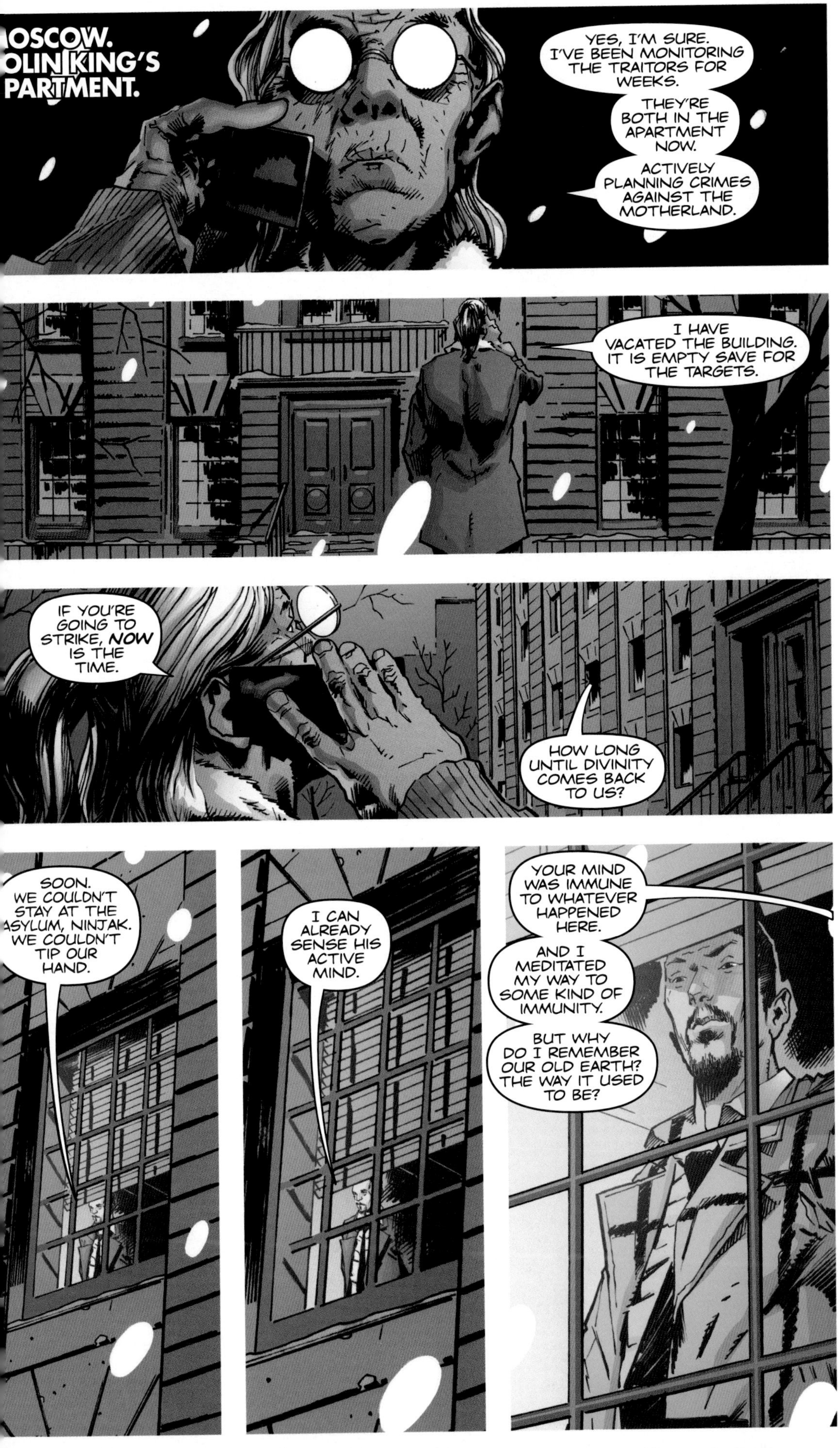
OSCOW. OLINKING'S PARTMENT.
YES, I'M SURE. I'VE BEEN MONITORING THE TRAITORS FOR WEEKS.
THEY'RE BOTH IN THE APARTMENT NOW.
ACTIVELY PLANNING CRIMES AGAINST THE MOTHERLAND.
I HAVE VACATED THE BUILDING. IT IS EMPTY SAVE FOR THE TARGETS.
IF YOU'RE GOING TO STRIKE, NOW IS THE TIME.
HOW LONG UNTIL DIVINITY COMES BACK TO US?
SOON. WE COULDN'T STAY AT THE ASYLUM, NINJAK. WE COULDN'T TIP OUR HAND.
I CAN ALREADY SENSE HIS ACTIVE MIND.
YOUR MIND WAS IMMUNE TO WHATEVER HAPPENED HERE.
AND I MEDITATED MY WAY TO SOME KIND OF IMMUNITY.
BUT WHY DO I REMEMBER OUR OLD EARTH? THE WAY IT USED TO BE?

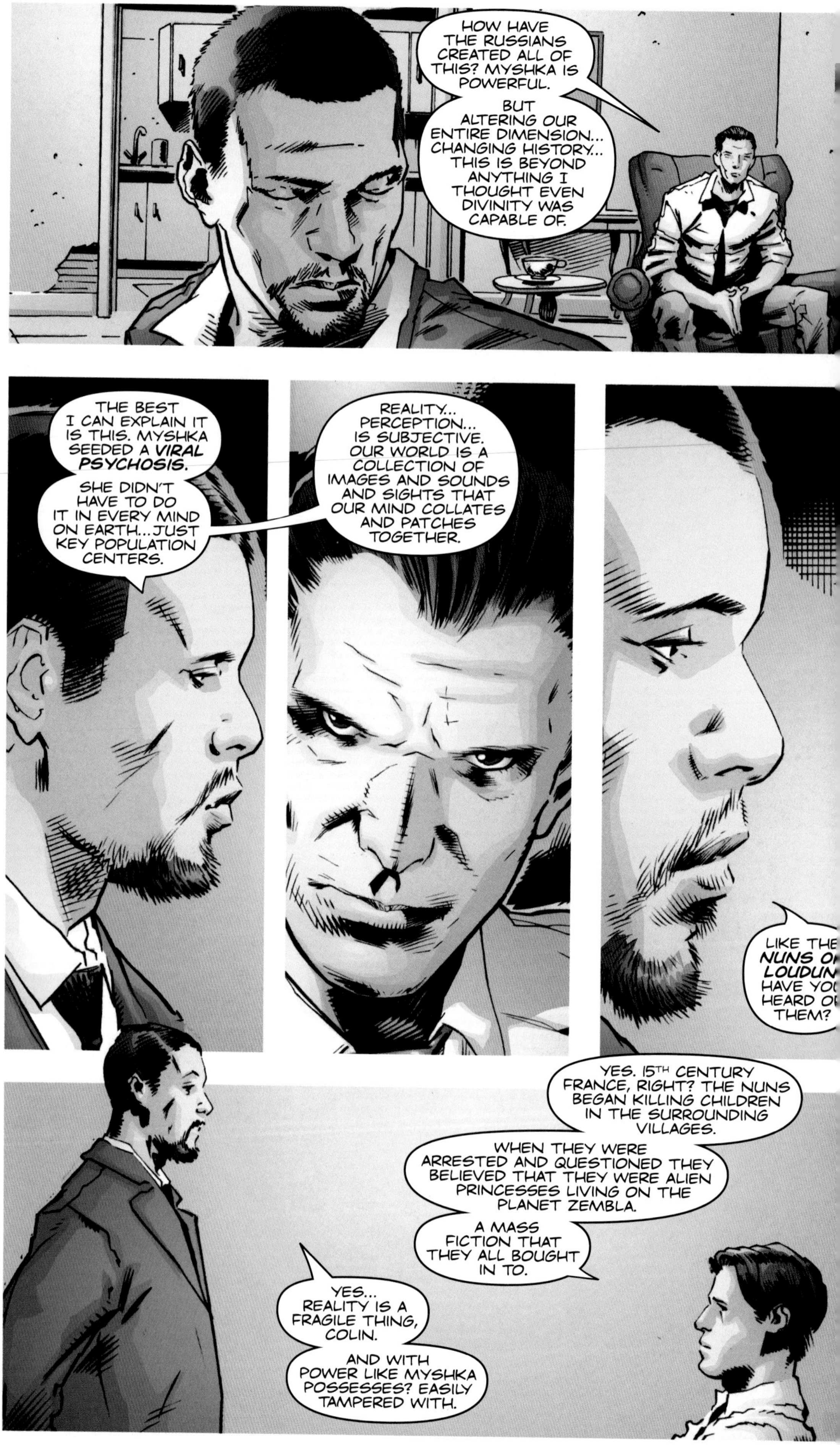
HOW HAVE THE RUSSIANS CREATED ALL OF THIS? MYSHKA IS POWERFUL.
BUT ALTERING OUR ENTIRE DIMENSION... CHANGING HISTORY... THIS IS BEYOND ANYTHING I THOUGHT EVEN DIVINITY WAS CAPABLE OF.
THE BEST I CAN EXPLAIN IT IS THIS. MYSHKA SEEDED A VIRAL PSYCHOSIS.
SHE DIDN'T HAVE TO DO IT IN EVERY MIND ON EARTH...JUST KEY POPULATION CENTERS.
REALITY... PERCEPTION... IS SUBJECTIVE. OUR WORLD IS A COLLECTION OF IMAGES AND SOUNDS AND SIGHTS THAT OUR MIND COLLATES AND PATCHES TOGETHER.
LIKE THE NUNS OF LOUDUN HAVE YOU HEARD OF THEM?
YES. 15TH CENTURY FRANCE, RIGHT? THE NUNS BEGAN KILLING CHILDREN IN THE SURROUNDING VILLAGES.
WHEN THEY WERE ARRESTED AND QUESTIONED THEY BELIEVED THAT THEY WERE ALIEN PRINCESSES LIVING ON THE PLANET ZEMBLA.
A MASS FICTION THAT THEY ALL BOUGHT IN TO.
YES... REALITY IS A FRAGILE THING, COLIN.
AND WITH POWER LIKE MYSHKA POSSESSES? EASILY TAMPERED WITH.

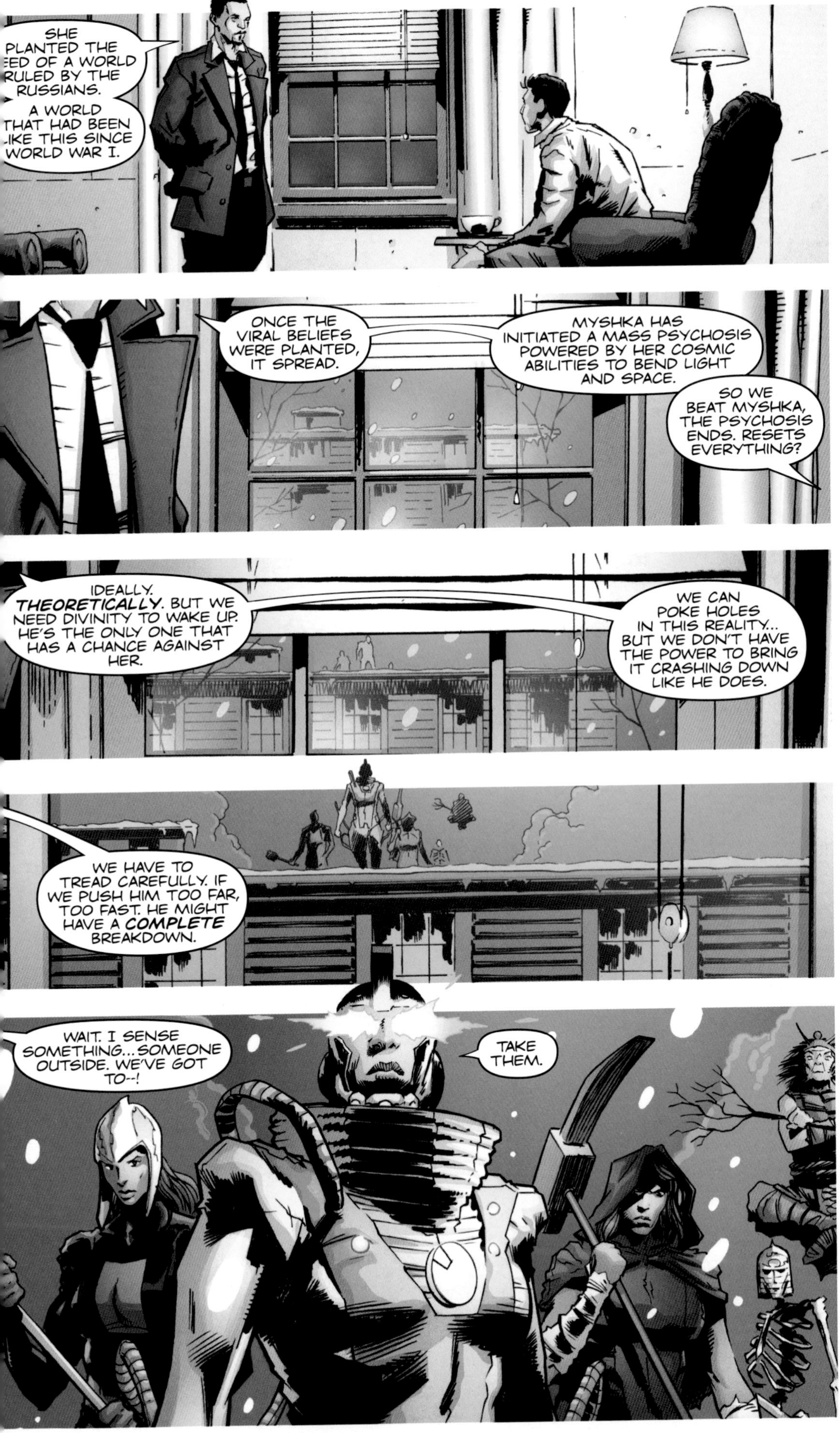
SHE PLANTED THE EED OF A WORLD RULED BY THE RUSSIANS.
A WORLD THAT HAD BEEN IKE THIS SINCE WORLD WAR I.
ONCE THE VIRAL BELIEFS WERE PLANTED, IT SPREAD.
MYSHKA HAS INITIATED A MASS PSYCHOSIS POWERED BY HER COSMIC ABILITIES TO BEND LIGHT AND SPACE.
SO WE BEAT MYSHKA, THE PSYCHOSIS ENDS. RESETS EVERYTHING?
IDEALLY. THEORETICALLY. BUT WE NEED DIVINITY TO WAKE UP. HE'S THE ONLY ONE THAT HAS A CHANCE AGAINST HER.
WE CAN POKE HOLES IN THIS REALITY... BUT WE DON'T HAVE THE POWER TO BRING IT CRASHING DOWN LIKE HE DOES.
WE HAVE TO TREAD CAREFULLY. IF WE PUSH HIM TOO FAR, TOO FAST. HE MIGHT HAVE A COMPLETE BREAKDOWN.
WAIT. I SENSE SOMETHING... SOMEONE OUTSIDE. WE'VE GOT TO--!
TAKE THEM.

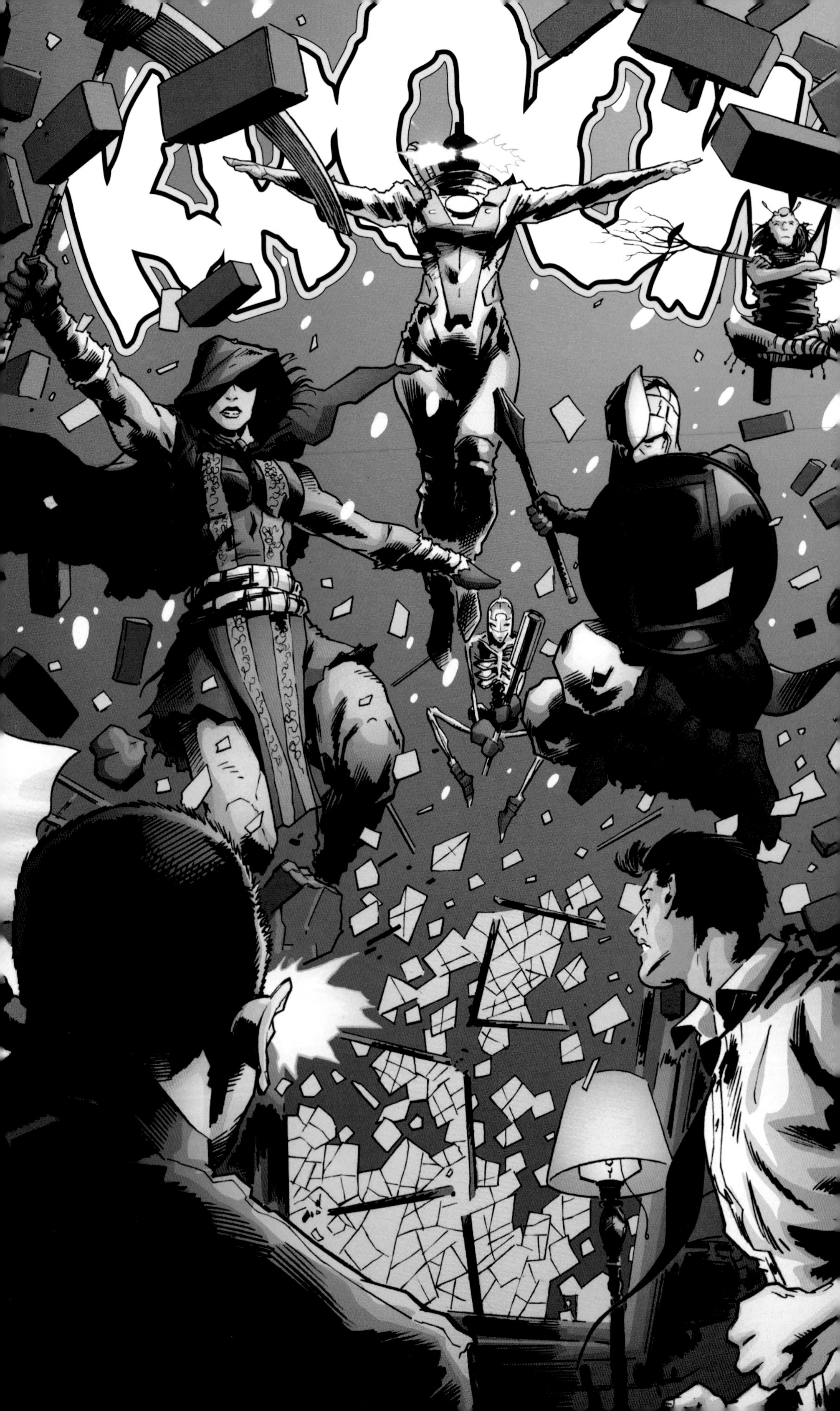

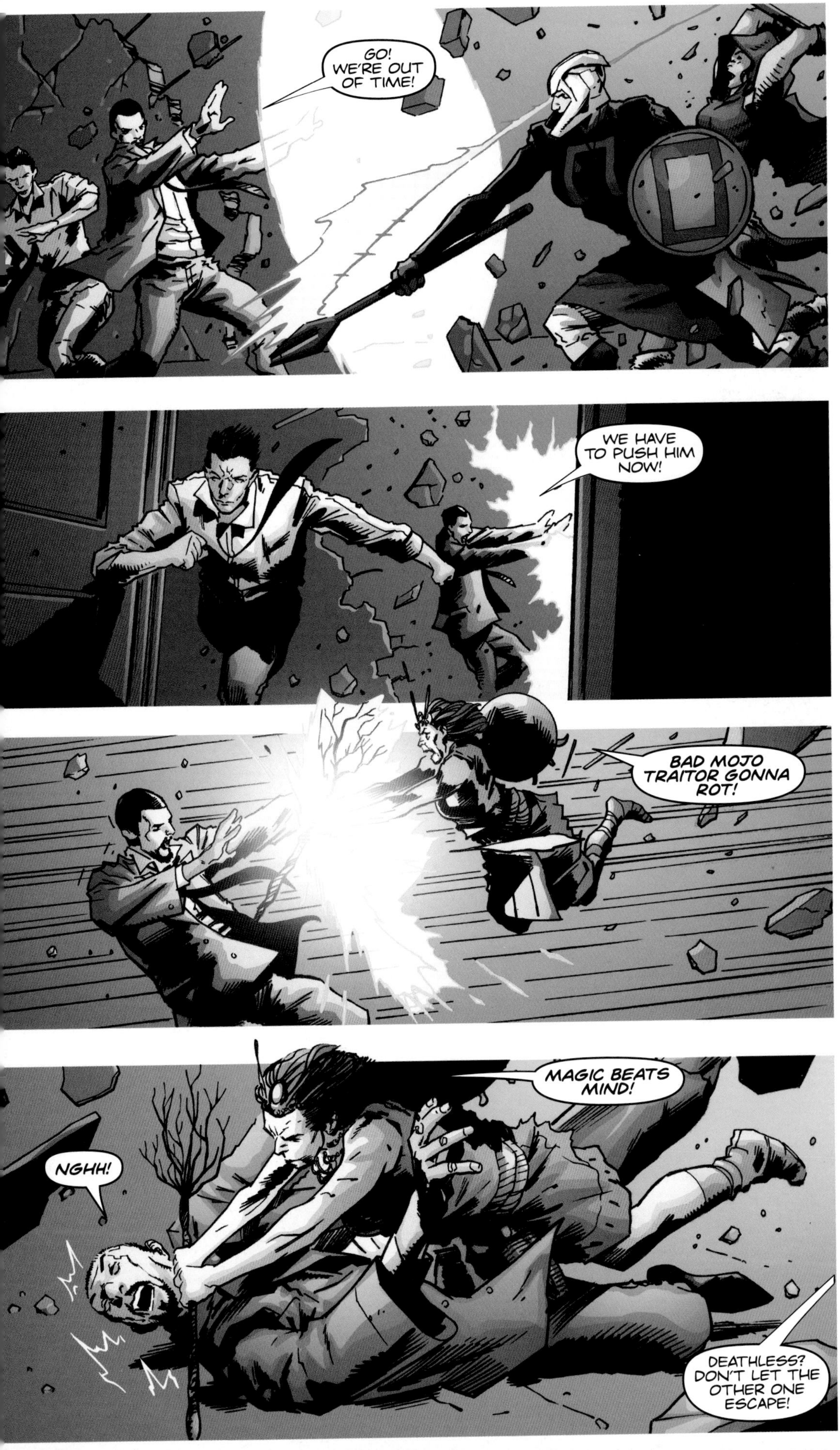
GO! WE'RE OUT OF TIME!
WE HAVE TO PUSH HIM NOW!
BAD MOJO TRAITOR GONNA ROT!
MAGIC BEATS MIND!
NGHH!
DEATHLESS? DON'T LET THE OTHER ONE ESCAPE!

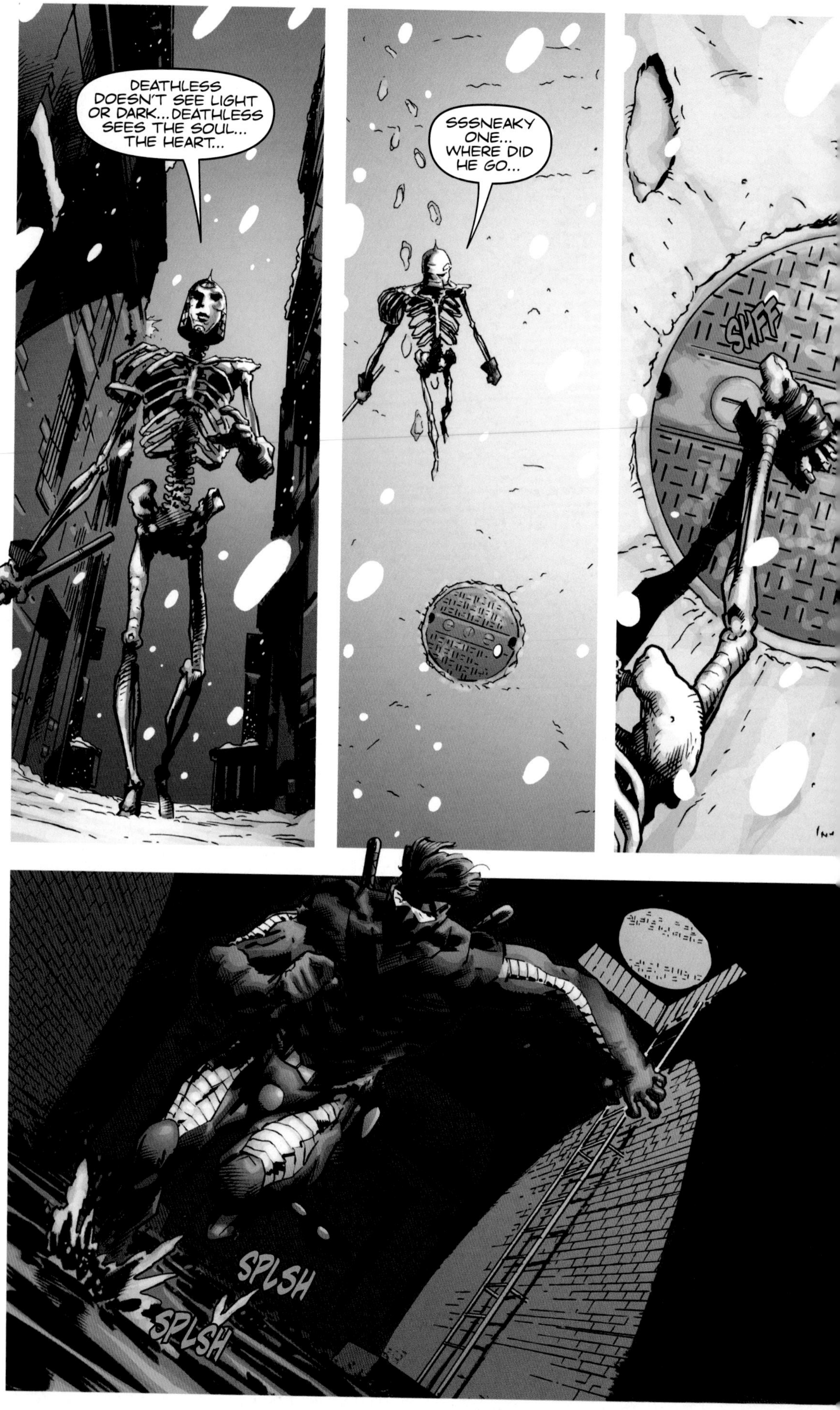
DEATHLESS DOESN'T SEE LIGHT OR DARK...DEATHLESS SEES THE SOUL... THE HEART...
SSSNEAKY ONE... WHERE DID HE GO...
SHFF
SPLSH
SPLSH

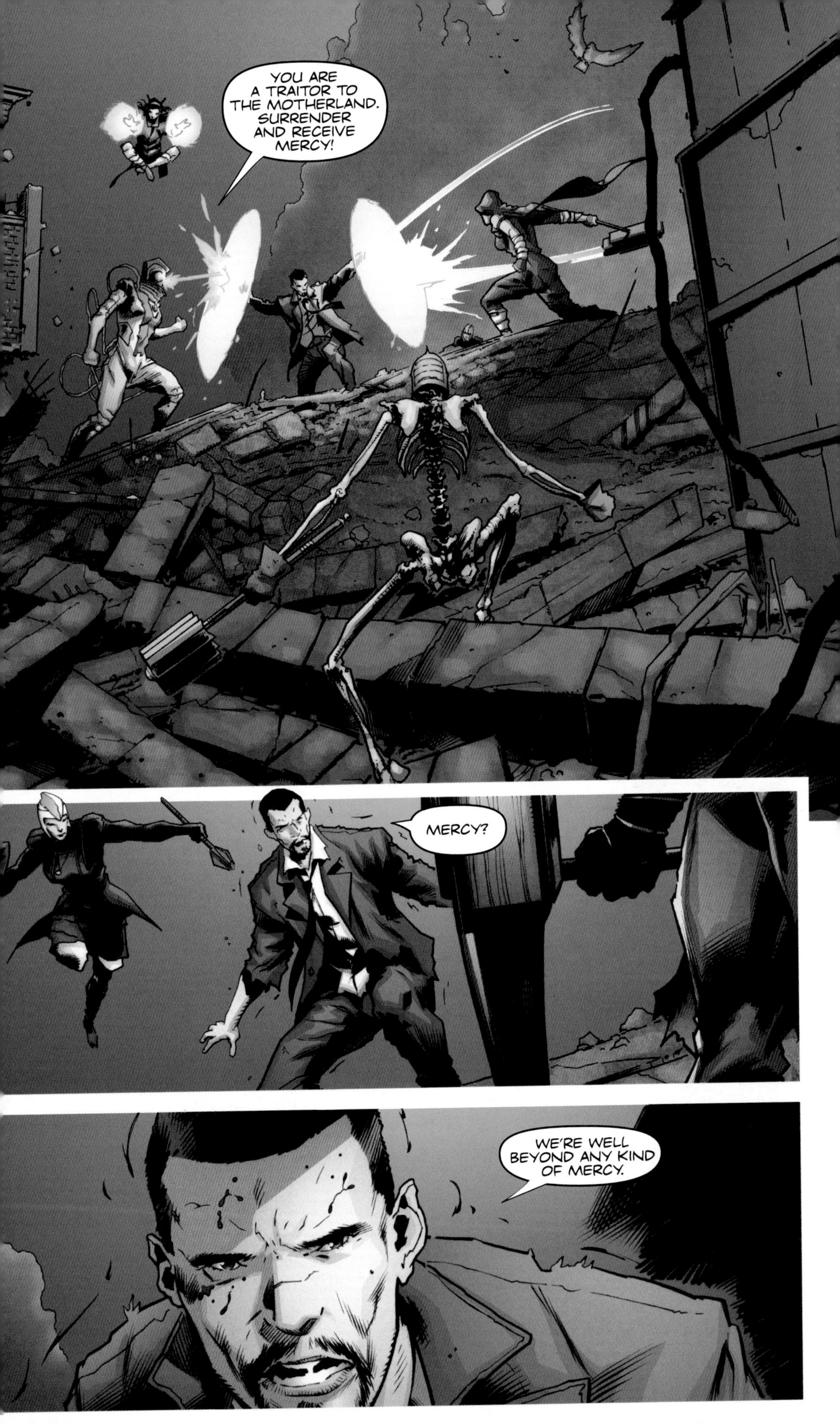

YOU ARE A TRAITOR TO THE MOTHERLAND. SURRENDER AND RECEIVE MERCY!
MERCY?
WE'RE WELL BEYOND ANY KIND OF MERCY.

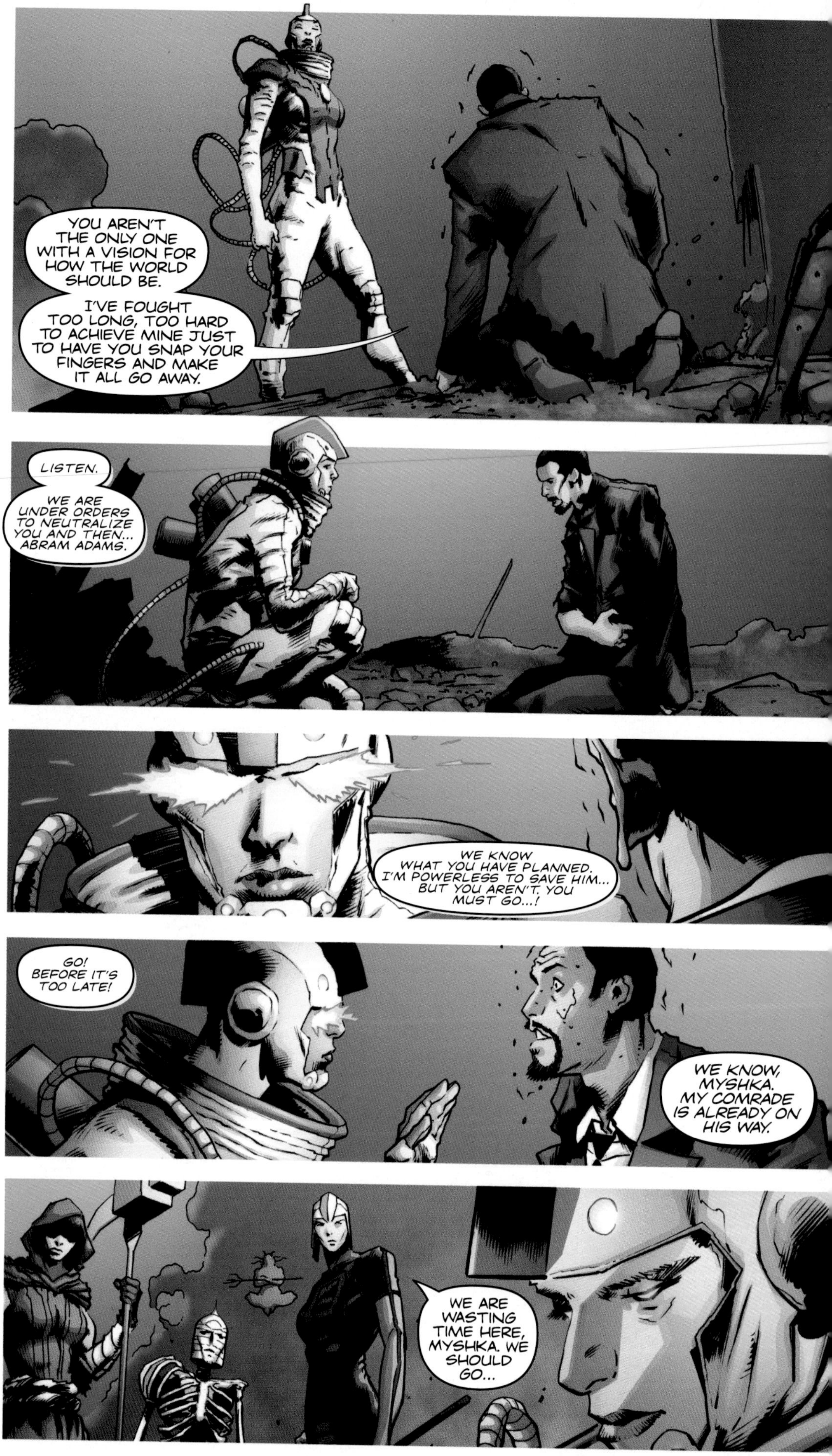
YOU AREN'T THE ONLY ONE WITH A VISION FOR HOW THE WORLD SHOULD BE.
I'VE FOUGHT TOO LONG, TOO HARD TO ACHIEVE MINE JUST TO HAVE YOU SNAP YOUR FINGERS AND MAKE IT ALL GO AWAY.
LISTEN.
WE ARE UNDER ORDERS TO NEUTRALIZE YOU AND THEN... ABRAM ADAMS.
WE KNOW WHAT YOU HAVE PLANNED. I'M POWERLESS TO SAVE HIM... BUT YOU AREN'T. YOU MUST GO...!
GO! BEFORE IT'S TOO LATE!
WE KNOW, MYSHKA. MY COMRADE IS ALREADY ON HIS WAY.
WE ARE WASTING TIME HERE, MYSHKA. WE SHOULD GO...

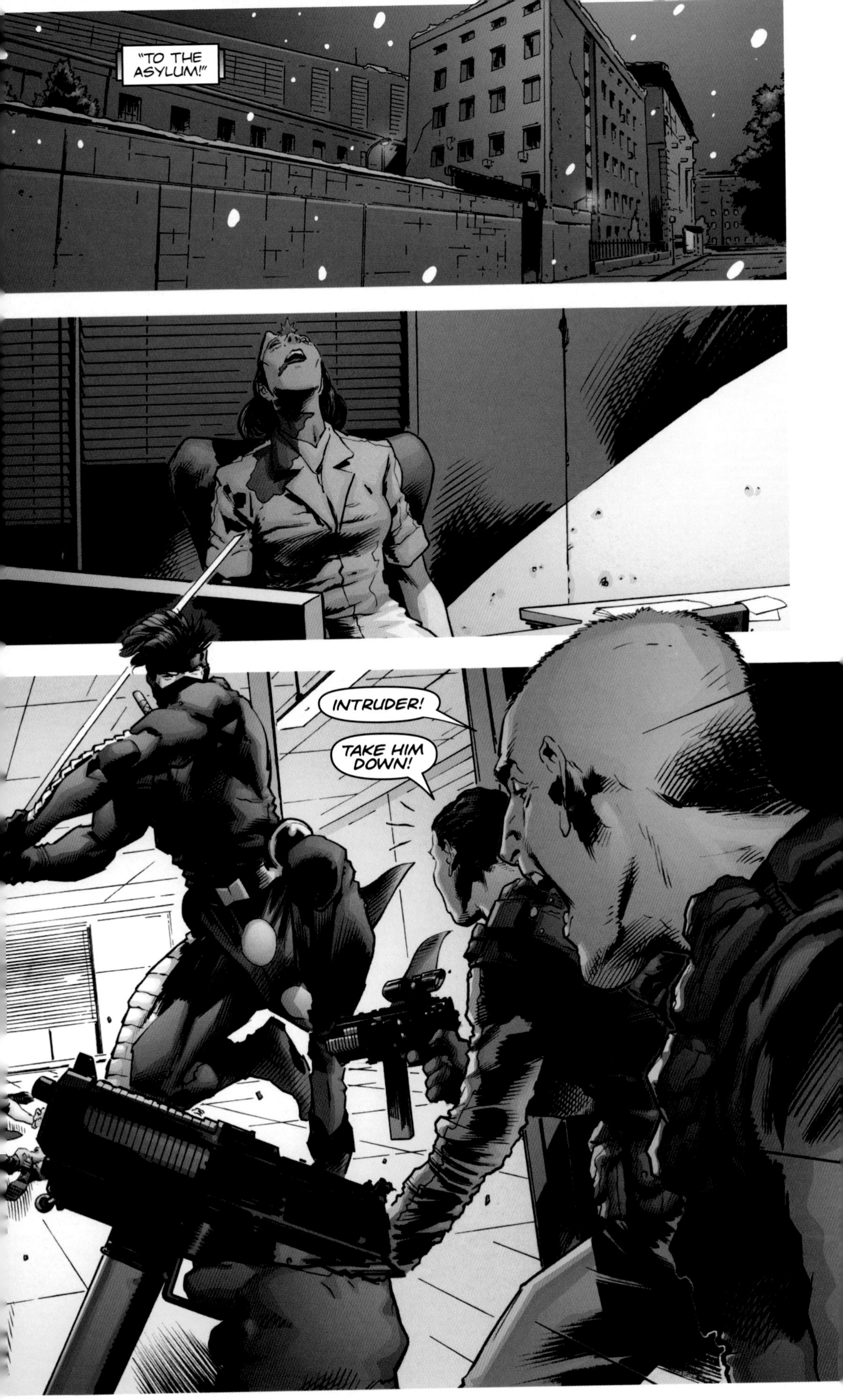
"TO THE ASYLUM!"
INTRUDER!
TAKE HIM DOWN!

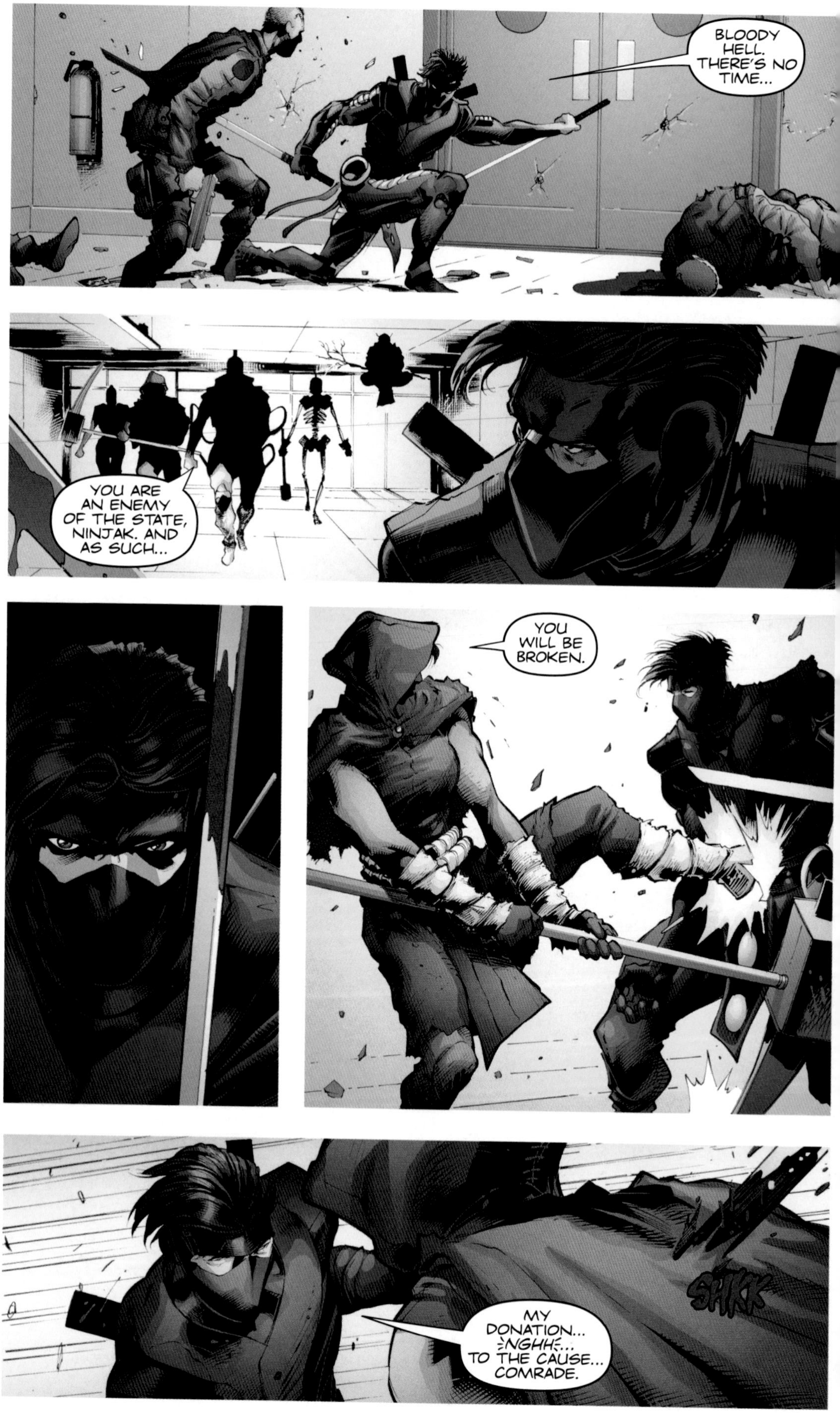
BLOODY HELL. THERE'S NO TIME...
YOU ARE AN ENEMY OF THE STATE, NINJAK. AND AS SUCH...
YOU WILL BE BROKEN.
SHKK
MY DONATION... NGHH... TO THE CAUSE... COMRADE.

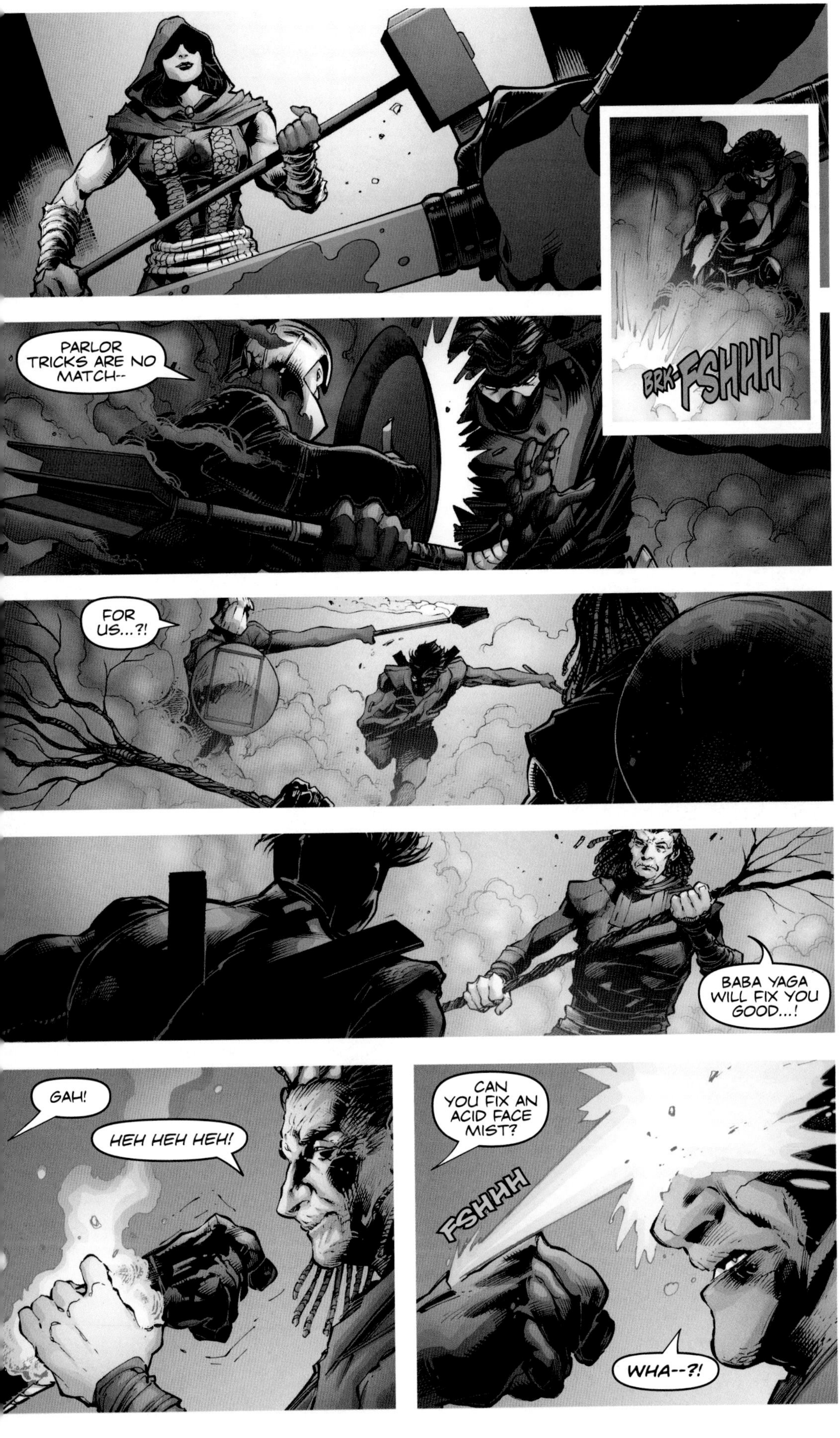
BRK-FSHHH
PARLOR TRICKS ARE NO MATCH--
FOR US...?!
BABA YAGA WILL FIX YOU GOOD...!
GAH!
HEH HEH HEH!
CAN YOU FIX AN ACID FACE MIST?
FSHHH
WHA--?!

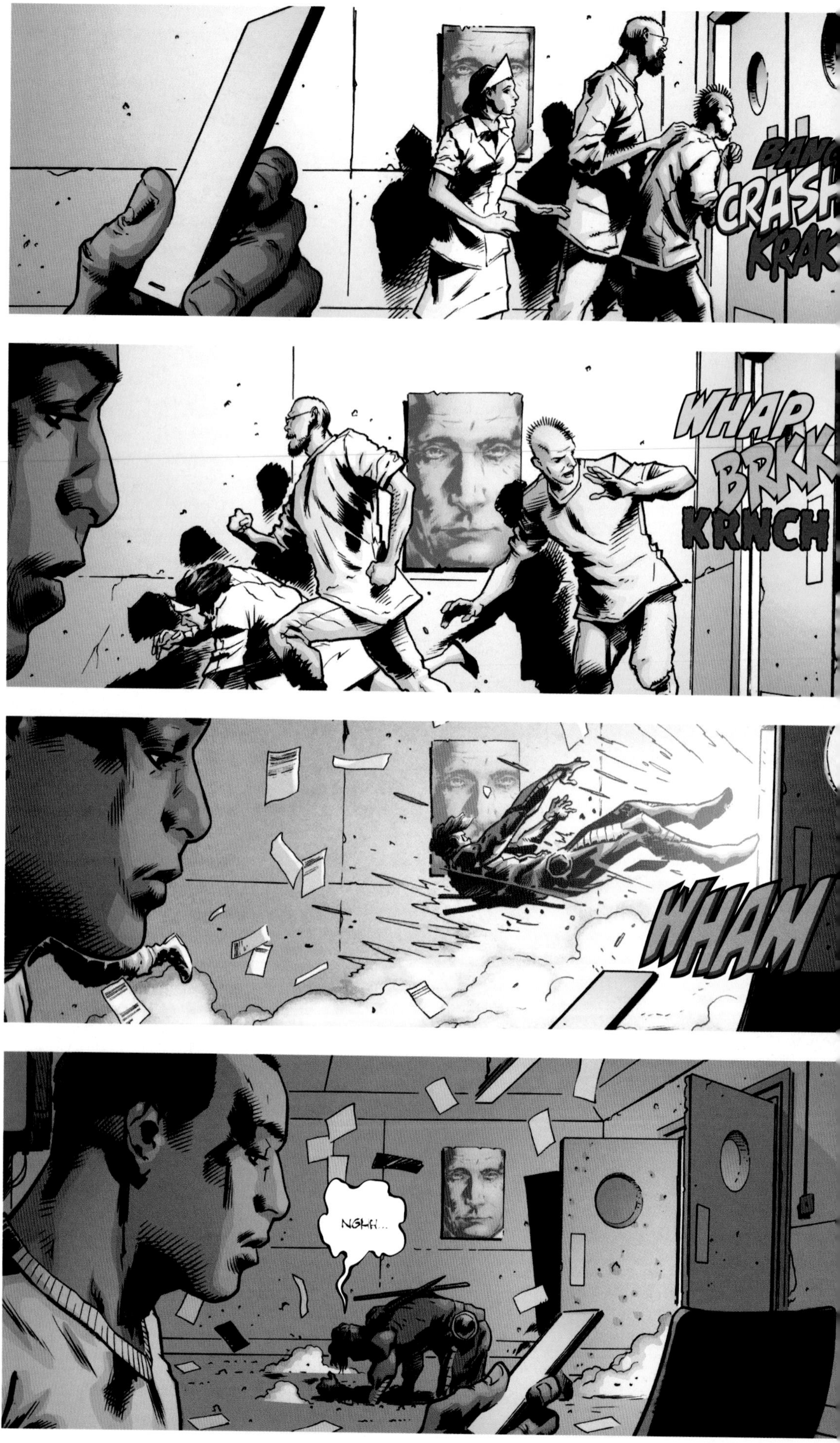
BANG
CRASH
KRAK
WHAP
BRKK
KRNCH
WHAM
NGHH...

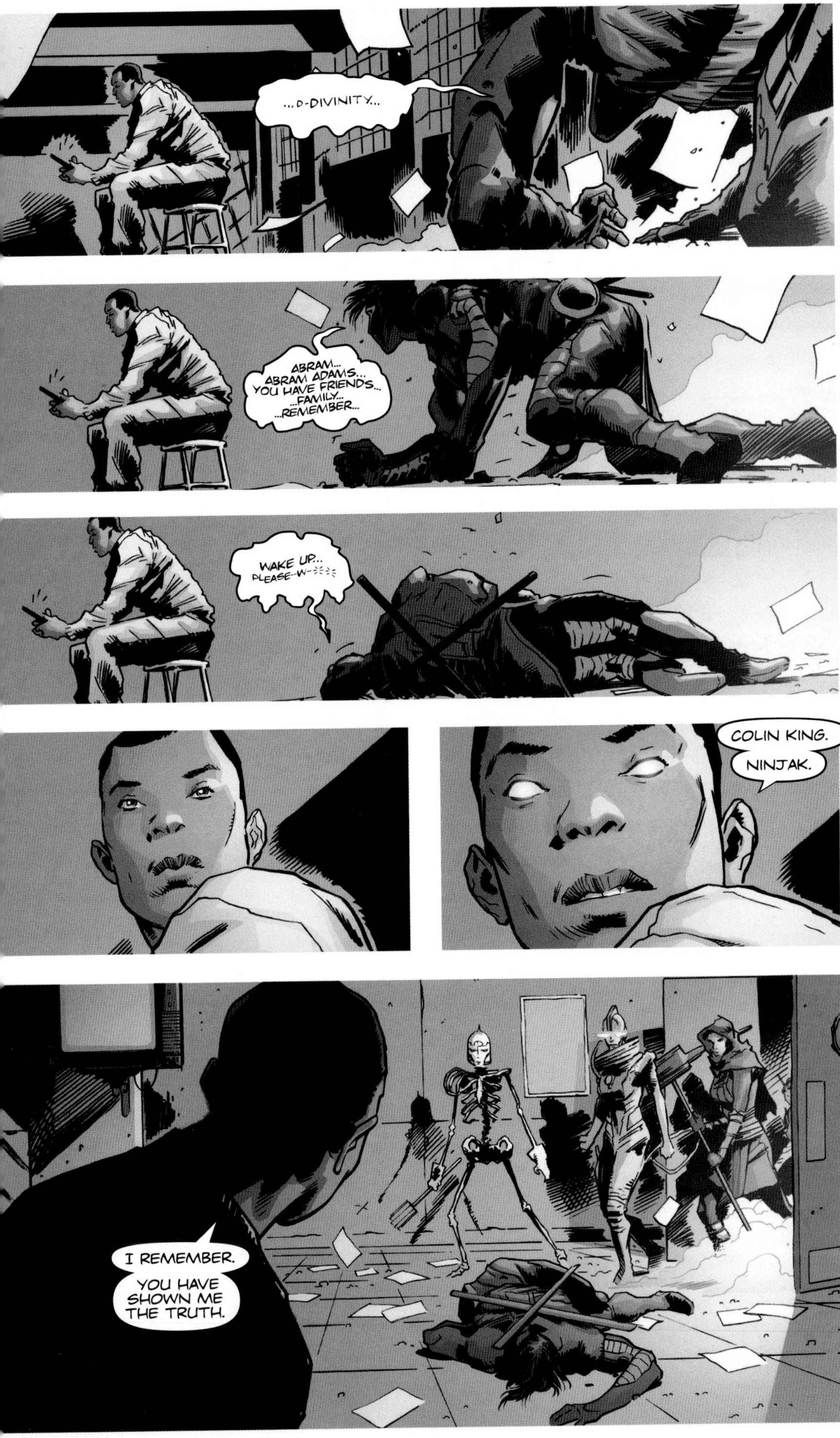
...D-DIVINITY...
ABRAM... ABRAM ADAMS... YOU HAVE FRIENDS... ...FAMILY... ...REMEMBER...
WAKE UP... PLEASE-W-
COLIN KING.
NINJAK.
I REMEMBER.
YOU HAVE SHOWN ME THE TRUTH.

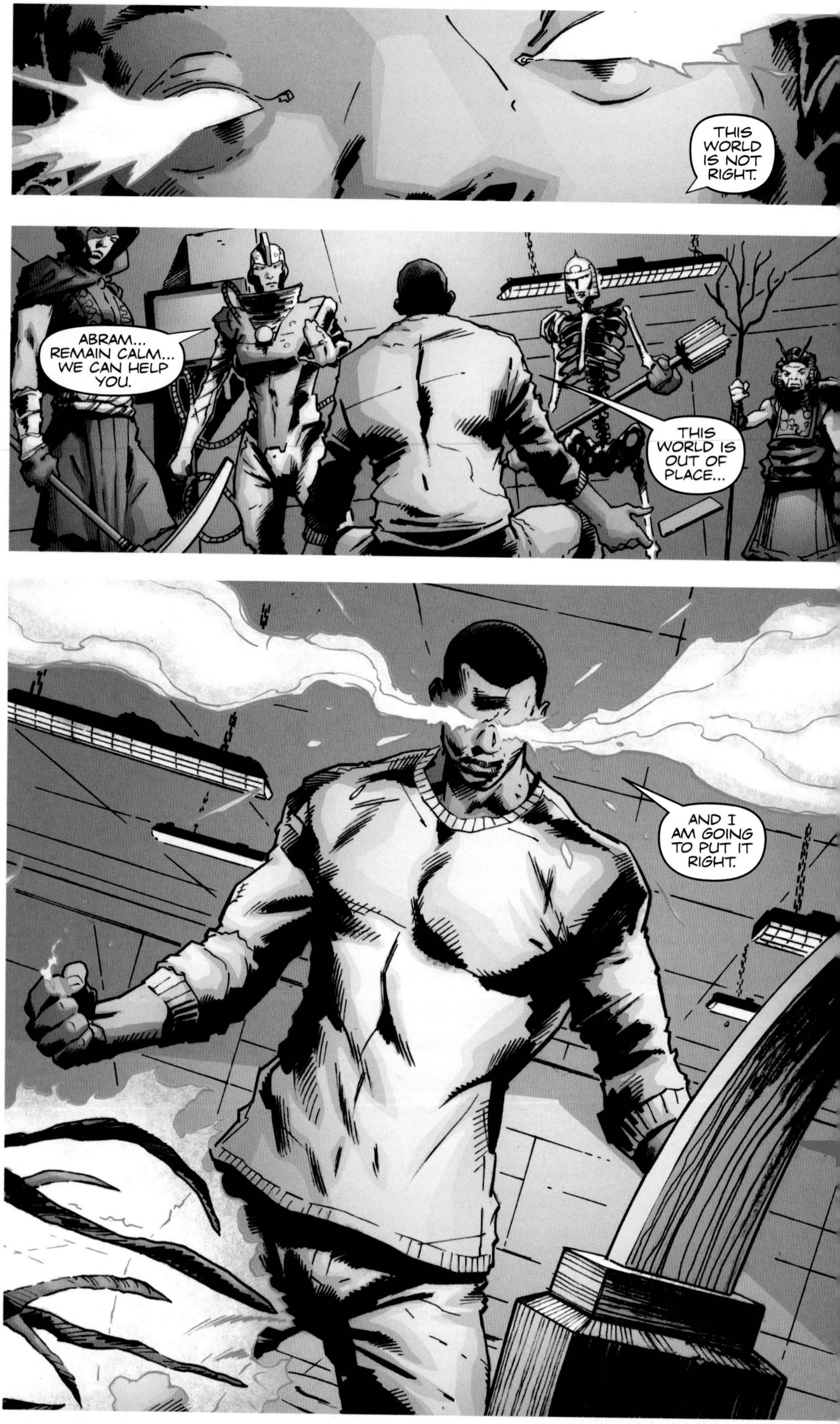
THIS WORLD IS NOT RIGHT.
ABRAM... REMAIN CALM... WE CAN HELP YOU.
THIS WORLD IS OUT OF PLACE...
AND I AM GOING TO PUT IT RIGHT.

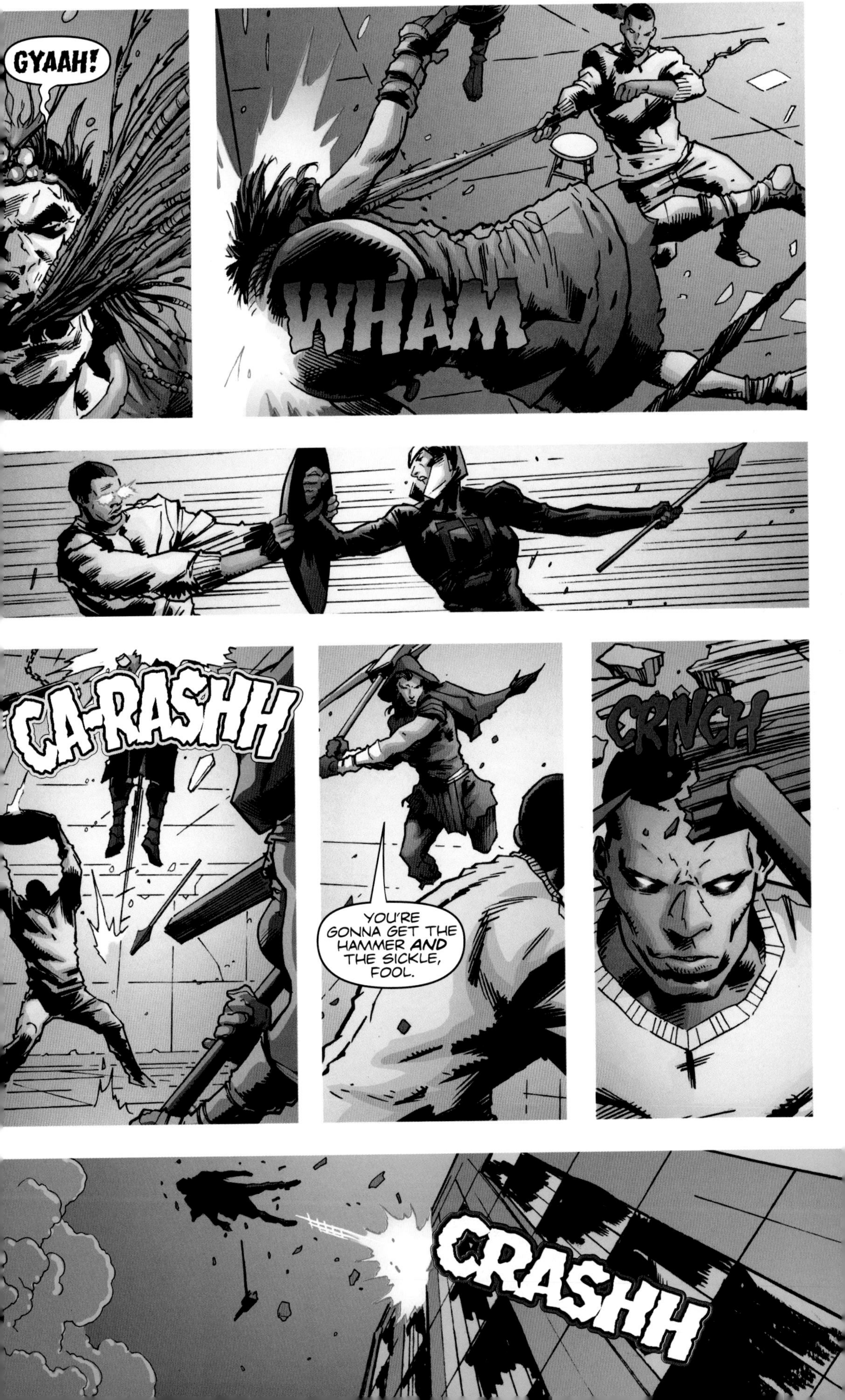
GYAAH!
WHAM
CA-RASHH
YOU'RE GONNA GET THE HAMMER AND THE SICKLE, FOOL.
CRNCH
CRASHH

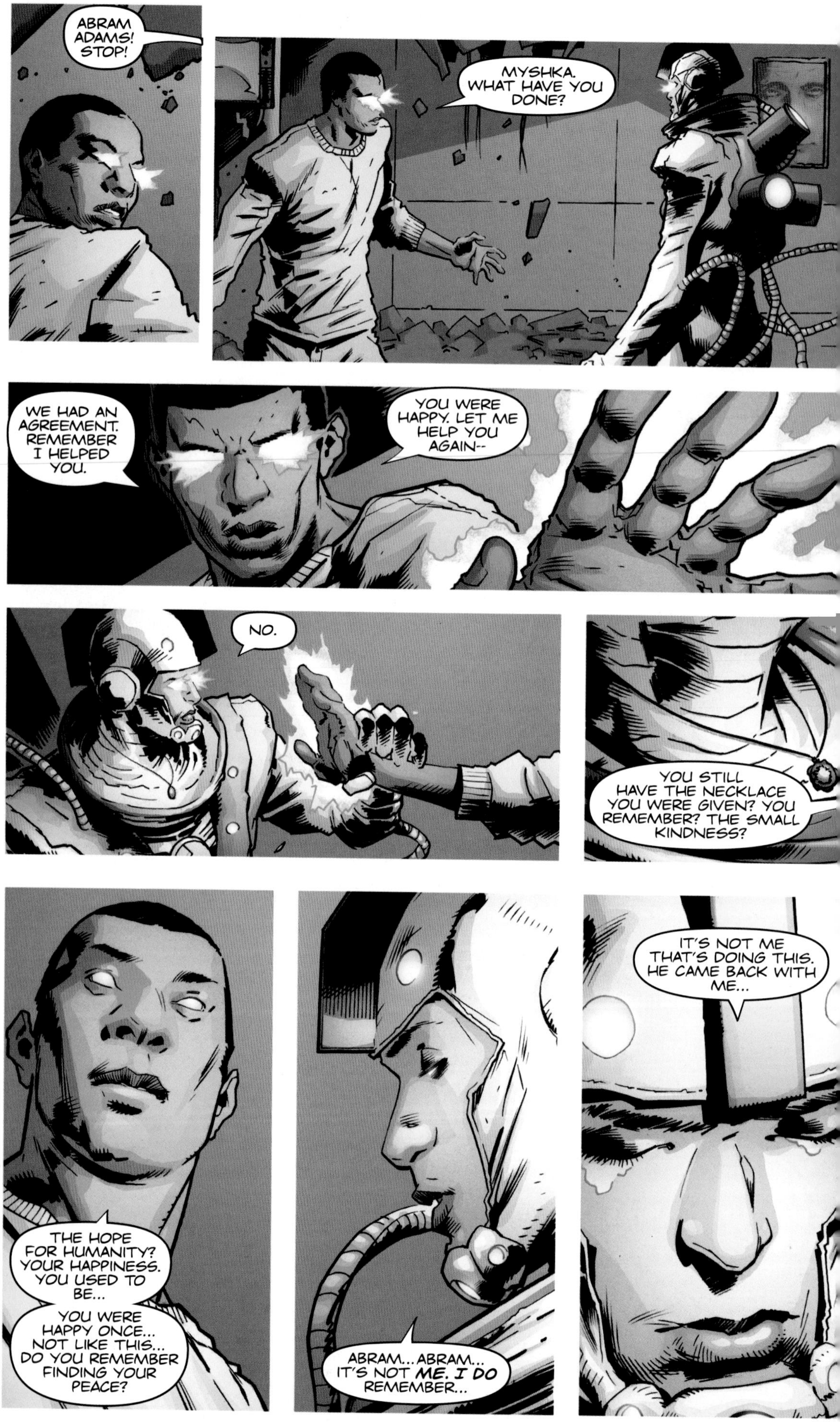
ABRAM ADAMS! STOP!
MYSHKA. WHAT HAVE YOU DONE?
WE HAD AN AGREEMENT. REMEMBER I HELPED YOU.
YOU WERE HAPPY. LET ME HELP YOU AGAIN--
NO.
YOU STILL HAVE THE NECKLACE YOU WERE GIVEN? YOU REMEMBER? THE SMALL KINDNESS?
THE HOPE FOR HUMANITY? YOUR HAPPINESS. YOU USED TO BE...
YOU WERE HAPPY ONCE... NOT LIKE THIS... DO YOU REMEMBER FINDING YOUR PEACE?
ABRAM... ABRAM... IT'S NOT ME. I DO REMEMBER...
IT'S NOT ME THAT'S DOING THIS. HE CAME BACK WITH ME...

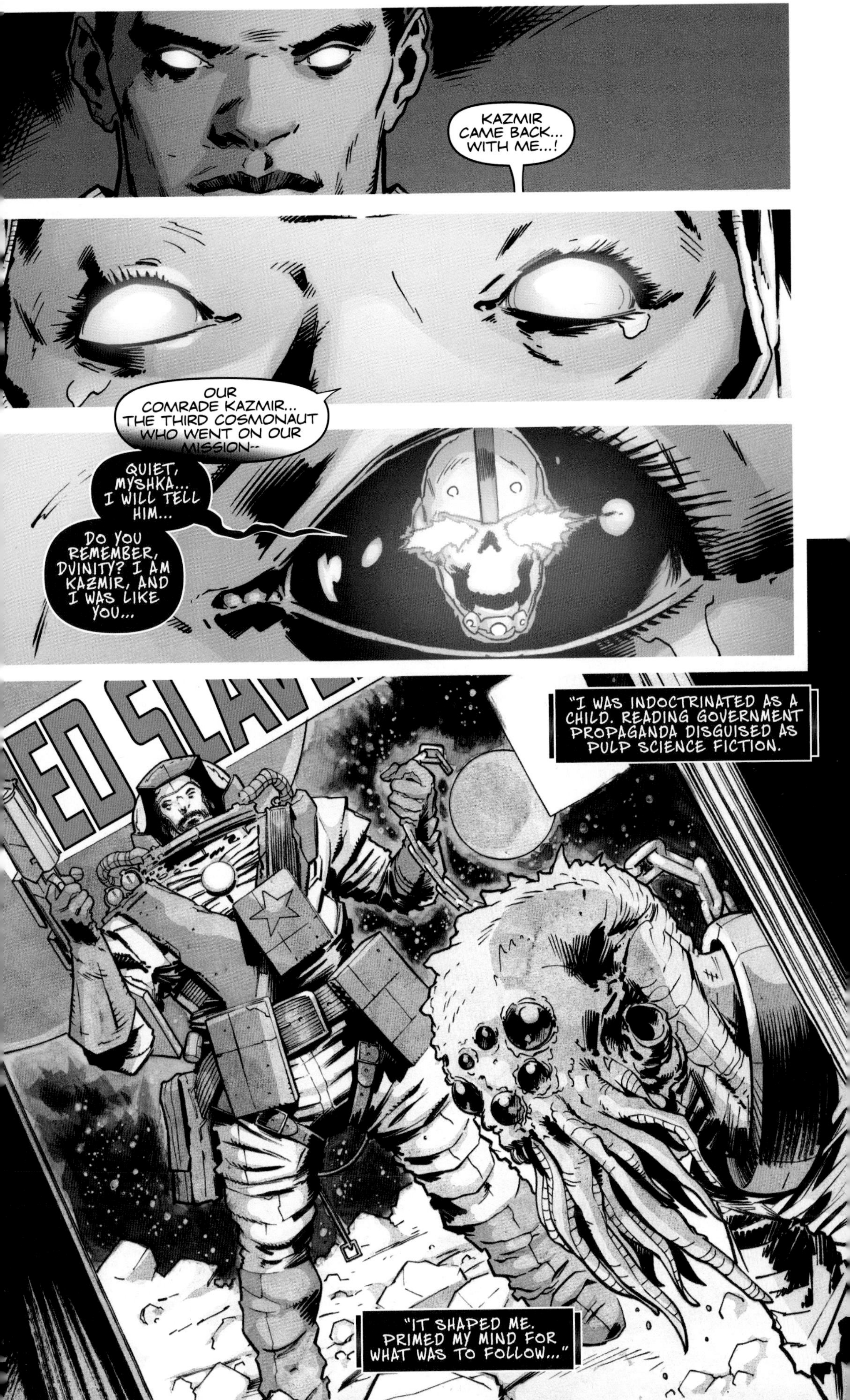

KAZMIR CAME BACK... WITH ME...!
OUR COMRADE KAZMIR... THE THIRD COSMONAUT WHO WENT ON OUR MISSION--
QUIET, MYSHKA... I WILL TELL HIM...
DO YOU REMEMBER, DVINITY? I AM KAZMIR, AND I WAS LIKE YOU...
"I WAS INDOCTRINATED AS A CHILD. READING GOVERNMENT PROPAGANDA DISGUISED AS PULP SCIENCE FICTION.
"IT SHAPED ME. PRIMED MY MIND FOR WHAT WAS TO FOLLOW..."

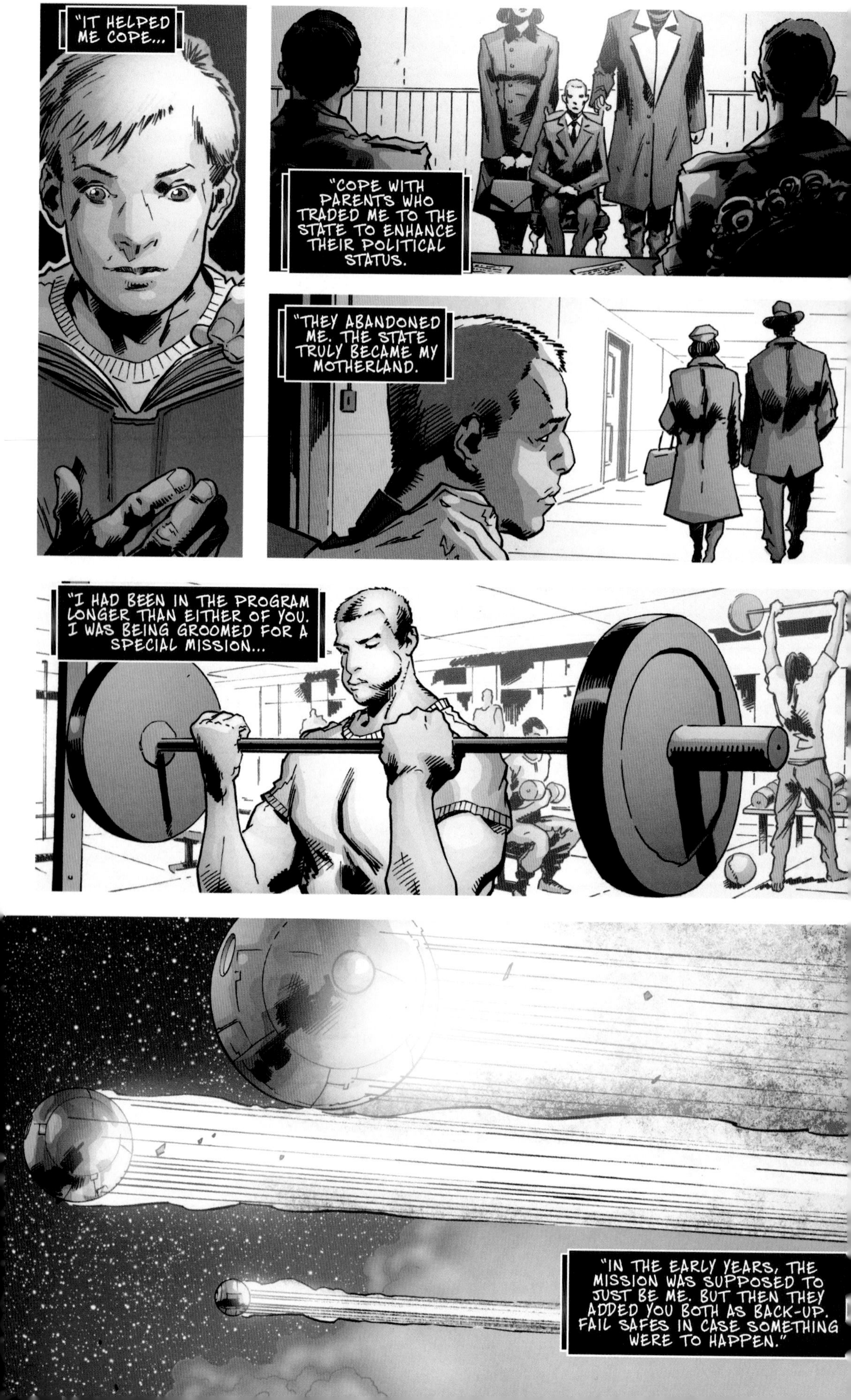
"IT HELPED ME COPE...
"COPE WITH PARENTS WHO TRADED ME TO THE STATE TO ENHANCE THEIR POLITICAL STATUS.
"THEY ABANDONED ME. THE STATE TRULY BECAME MY MOTHERLAND.
"I HAD BEEN IN THE PROGRAM LONGER THAN EITHER OF YOU. I WAS BEING GROOMED FOR A SPECIAL MISSION...
"IN THE EARLY YEARS, THE MISSION WAS SUPPOSED TO JUST BE ME. BUT THEN THEY ADDED YOU BOTH AS BACK-UP. FAIL SAFES IN CASE SOMETHING WERE TO HAPPEN."

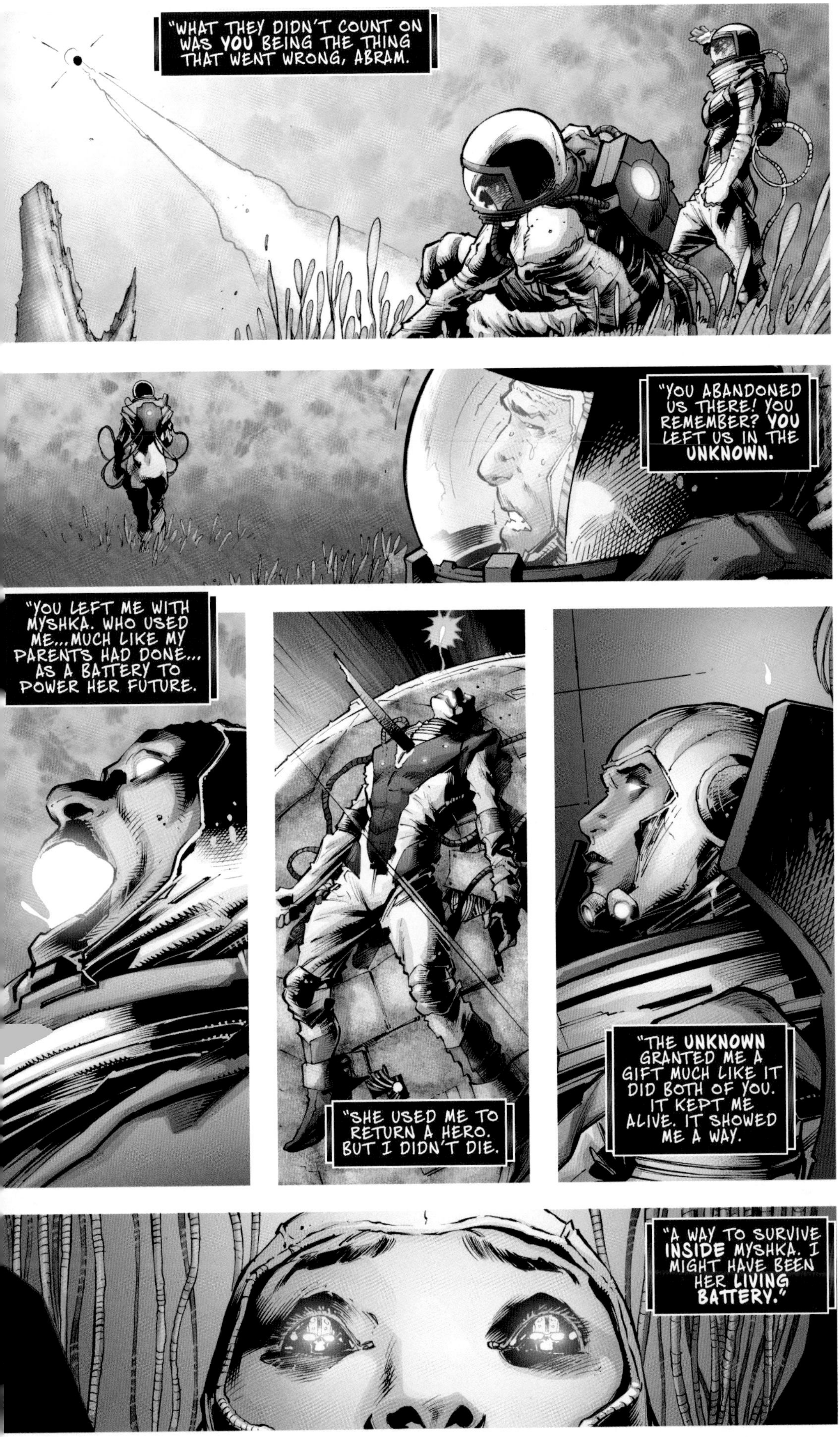
"WHAT THEY DIDN'T COUNT ON WAS YOU BEING THE THING THAT WENT WRONG, ABRAM.
"YOU ABANDONED US THERE! YOU REMEMBER? YOU LEFT US IN THE UNKNOWN.
"YOU LEFT ME WITH MYSHKA. WHO USED ME...MUCH LIKE MY PARENTS HAD DONE... AS A BATTERY TO POWER HER FUTURE.
"SHE USED ME TO RETURN A HERO. BUT I DIDN'T DIE.
"THE UNKNOWN GRANTED ME A GIFT MUCH LIKE IT DID BOTH OF YOU. IT KEPT ME ALIVE. IT SHOWED ME A WAY.
"A WAY TO SURVIVE INSIDE MYSHKA. I MIGHT HAVE BEEN HER LIVING BATTERY."

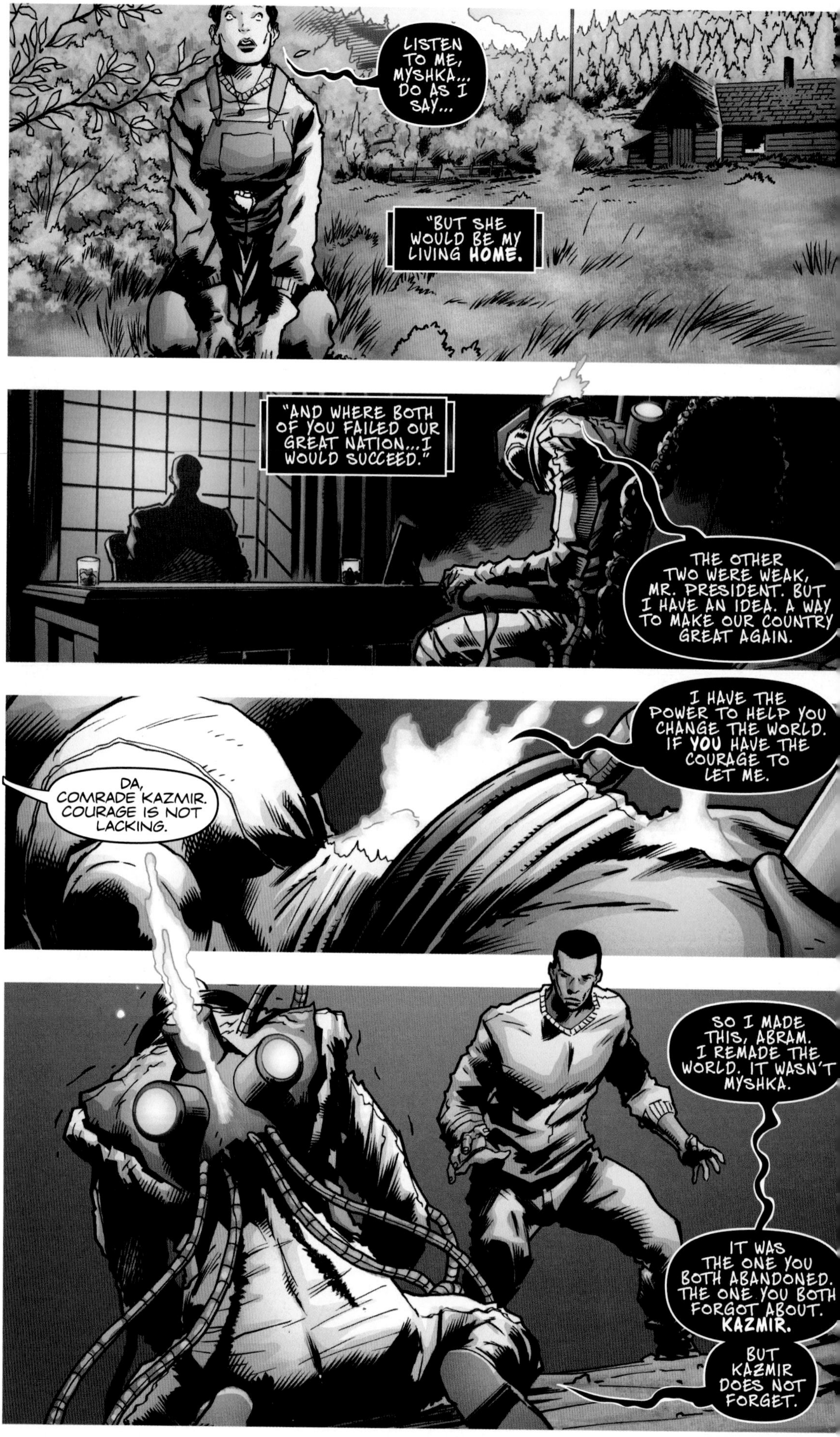
LISTEN TO ME, MYSHKA... DO AS I SAY...
"BUT SHE WOULD BE MY LIVING **HOME.**
"AND WHERE BOTH OF YOU FAILED OUR GREAT NATION...I WOULD SUCCEED."
THE OTHER TWO WERE WEAK, MR. PRESIDENT. BUT I HAVE AN IDEA. A WAY TO MAKE OUR COUNTRY GREAT AGAIN.
I HAVE THE POWER TO HELP YOU CHANGE THE WORLD. IF **YOU** HAVE THE COURAGE TO LET ME.
DA, COMRADE KAZMIR. COURAGE IS NOT LACKING.
SO I MADE THIS, ABRAM. I REMADE THE WORLD. IT WASN'T MYSHKA.
IT WAS THE ONE YOU BOTH ABANDONED. THE ONE YOU BOTH FORGOT ABOUT. **KAZMIR.**
BUT KAZMIR DOES NOT FORGET.

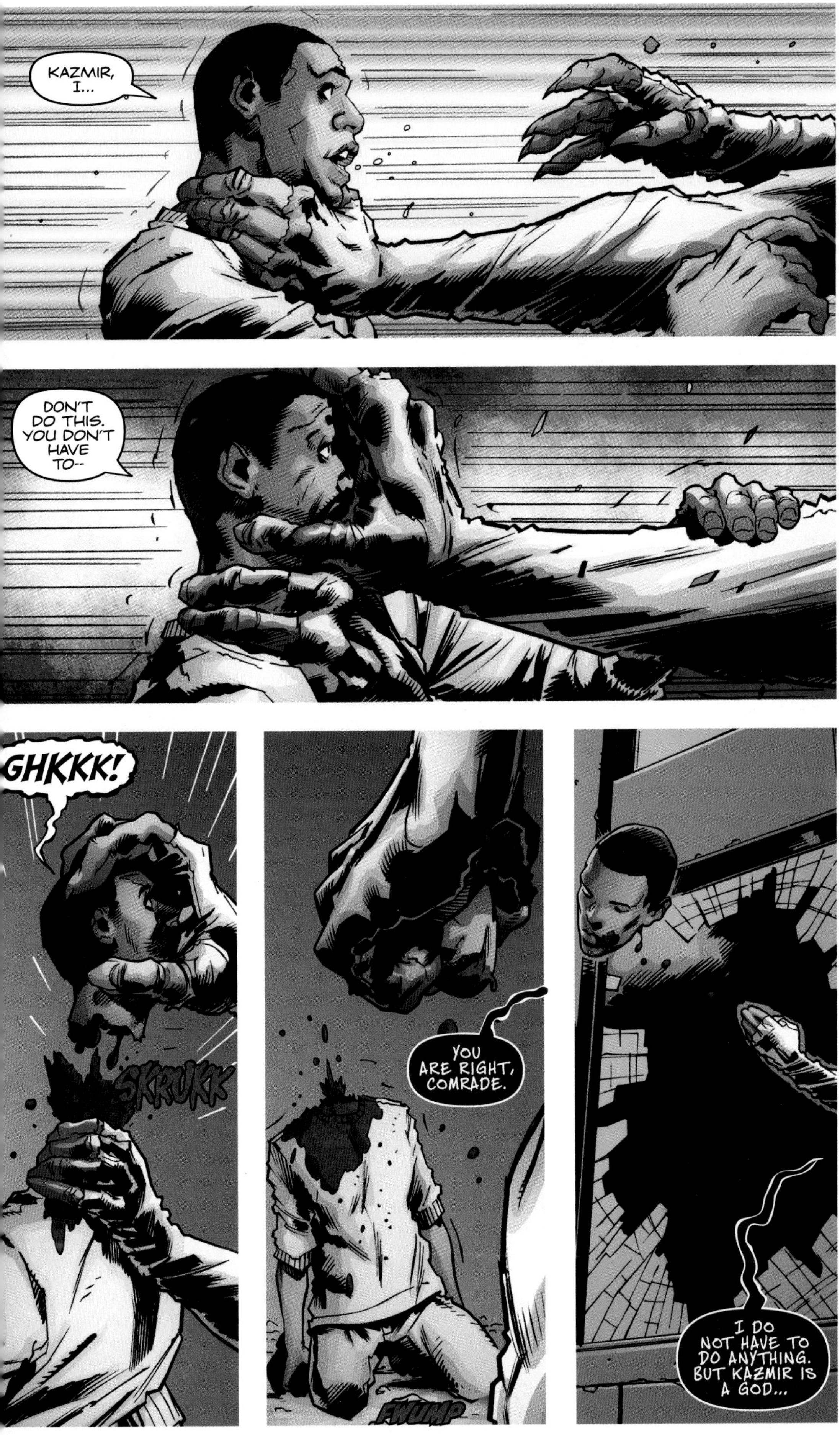
KAZMIR, I...
DON'T DO THIS. YOU DON'T HAVE TO--
GHKKK!
SKRUKK
YOU ARE RIGHT, COMRADE.
FWUMP
I DO NOT HAVE TO DO ANYTHING. BUT KAZMIR IS A GOD...

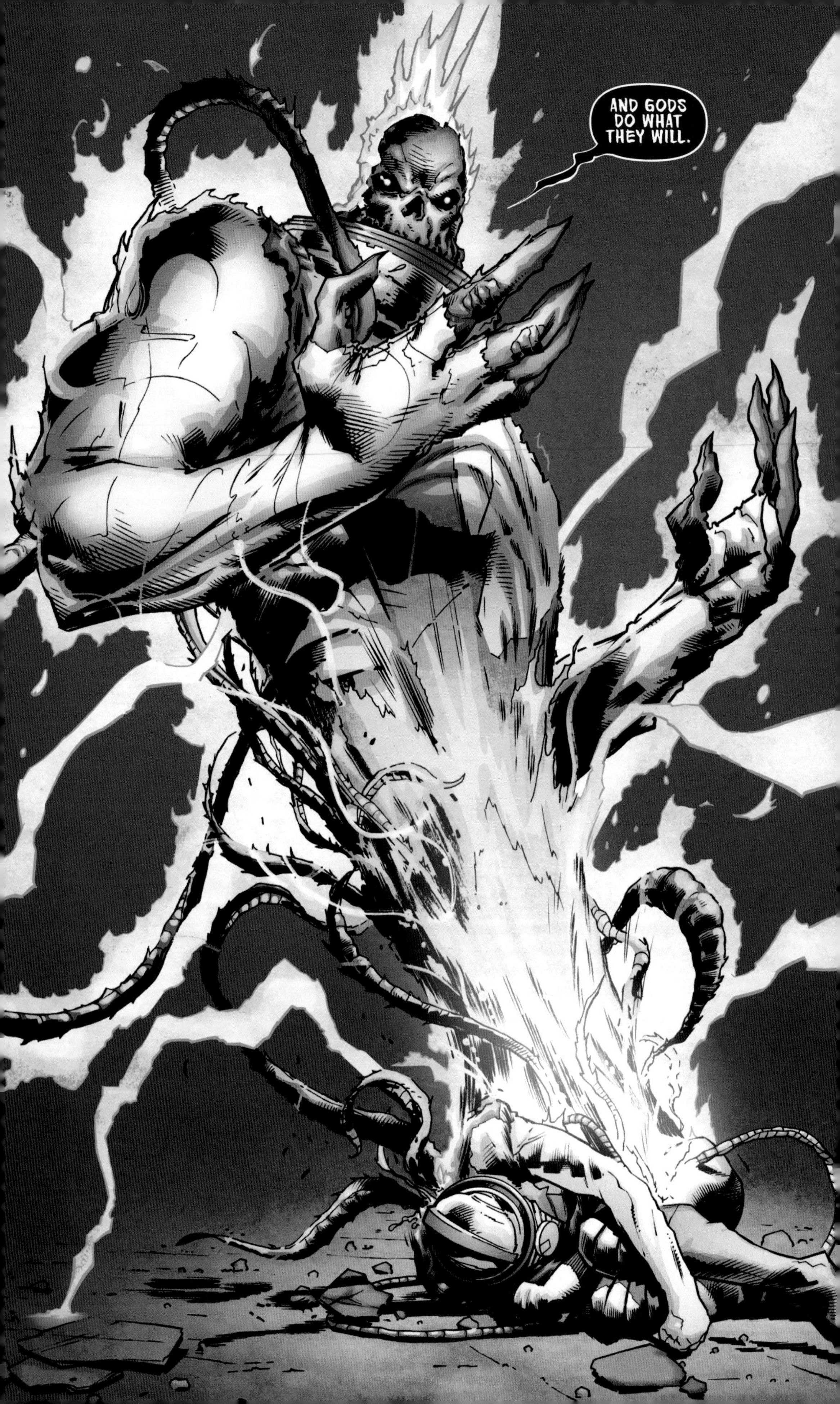
AND GODS DO WHAT THEY WILL.

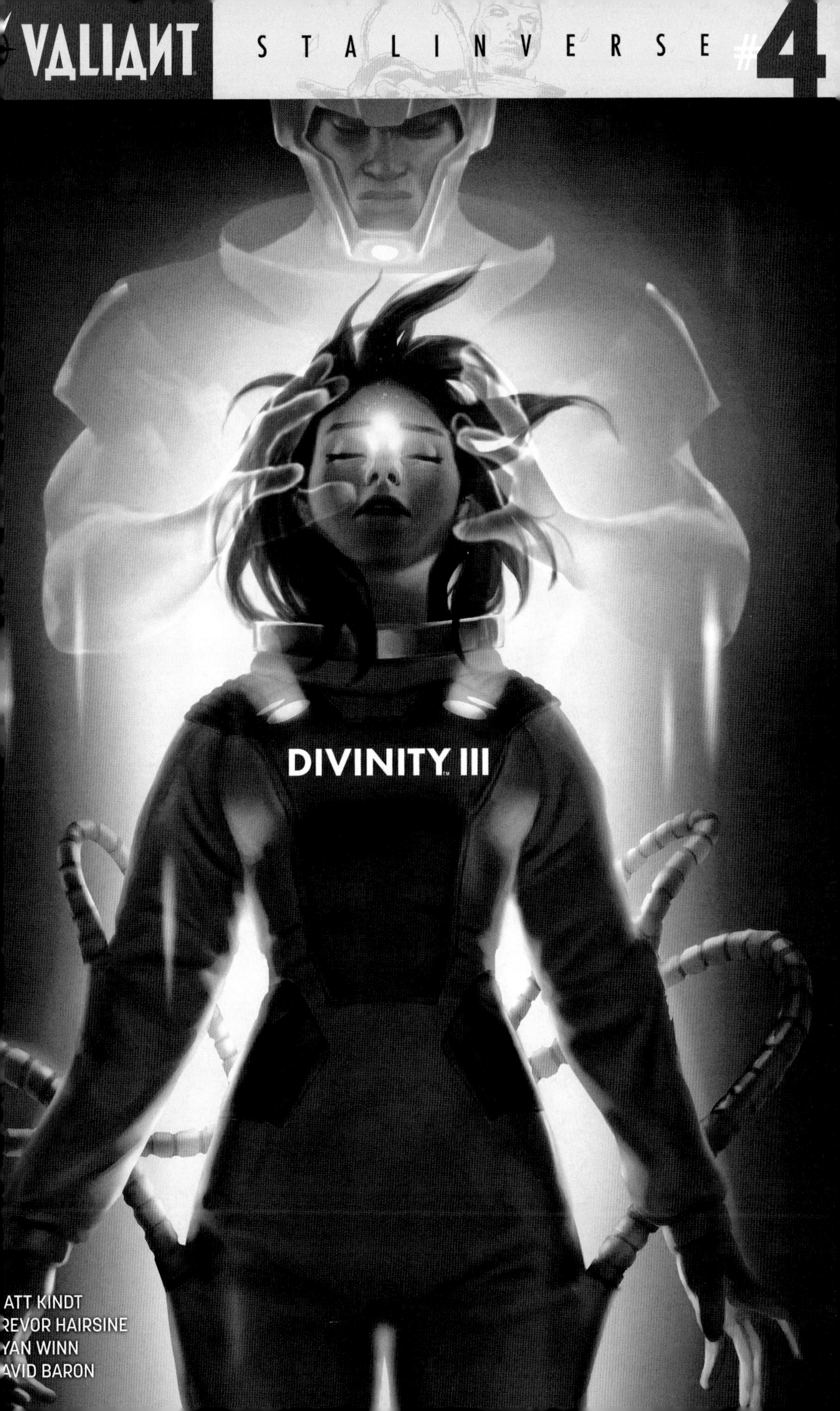
VALIANT
STALINVERSE
#4
DIVINITY III
ATT KINDT
REVOR HAIRSINE
YAN WINN
AVID BARON

T THE BOTTOM OF THE CASPIAN SEA...
SLRSH
FLRP
SHKK

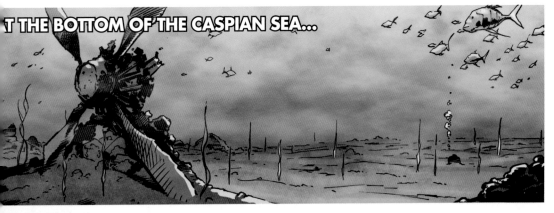

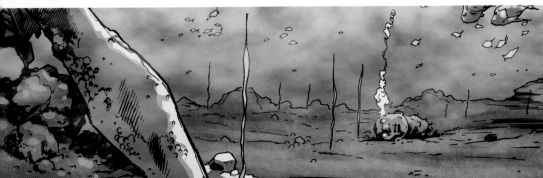

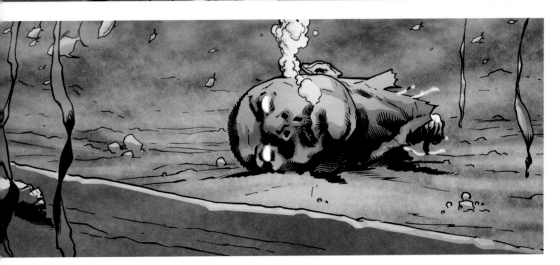

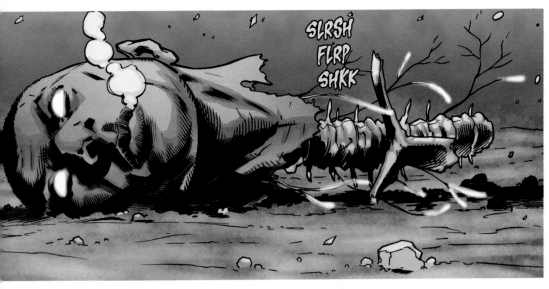

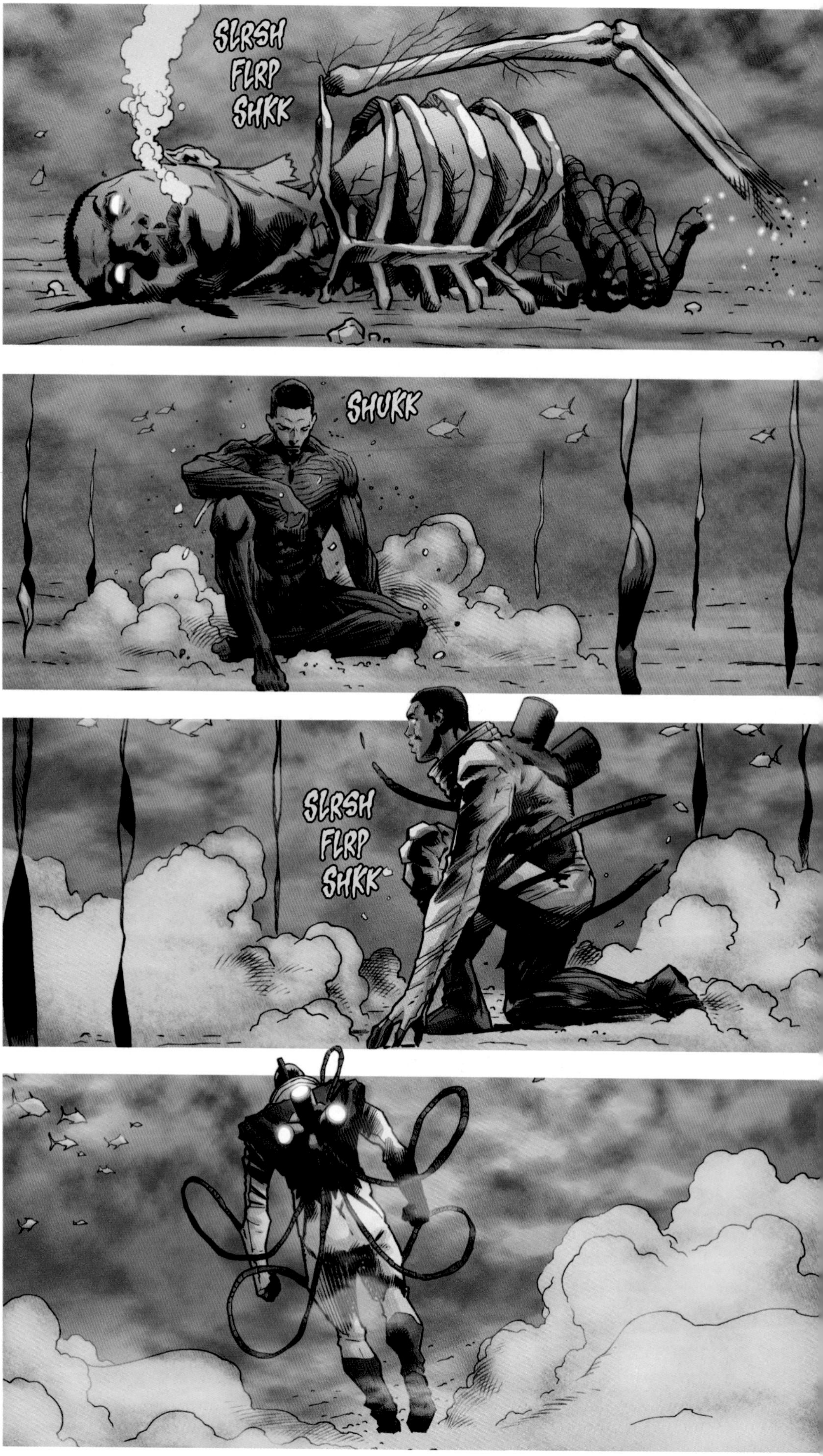
SLRSH
FLRP
SHKK
SHUKK
SLRSH
FLRP
SHKK

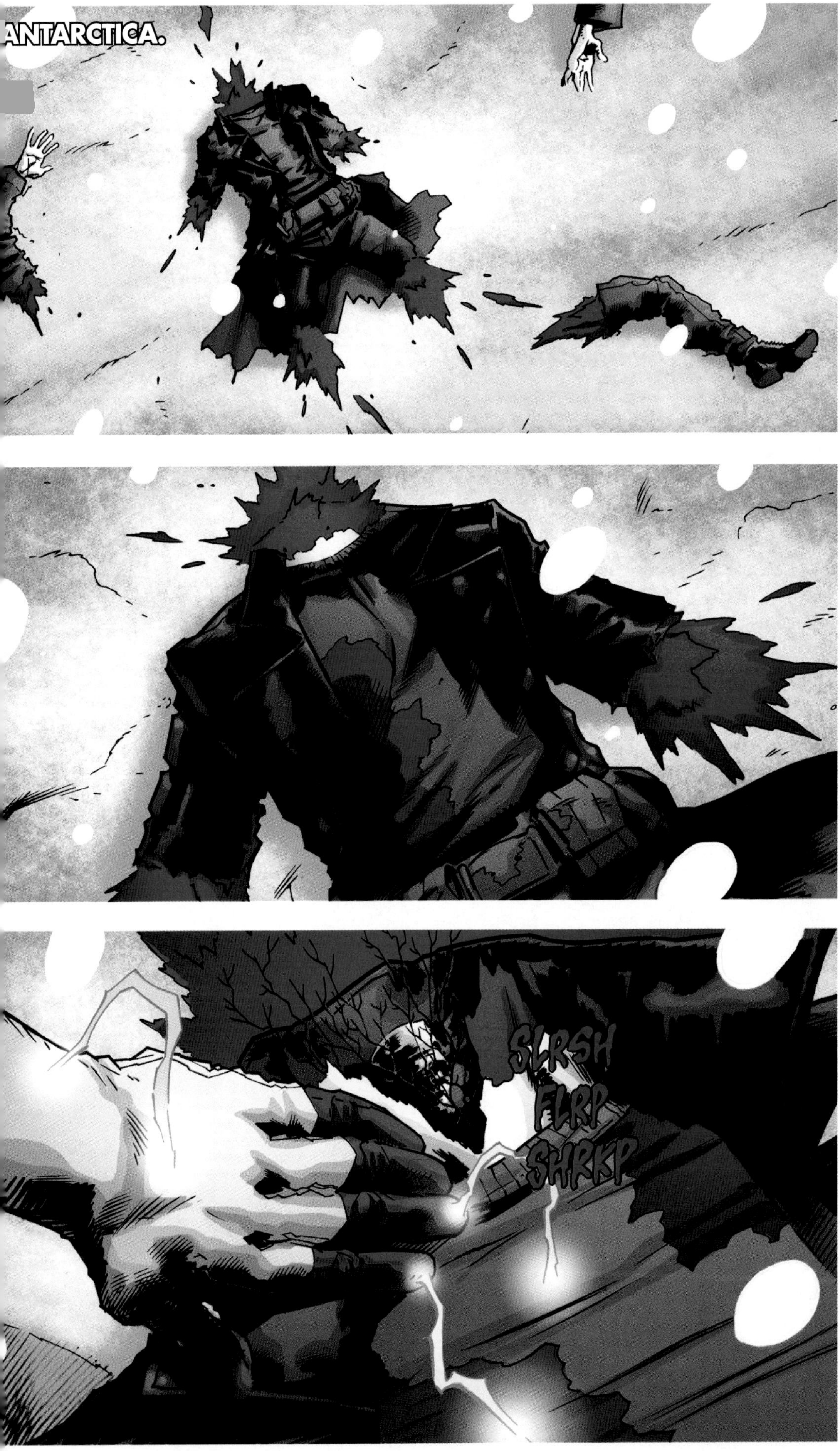
ANTARCTICA.
SLRSH
FLRP
SHRKP

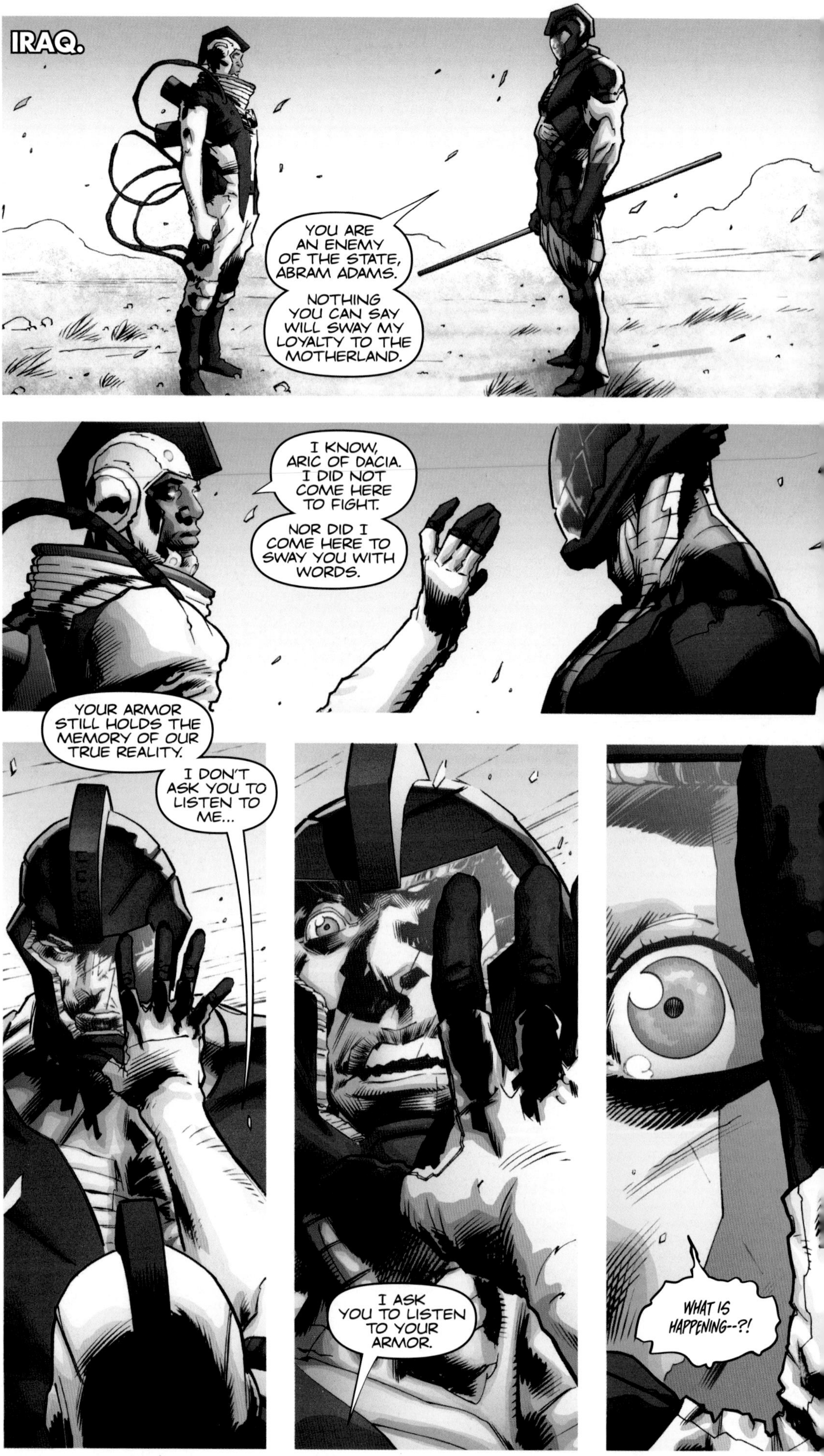
IRAQ.
YOU ARE AN ENEMY OF THE STATE, ABRAM ADAMS.
NOTHING YOU CAN SAY WILL SWAY MY LOYALTY TO THE MOTHERLAND.
I KNOW, ARIC OF DACIA. I DID NOT COME HERE TO FIGHT.
NOR DID I COME HERE TO SWAY YOU WITH WORDS.
YOUR ARMOR STILL HOLDS THE MEMORY OF OUR TRUE REALITY.
I DON'T ASK YOU TO LISTEN TO ME...
I ASK YOU TO LISTEN TO YOUR ARMOR.
WHAT IS HAPPENING--?!

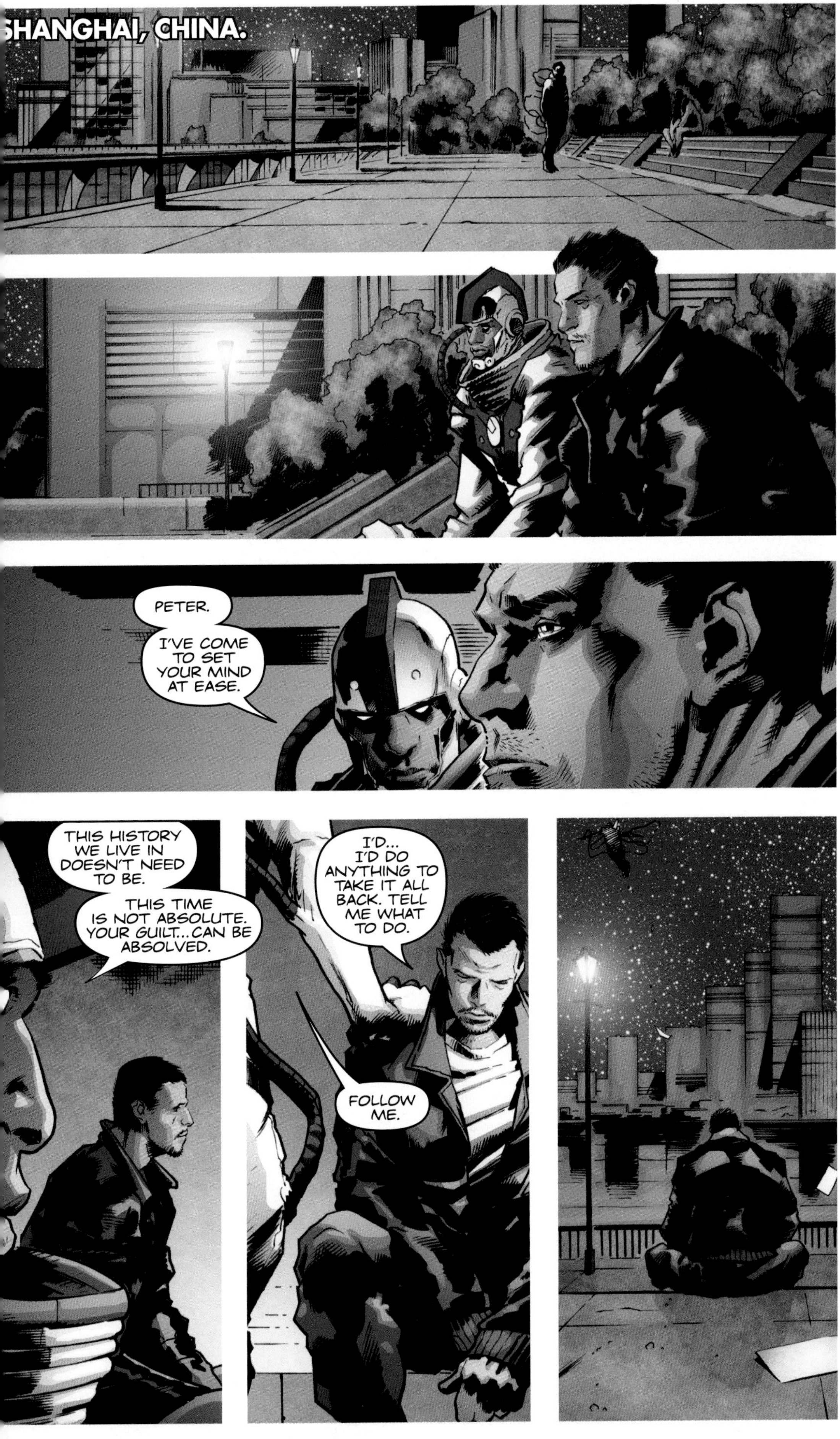
SHANGHAI, CHINA.
PETER.
I'VE COME TO SET YOUR MIND AT EASE.
THIS HISTORY WE LIVE IN DOESN'T NEED TO BE.
THIS TIME IS NOT ABSOLUTE. YOUR GUILT...CAN BE ABSOLVED.
I'D... I'D DO ANYTHING TO TAKE IT ALL BACK. TELL ME WHAT TO DO.
FOLLOW ME.

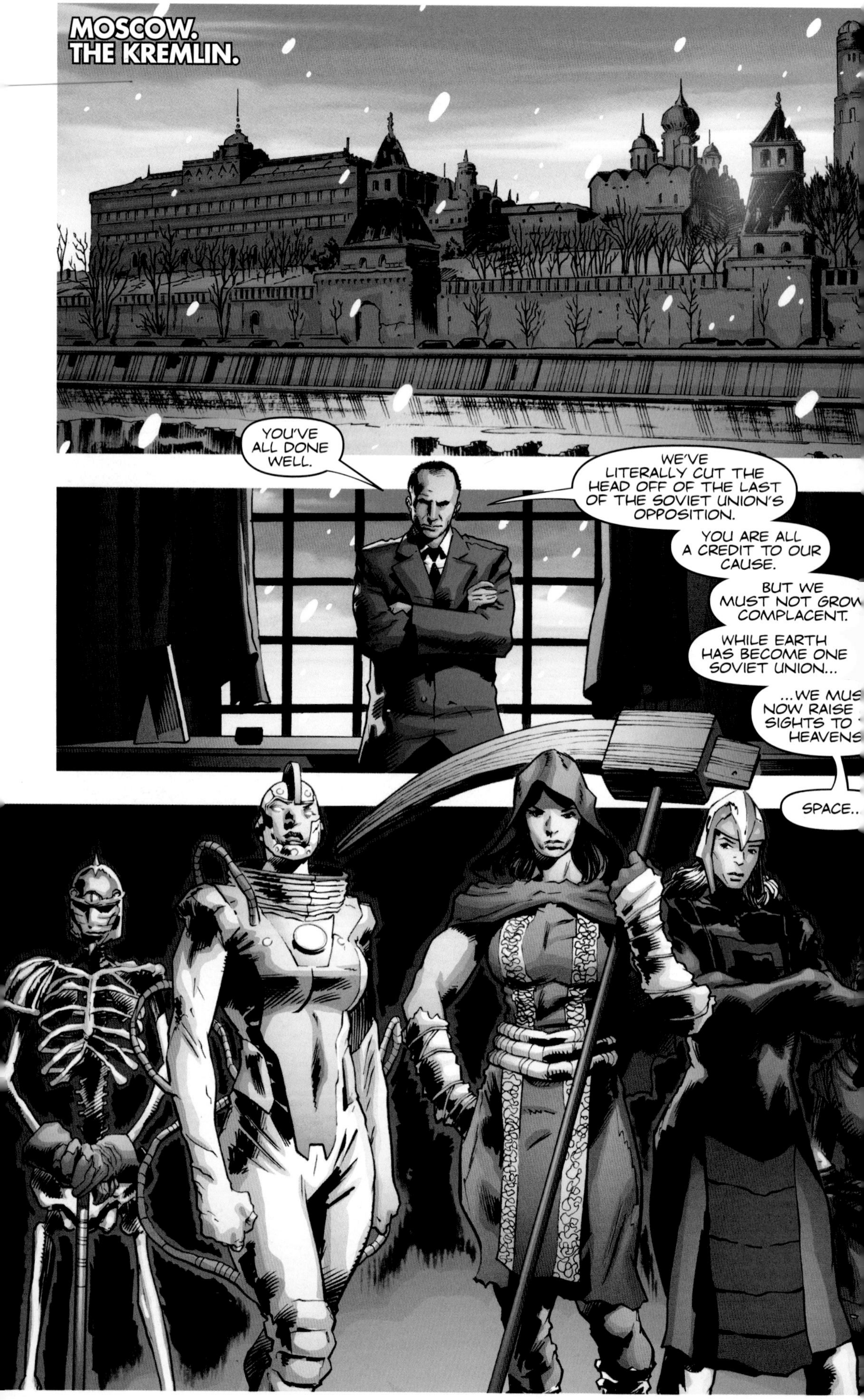
MOSCOW. THE KREMLIN.
YOU'VE ALL DONE WELL.
WE'VE LITERALLY CUT THE HEAD OFF OF THE LAST OF THE SOVIET UNION'S OPPOSITION.
YOU ARE ALL A CREDIT TO OUR CAUSE.
BUT WE MUST NOT GROW COMPLACENT.
WHILE EARTH HAS BECOME ONE SOVIET UNION...
...WE MUS NOW RAISE SIGHTS TO HEAVENS
SPACE..

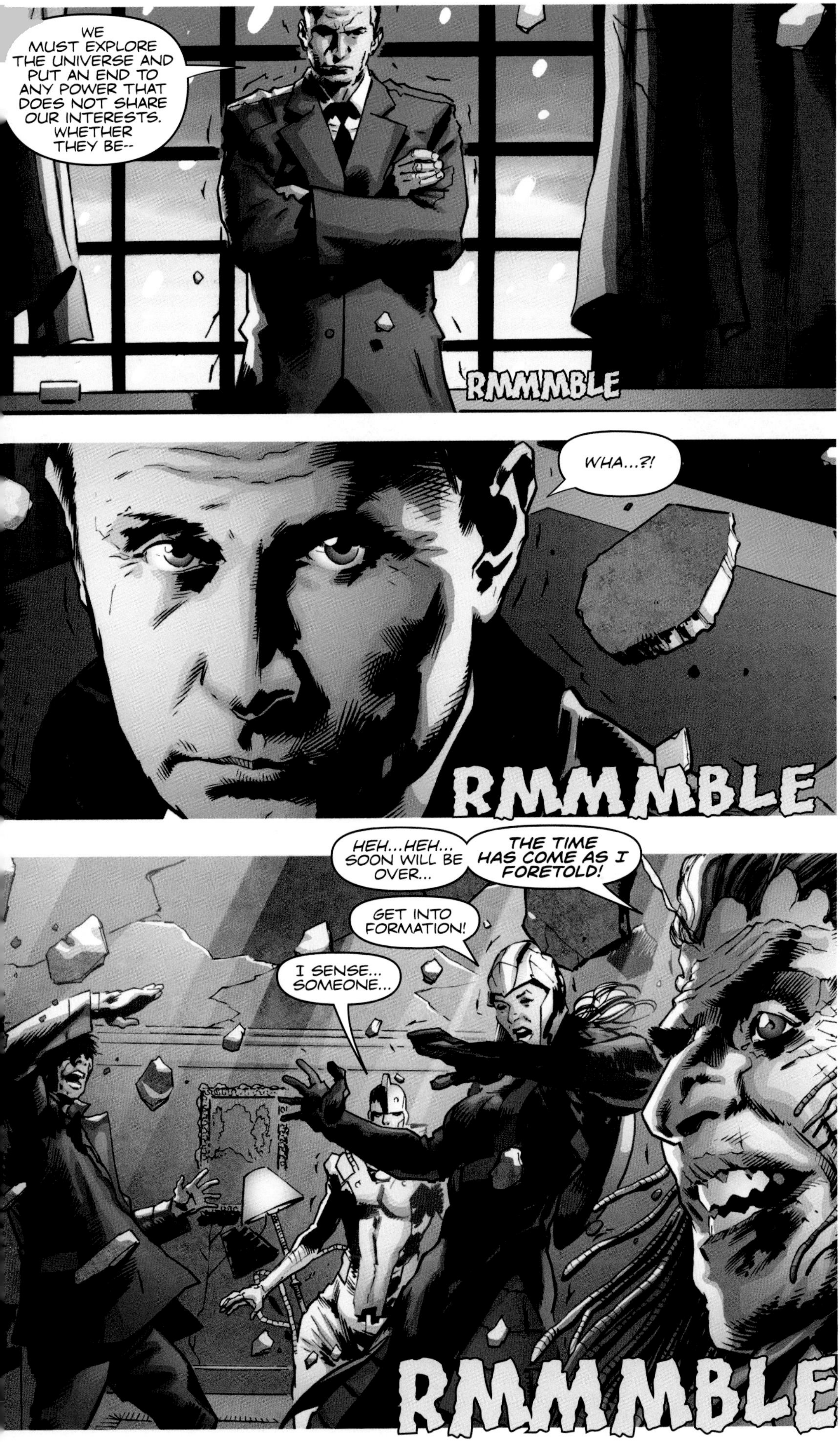
WE MUST EXPLORE THE UNIVERSE AND PUT AN END TO ANY POWER THAT DOES NOT SHARE OUR INTERESTS. WHETHER THEY BE--
RMMMBLE
WHA...?!
RMMMBLE
HEH...HEH... SOON WILL BE OVER...
THE TIME HAS COME AS I FORETOLD!
GET INTO FORMATION!
I SENSE... SOMEONE...
RMMMBLE

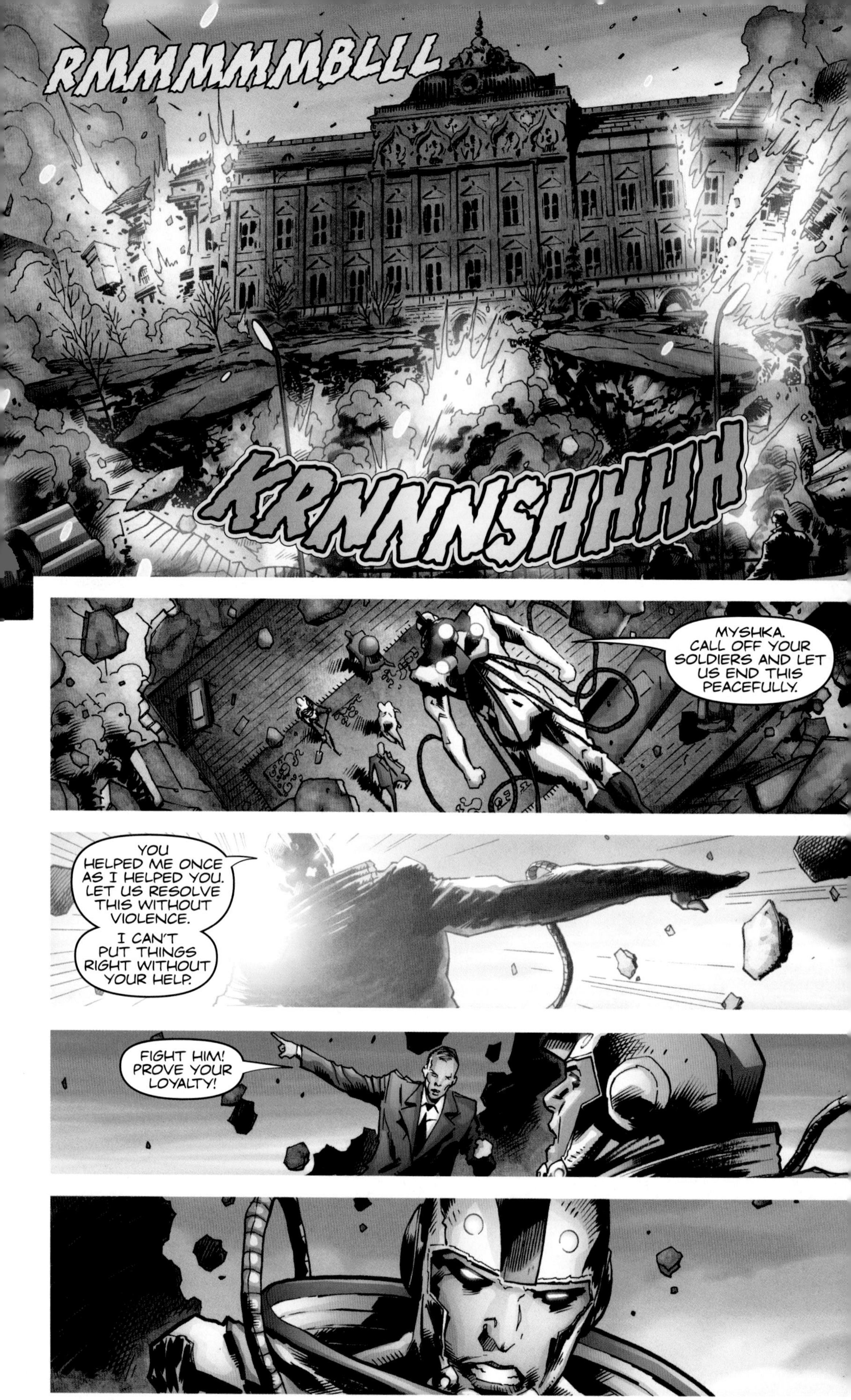
RMMMMMMBLLL
KRNNNSHHHH
MYSHKA. CALL OFF YOUR SOLDIERS AND LET US END THIS PEACEFULLY.
YOU HELPED ME ONCE AS I HELPED YOU. LET US RESOLVE THIS WITHOUT VIOLENCE.
I CAN'T PUT THINGS RIGHT WITHOUT YOUR HELP.
FIGHT HIM! PROVE YOUR LOYALTY!

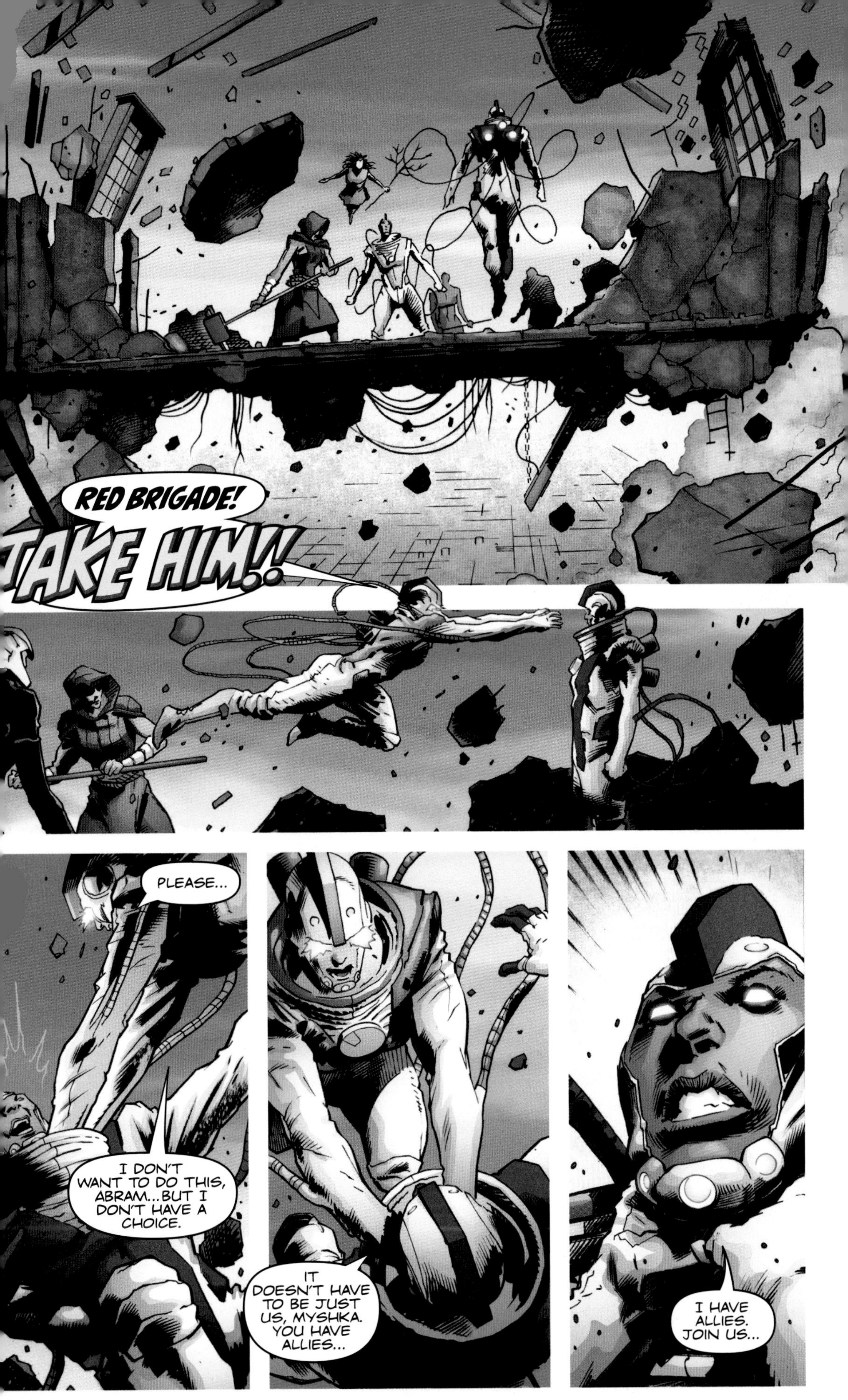
RED BRIGADE!
TAKE HIM!!
PLEASE...
I DON'T WANT TO DO THIS, ABRAM...BUT I DON'T HAVE A CHOICE.
IT DOESN'T HAVE TO BE JUST US, MYSHKA. YOU HAVE ALLIES...
I HAVE ALLIES. JOIN US...

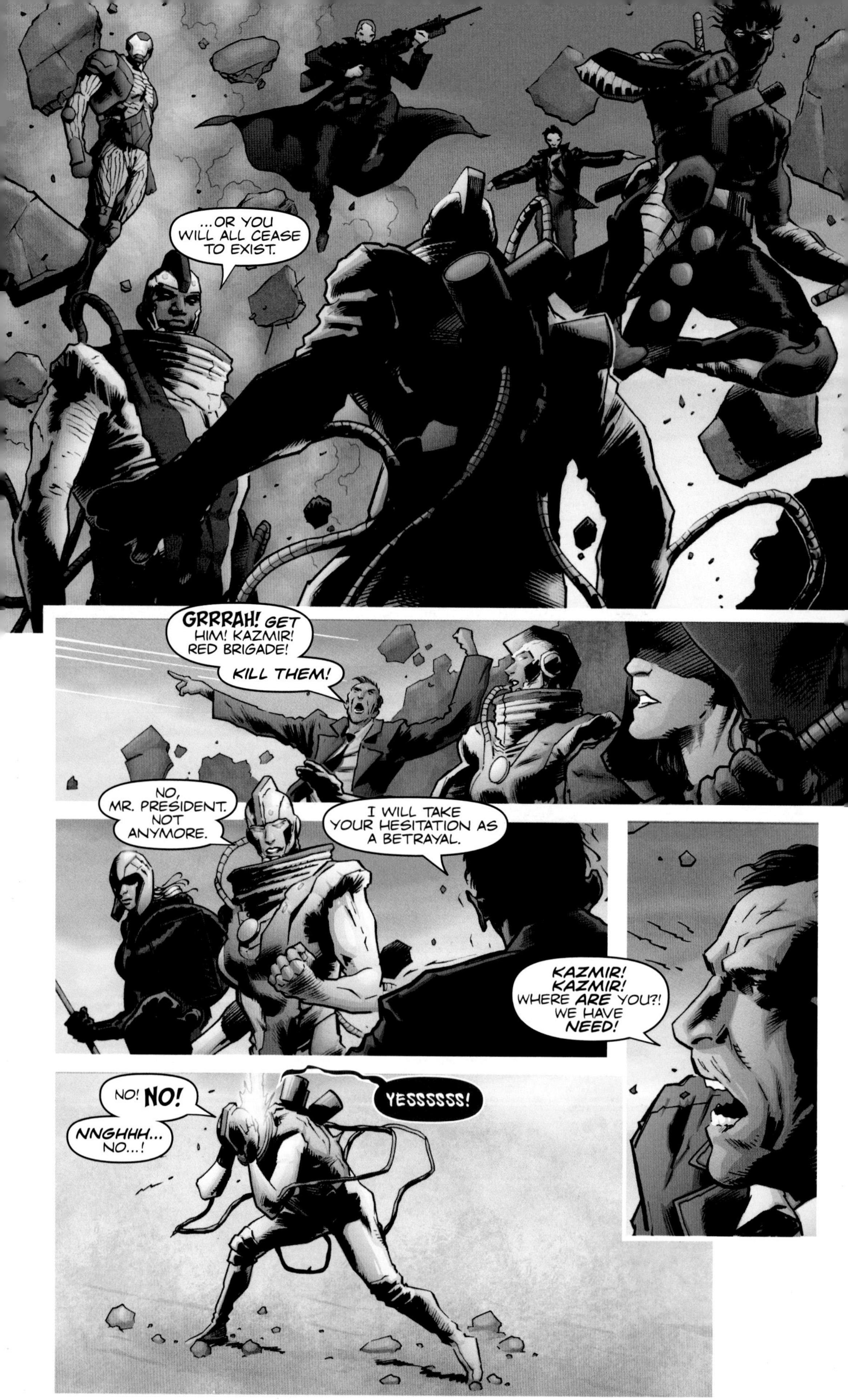
...OR YOU WILL ALL CEASE TO EXIST.
GRRRAH! GET HIM! KAZMIR! RED BRIGADE!
KILL THEM!
NO, MR. PRESIDENT. NOT ANYMORE.
I WILL TAKE YOUR HESITATION AS A BETRAYAL.
KAZMIR! KAZMIR! WHERE ARE YOU?! WE HAVE NEED!
NO! NO!
NNGHHH... NO...!
YESSSSSS!

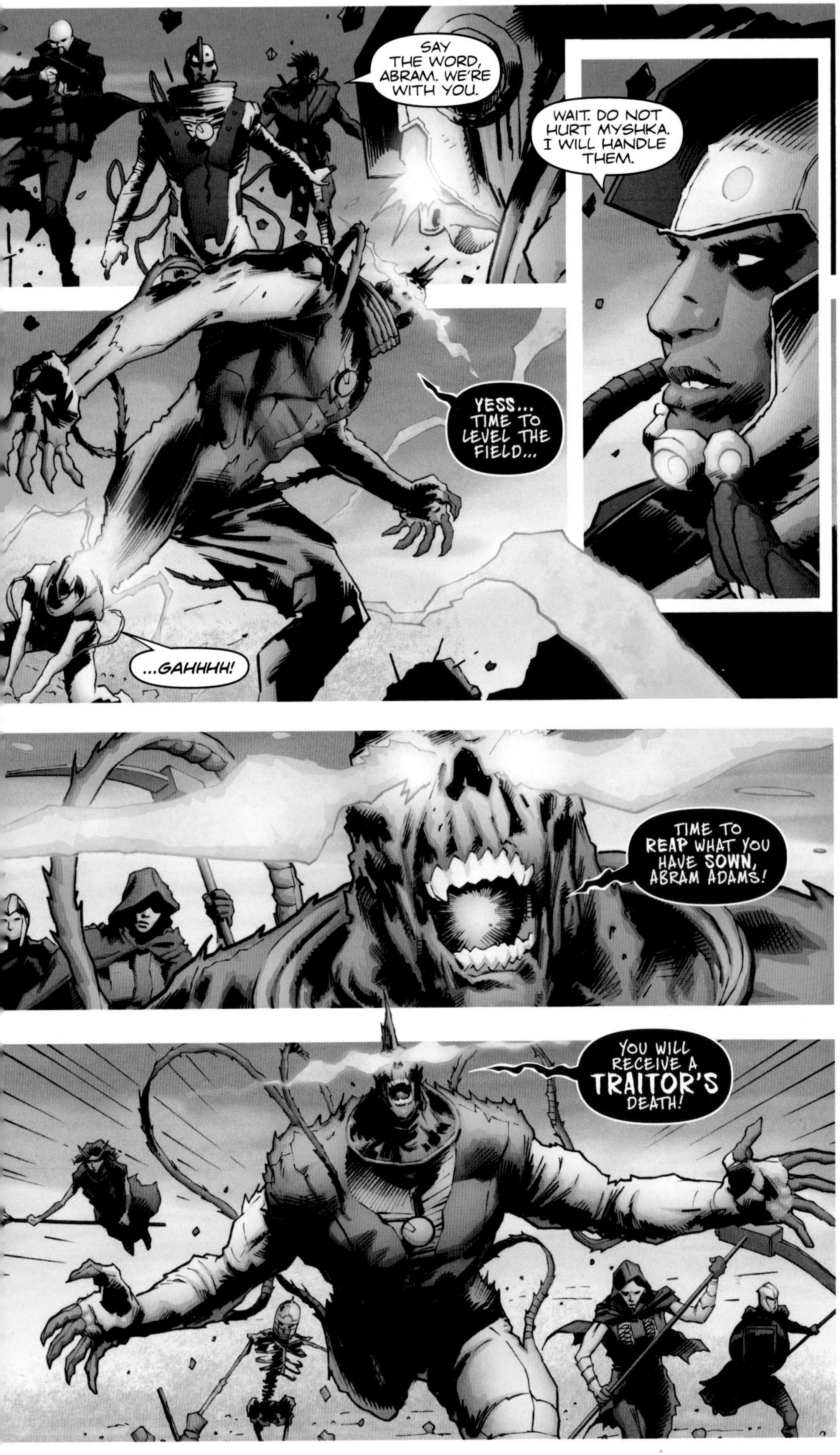
SAY THE WORD, ABRAM. WE'RE WITH YOU.
WAIT. DO NOT HURT MYSHKA. I WILL HANDLE THEM.
YESS... TIME TO LEVEL THE FIELD...
...GAHHHH!
TIME TO REAP WHAT YOU HAVE SOWN, ABRAM ADAMS!
YOU WILL RECEIVE A TRAITOR'S DEATH!

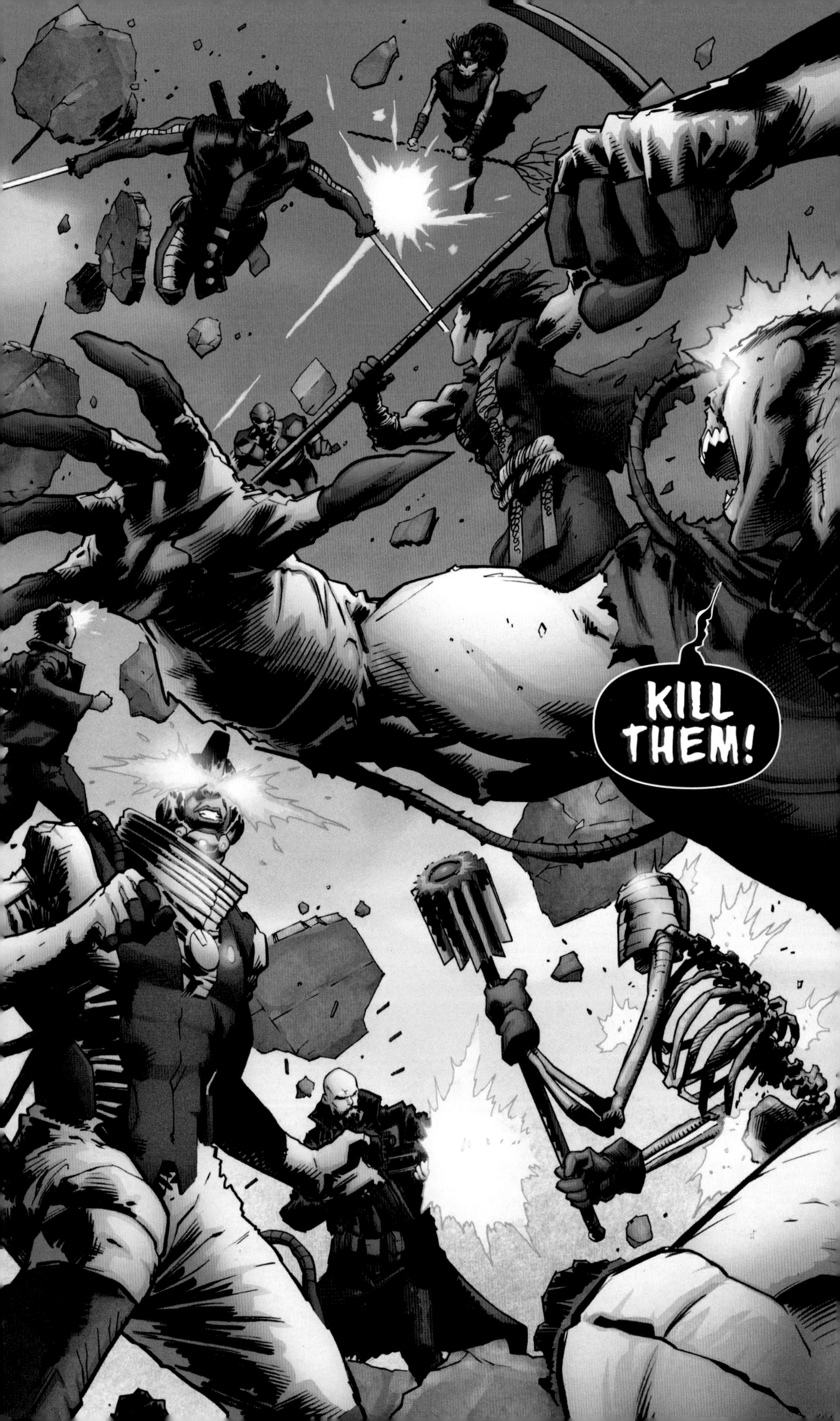
KILL THEM!

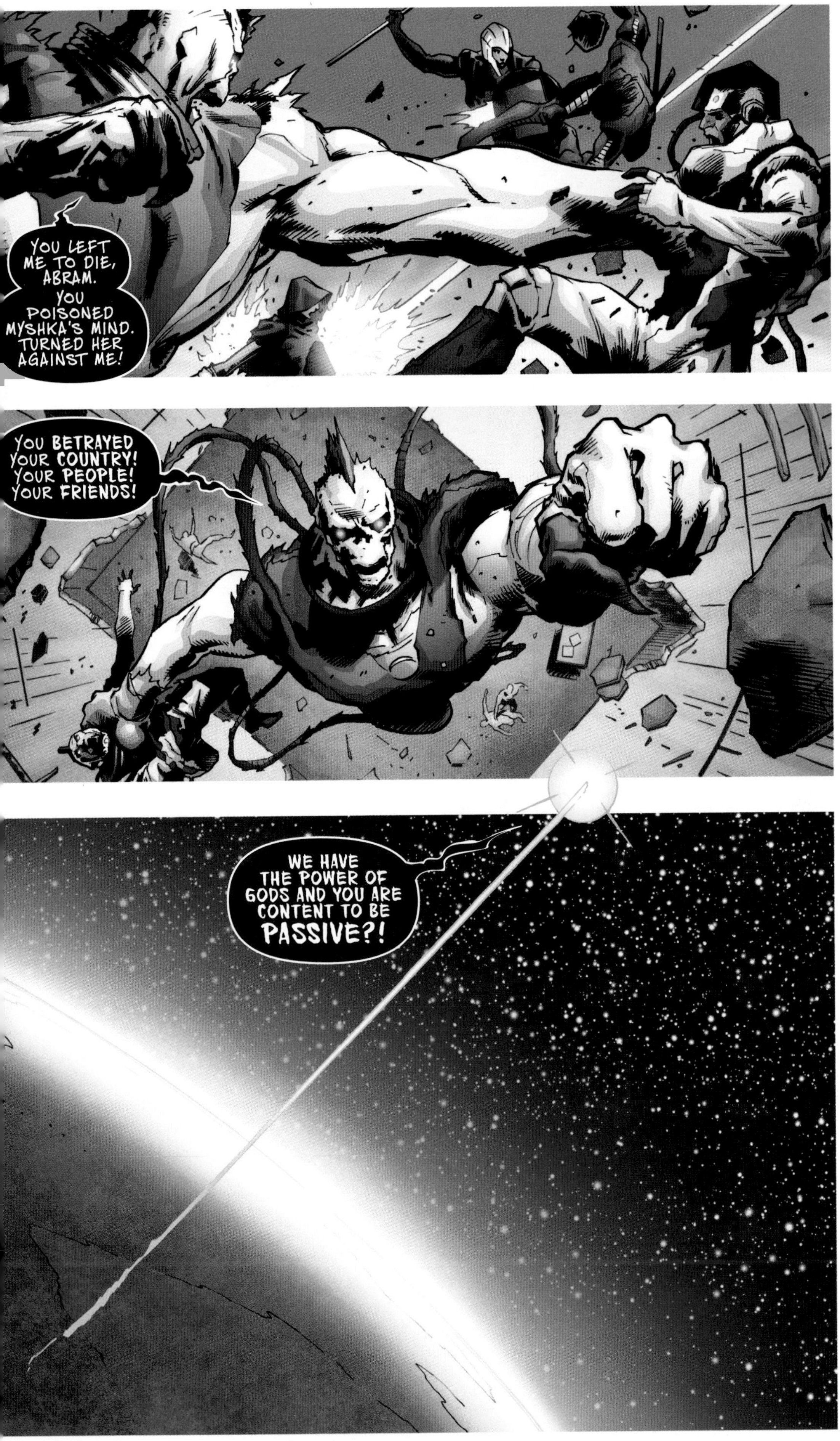
YOU LEFT ME TO DIE, ABRAM.
YOU POISONED MYSHKA'S MIND. TURNED HER AGAINST ME!
YOU BETRAYED YOUR COUNTRY! YOUR PEOPLE! YOUR FRIENDS!
WE HAVE THE POWER OF GODS AND YOU ARE CONTENT TO BE PASSIVE?!

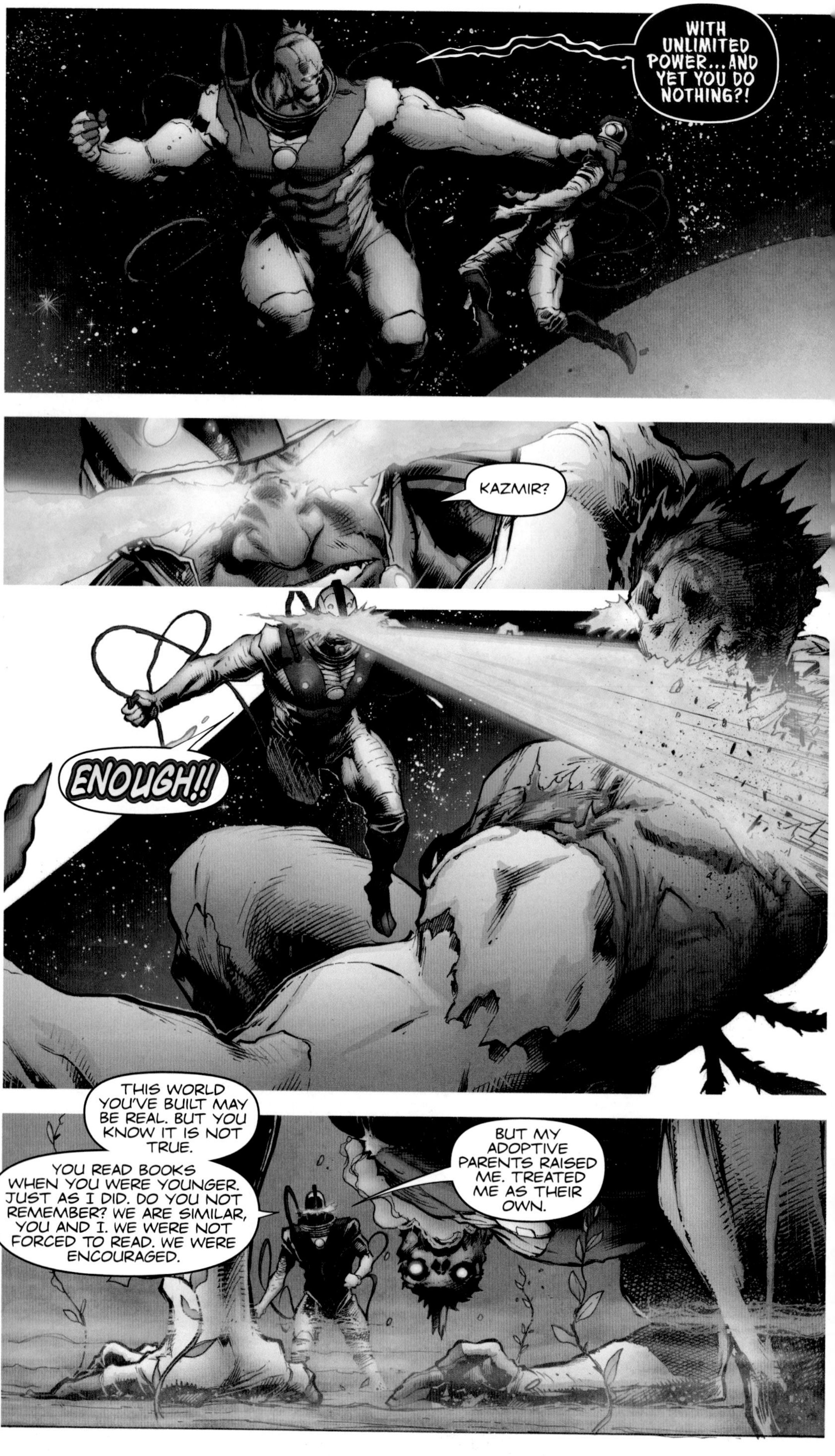
WITH UNLIMITED POWER... AND YET YOU DO NOTHING?!
KAZMIR?
ENOUGH!!
THIS WORLD YOU'VE BUILT MAY BE REAL. BUT YOU KNOW IT IS NOT TRUE.
YOU READ BOOKS WHEN YOU WERE YOUNGER. JUST AS I DID. DO YOU NOT REMEMBER? WE ARE SIMILAR, YOU AND I. WE WERE NOT FORCED TO READ. WE WERE ENCOURAGED.
BUT MY ADOPTIVE PARENTS RAISED ME. TREATED ME AS THEIR OWN.

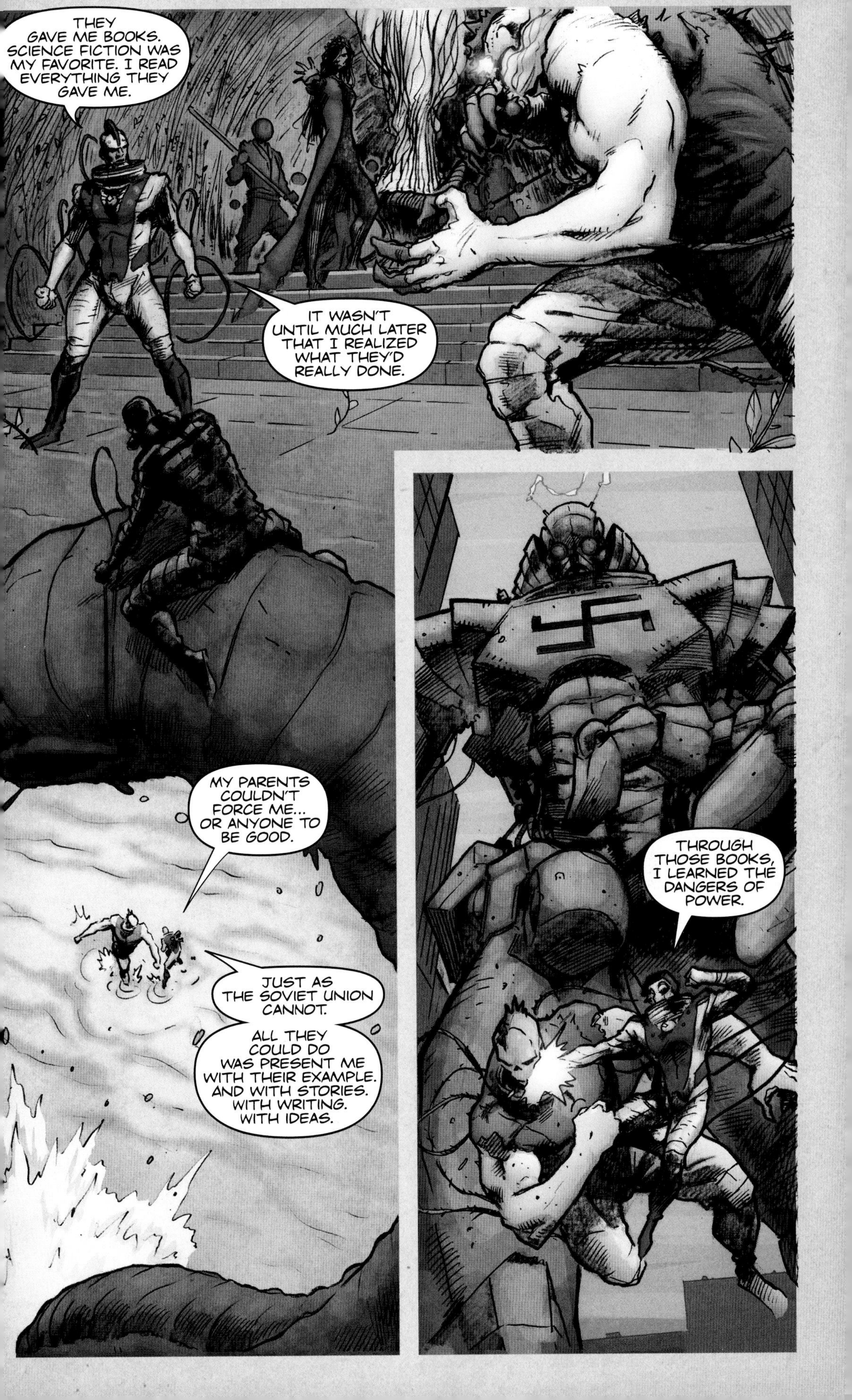
THEY GAVE ME BOOKS. SCIENCE FICTION WAS MY FAVORITE. I READ EVERYTHING THEY GAVE ME.
IT WASN'T UNTIL MUCH LATER THAT I REALIZED WHAT THEY'D REALLY DONE.
MY PARENTS COULDN'T FORCE ME... OR ANYONE TO BE GOOD.
JUST AS THE SOVIET UNION CANNOT.
ALL THEY COULD DO WAS PRESENT ME WITH THEIR EXAMPLE. AND WITH STORIES. WITH WRITING. WITH IDEAS.
THROUGH THOSE BOOKS, I LEARNED THE DANGERS OF POWER.

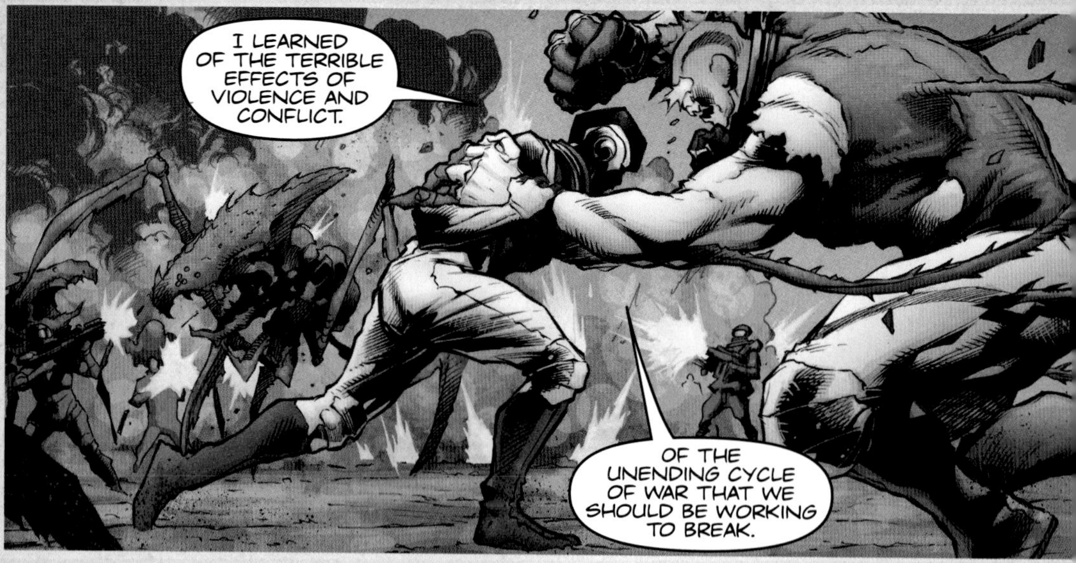
I LEARNED OF THE TERRIBLE EFFECTS OF VIOLENCE AND CONFLICT.
OF THE UNENDING CYCLE OF WAR THAT WE SHOULD BE WORKING TO BREAK.

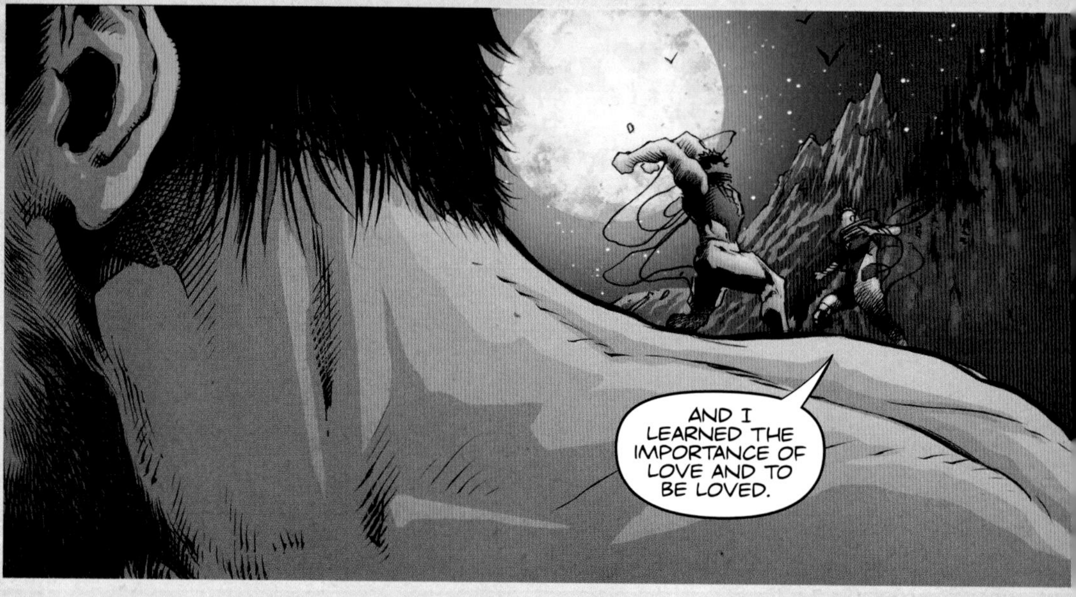
AND I LEARNED THE IMPORTANCE OF LOVE AND TO BE LOVED.

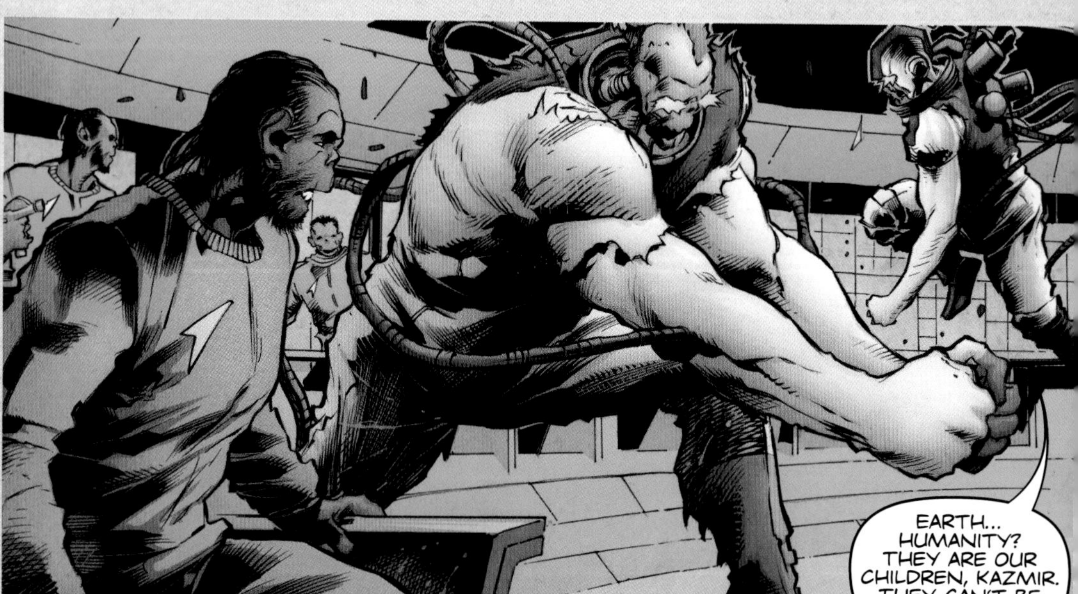
EARTH... HUMANITY? THEY ARE OUR CHILDREN, KAZMIR. THEY CAN'T BE FORCED TO LEARN.

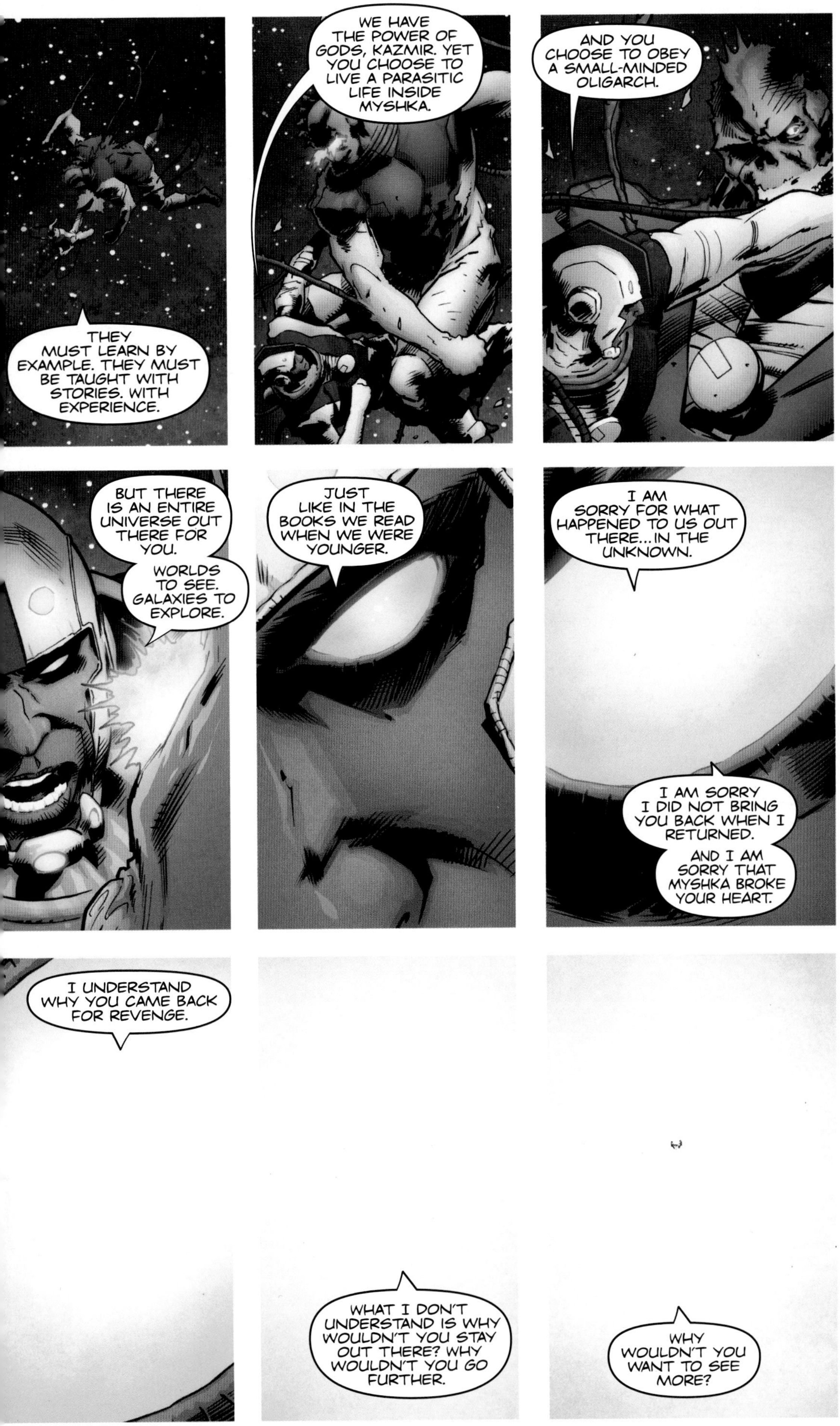
THEY MUST LEARN BY EXAMPLE. THEY MUST BE TAUGHT WITH STORIES. WITH EXPERIENCE.
WE HAVE THE POWER OF GODS, KAZMIR. YET YOU CHOOSE TO LIVE A PARASITIC LIFE INSIDE MYSHKA.
AND YOU CHOOSE TO OBEY A SMALL-MINDED OLIGARCH.
BUT THERE IS AN ENTIRE UNIVERSE OUT THERE FOR YOU.
WORLDS TO SEE. GALAXIES TO EXPLORE.
JUST LIKE IN THE BOOKS WE READ WHEN WE WERE YOUNGER.
I AM SORRY FOR WHAT HAPPENED TO US OUT THERE... IN THE UNKNOWN.
I AM SORRY I DID NOT BRING YOU BACK WHEN I RETURNED.
AND I AM SORRY THAT MYSHKA BROKE YOUR HEART.
I UNDERSTAND WHY YOU CAME BACK FOR REVENGE.
WHAT I DON'T UNDERSTAND IS WHY WOULDN'T YOU STAY OUT THERE? WHY WOULDN'T YOU GO FURTHER.
WHY WOULDN'T YOU WANT TO SEE MORE?

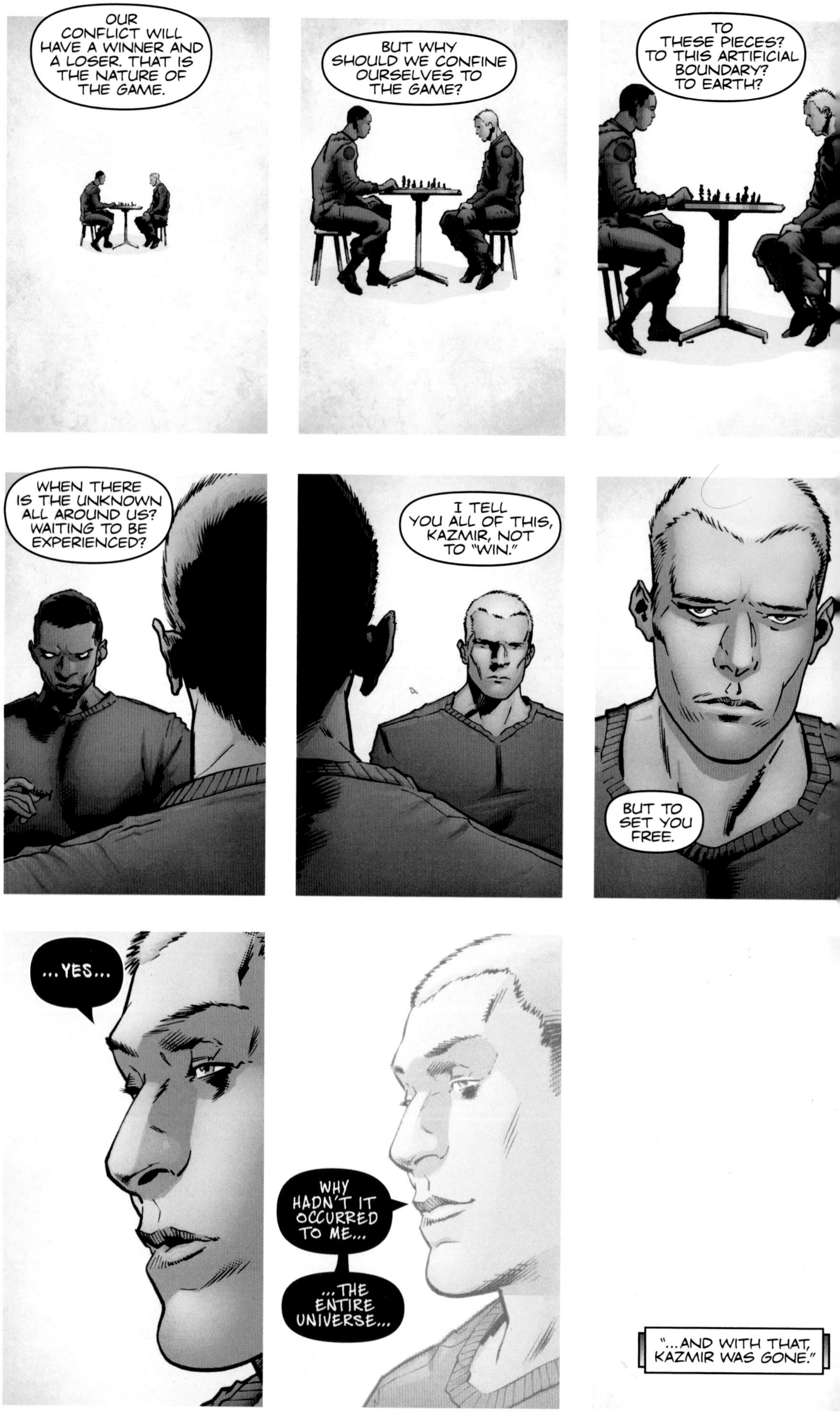
OUR CONFLICT WILL HAVE A WINNER AND A LOSER. THAT IS THE NATURE OF THE GAME.
BUT WHY SHOULD WE CONFINE OURSELVES TO THE GAME?
TO THESE PIECES? TO THIS ARTIFICIAL BOUNDARY? TO EARTH?
WHEN THERE IS THE UNKNOWN ALL AROUND US? WAITING TO BE EXPERIENCED?
I TELL YOU ALL OF THIS, KAZMIR, NOT TO "WIN."
BUT TO SET YOU FREE.
...YES...
WHY HADN'T IT OCCURRED TO ME...
...THE ENTIRE UNIVERSE...
"...AND WITH THAT, KAZMIR WAS GONE."

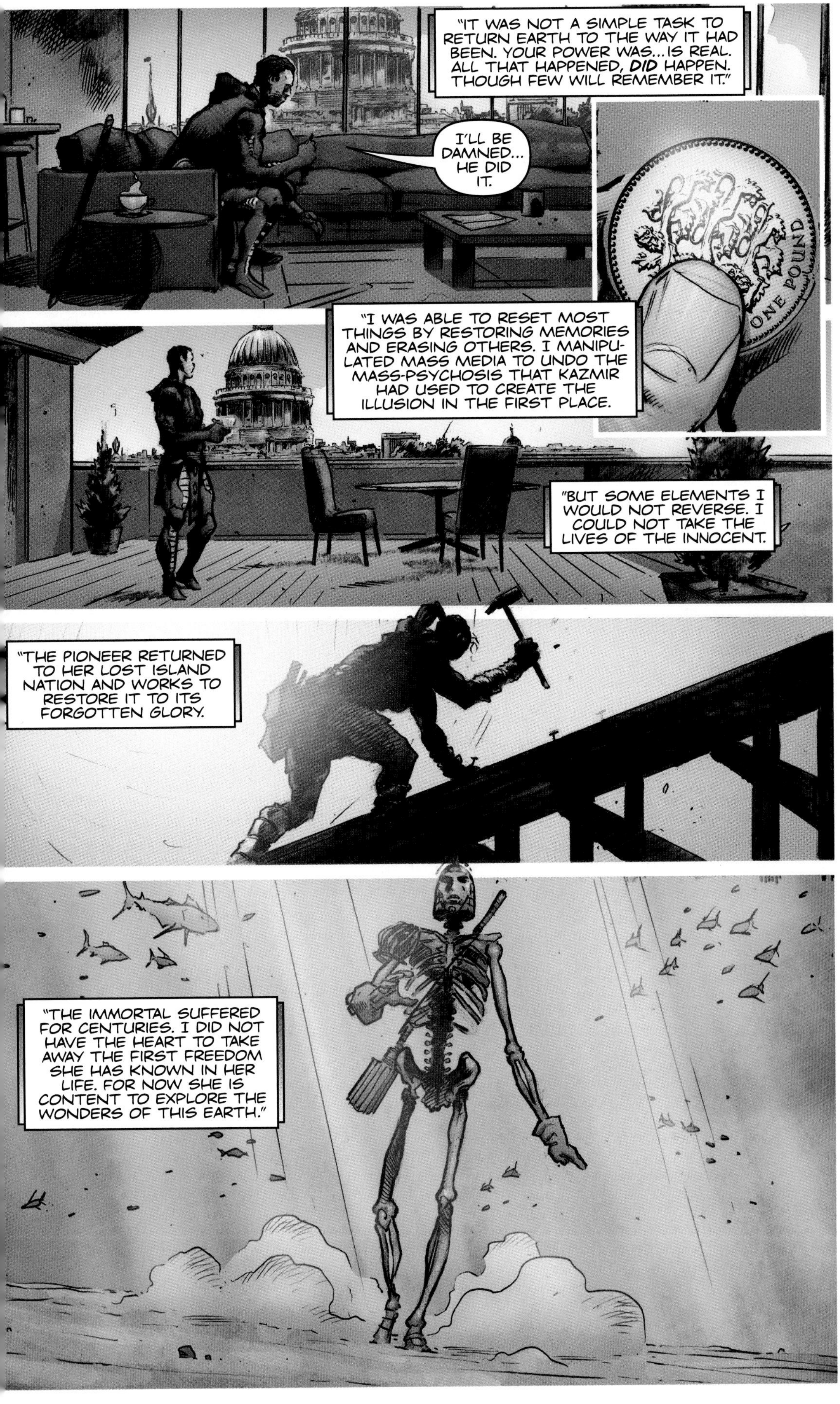
"IT WAS NOT A SIMPLE TASK TO RETURN EARTH TO THE WAY IT HAD BEEN. YOUR POWER WAS...IS REAL. ALL THAT HAPPENED, **DID** HAPPEN. THOUGH FEW WILL REMEMBER IT."
I'LL BE DAMNED... HE DID IT.
ONE POUND
"I WAS ABLE TO RESET MOST THINGS BY RESTORING MEMORIES AND ERASING OTHERS. I MANIPULATED MASS MEDIA TO UNDO THE MASS-PSYCHOSIS THAT KAZMIR HAD USED TO CREATE THE ILLUSION IN THE FIRST PLACE.
"BUT SOME ELEMENTS I WOULD NOT REVERSE. I COULD NOT TAKE THE LIVES OF THE INNOCENT.
"THE PIONEER RETURNED TO HER LOST ISLAND NATION AND WORKS TO RESTORE IT TO ITS FORGOTTEN GLORY.
"THE IMMORTAL SUFFERED FOR CENTURIES. I DID NOT HAVE THE HEART TO TAKE AWAY THE FIRST FREEDOM SHE HAS KNOWN IN HER LIFE. FOR NOW SHE IS CONTENT TO EXPLORE THE WONDERS OF THIS EARTH."

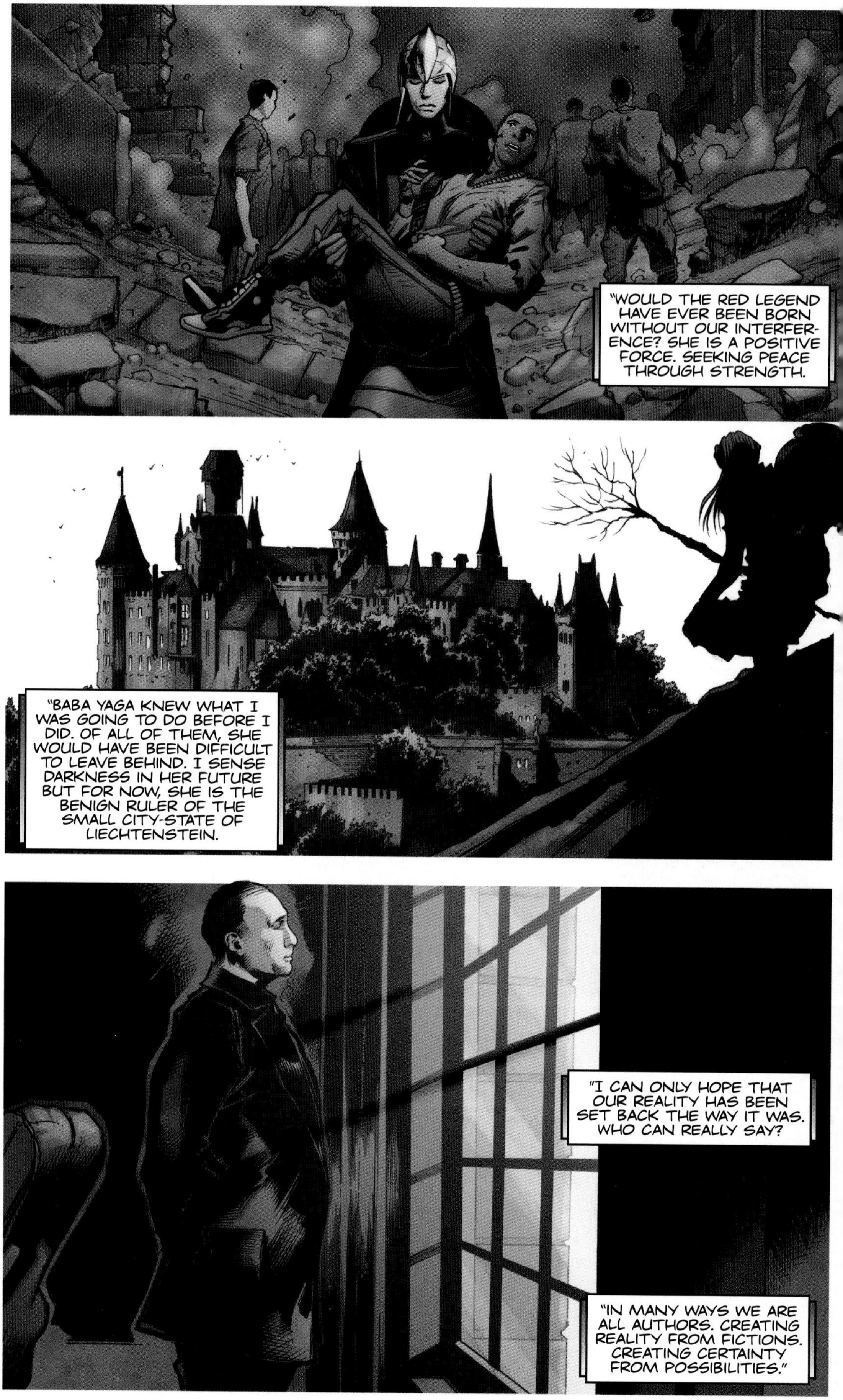
"WOULD THE RED LEGEND HAVE EVER BEEN BORN WITHOUT OUR INTERFERENCE? SHE IS A POSITIVE FORCE. SEEKING PEACE THROUGH STRENGTH.
"BABA YAGA KNEW WHAT I WAS GOING TO DO BEFORE I DID. OF ALL OF THEM, SHE WOULD HAVE BEEN DIFFICULT TO LEAVE BEHIND. I SENSE DARKNESS IN HER FUTURE BUT FOR NOW, SHE IS THE BENIGN RULER OF THE SMALL CITY-STATE OF LIECHTENSTEIN.
"I CAN ONLY HOPE THAT OUR REALITY HAS BEEN SET BACK THE WAY IT WAS. WHO CAN REALLY SAY?
"IN MANY WAYS WE ARE ALL AUTHORS. CREATING REALITY FROM FICTIONS. CREATING CERTAINTY FROM POSSIBILITIES."

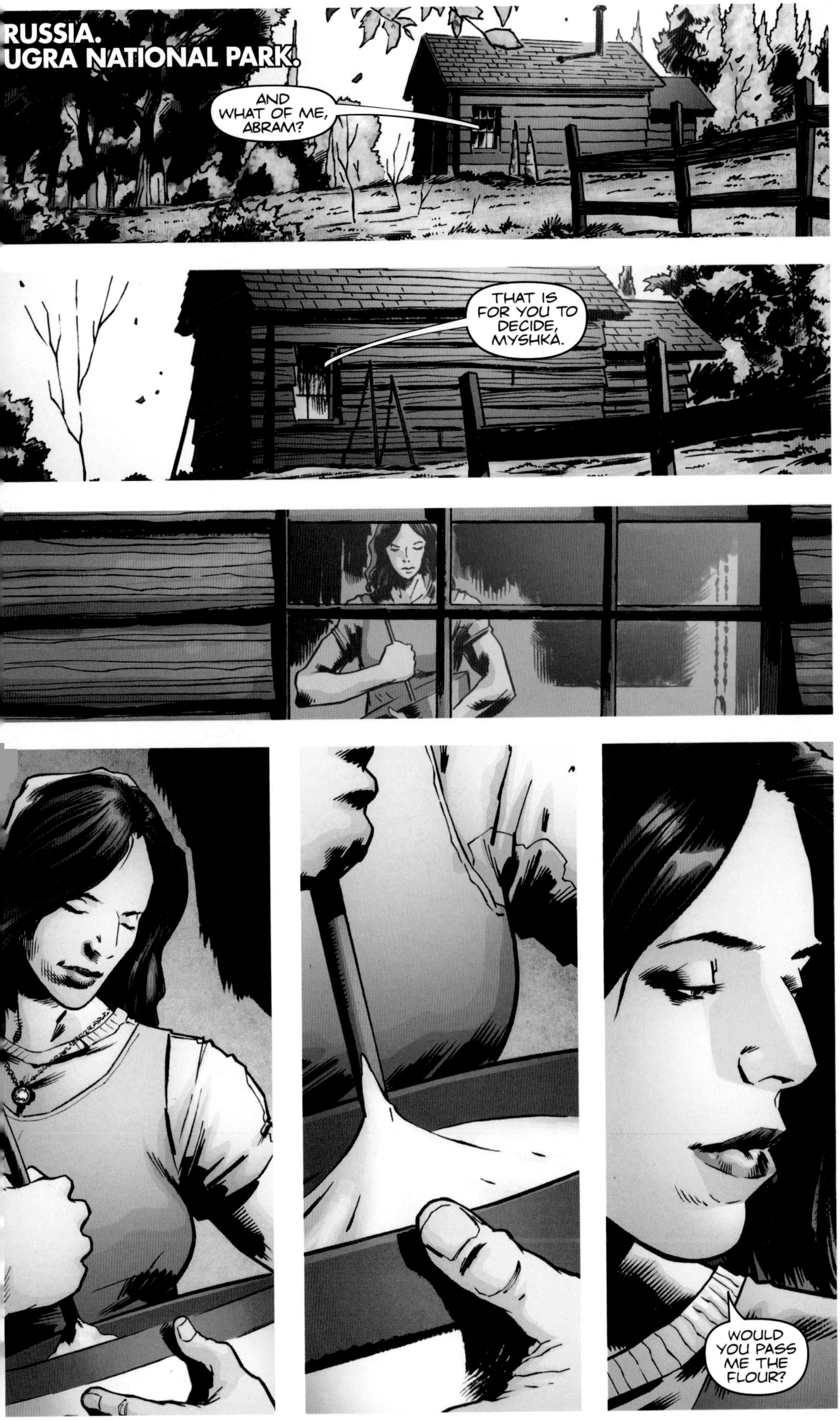
RUSSIA.
UGRA NATIONAL PARK.
AND WHAT OF ME, ABRAM?
THAT IS FOR YOU TO DECIDE, MYSHKA.
WOULD YOU PASS ME THE FLOUR?

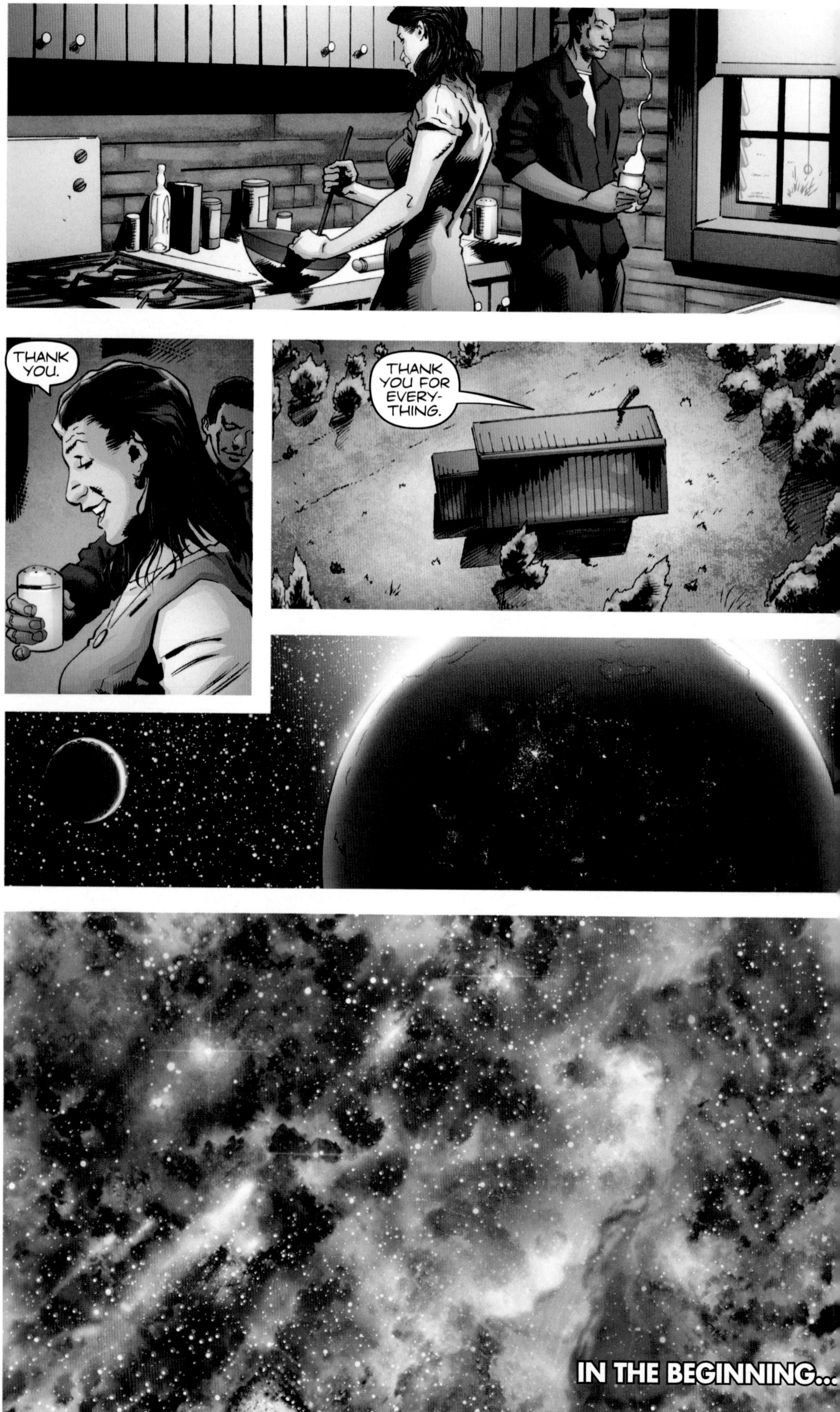
THANK YOU.
THANK YOU FOR EVERY-THING.
IN THE BEGINNING...

GALLERY

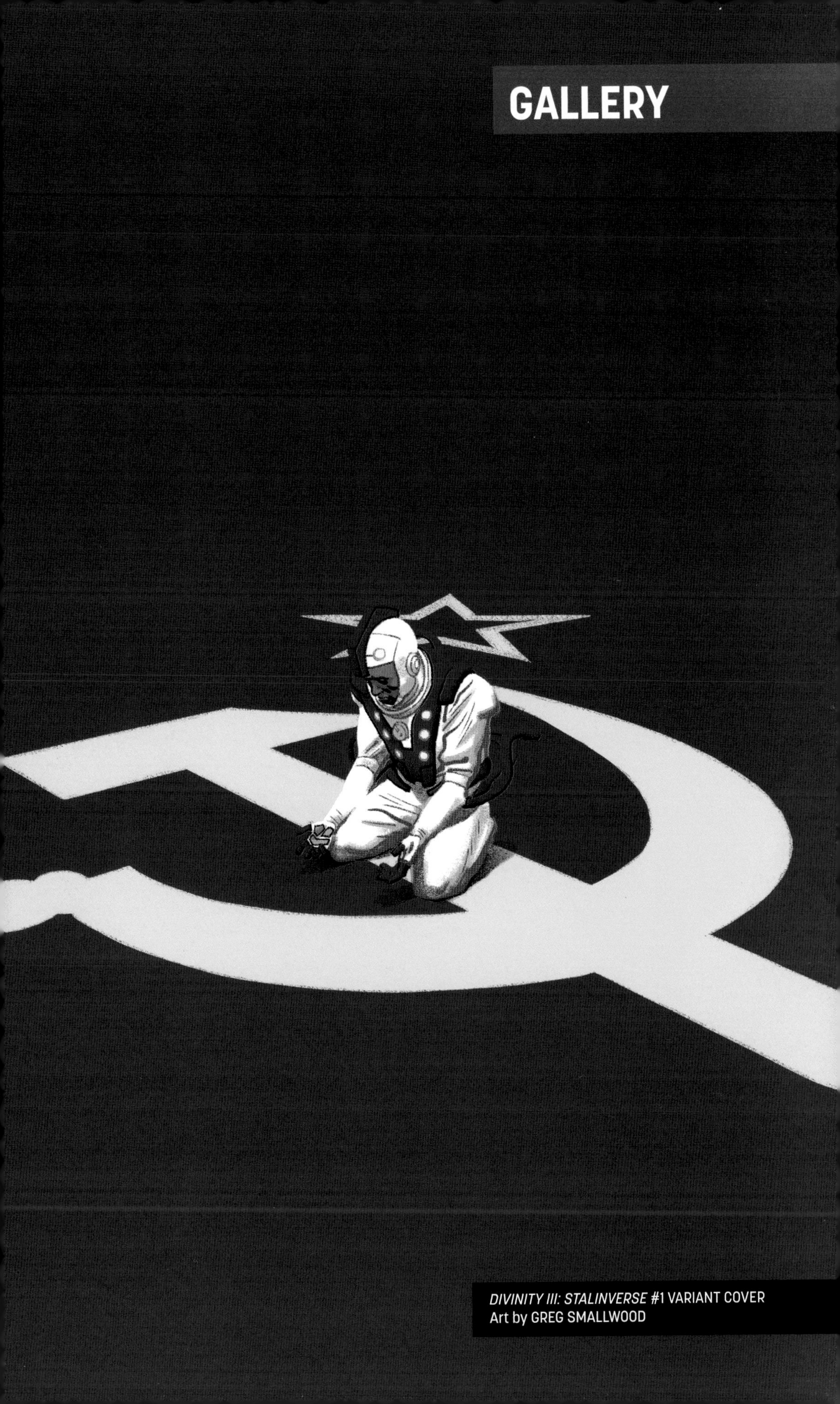

DIVINITY III: STALINVERSE #1 VARIANT COVER
Art by GREG SMALLWOOD

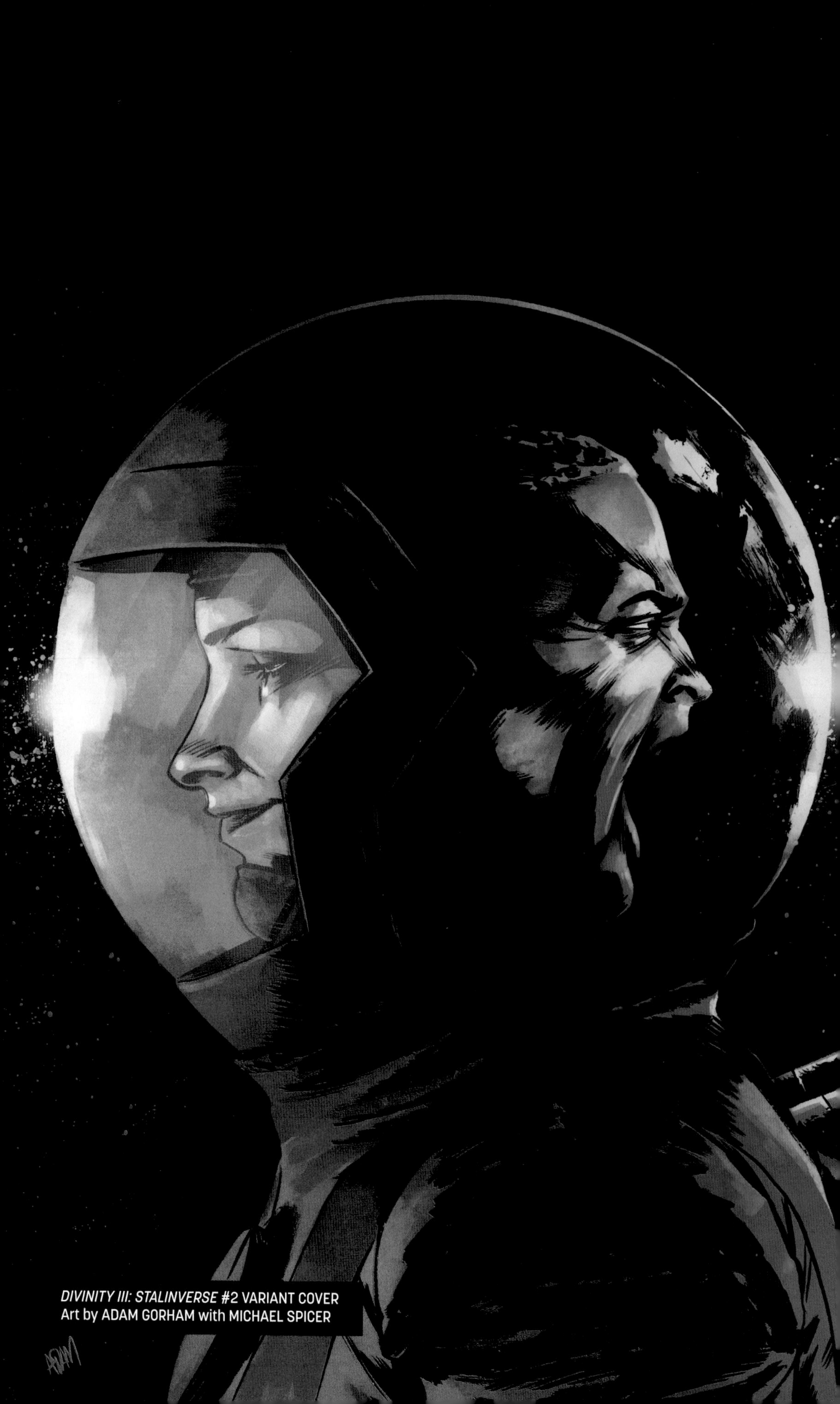

DIVINITY III: STALINVERSE #2 VARIANT COVER
Art by ADAM GORHAM with MICHAEL SPICER

DIVINITY III: STALINVERSE #3 VARIANT COVER
Art by ADAM GORHAM with ULISES ARREOLA

DIVINITY III: STALINVERSE #4 VARIANT COVER
Art by ADAM GORHAM with ULISES ARREOLA

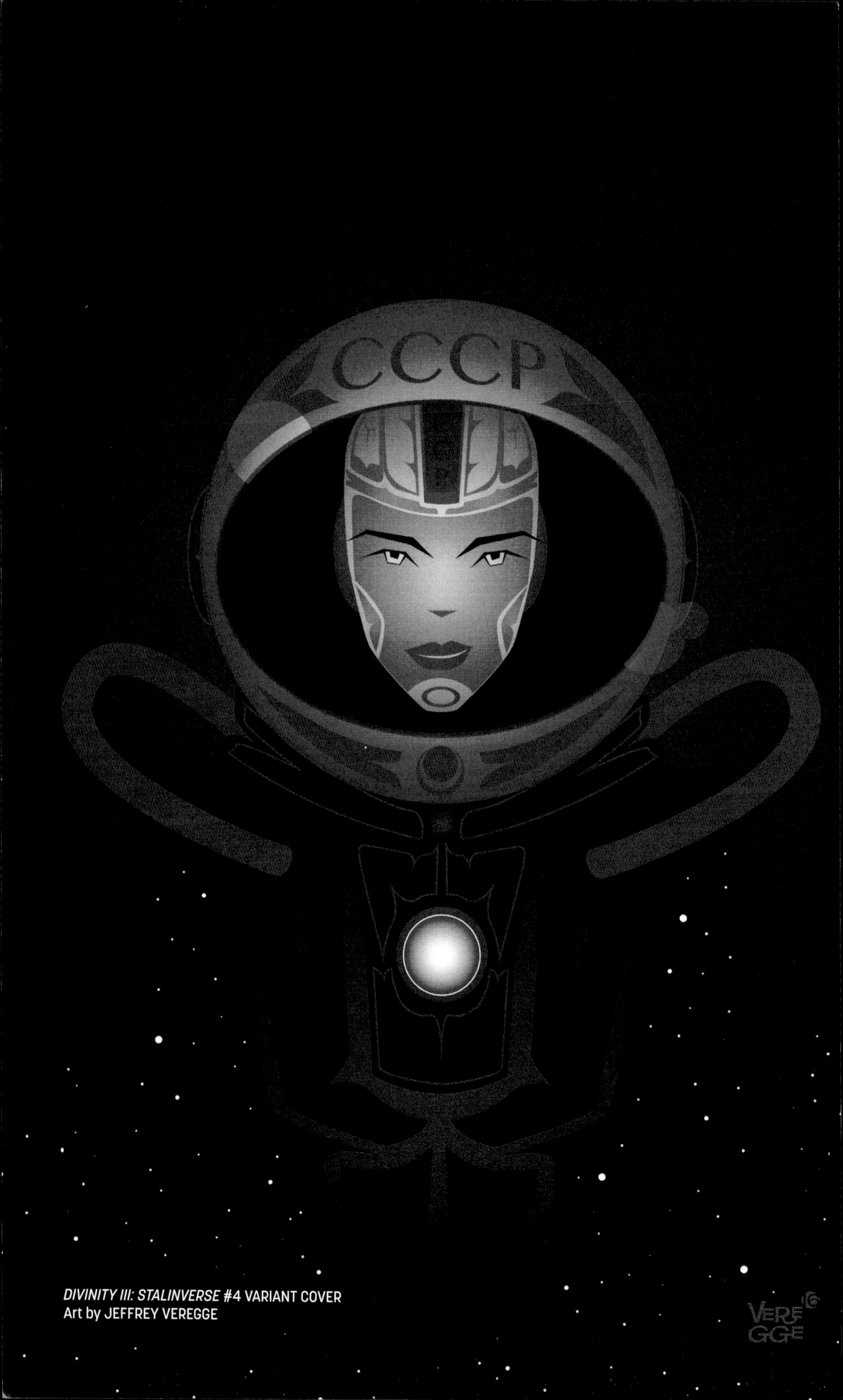
CCCP
VEREGGE
'16

DIVINITY III: STALINVERSE #4 VARIANT COVER
Art by JEFFREY VEREGGE

DIVINITY III: STALINVERSE #1, p. 2
Pencils by TREVOR HAIRSINE
Inks by RYAN WINN

DIVINITY III: STALINVERSE #1, p. 12
Pencils by TREVOR HAIRSINE
Inks by RYAN WINN

DIVINITY III: STALINVERSE #2, p. 19
Pencils by TREVOR HAIRSINE
Inks by RYAN WINN

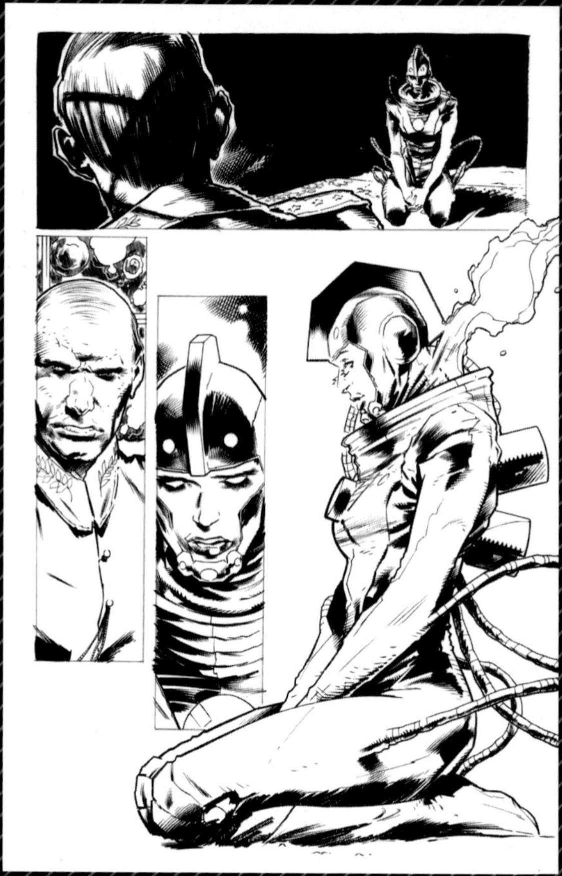

DIVINITY III: STALINVERSE #2, p. 20
Pencils by TREVOR HAIRSINE
Inks by RYAN WINN

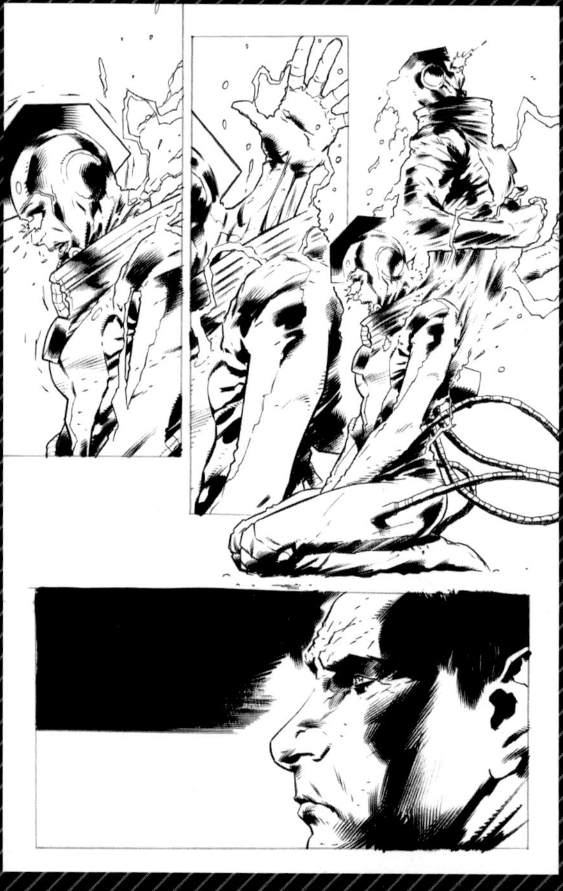

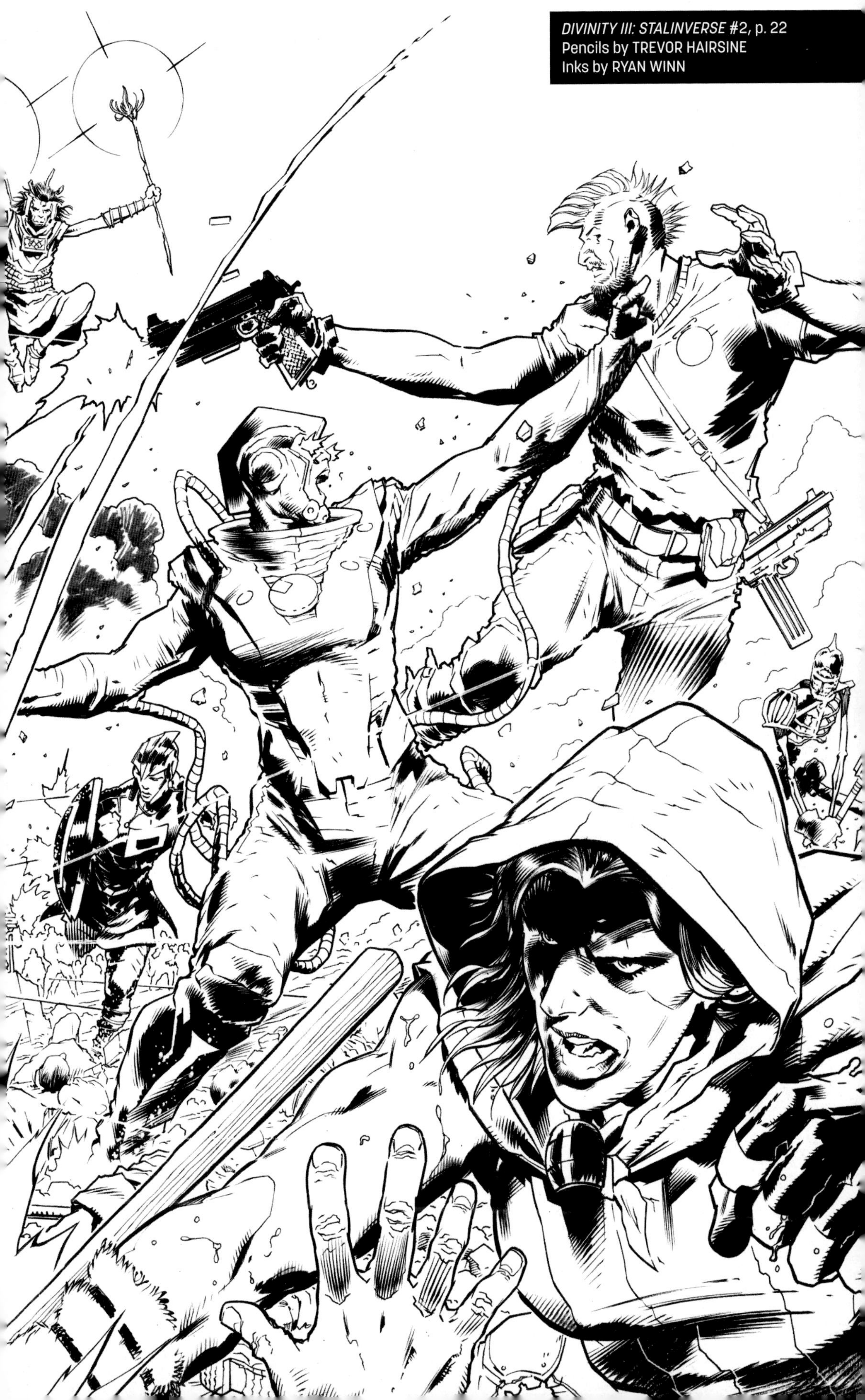

DIVINITY III: STALINVERSE #2, p. 22
Pencils by TREVOR HAIRSINE
Inks by RYAN WINN

DIVINITY III: STALINVERSE #3, p. 4
Pencils by TREVOR HAIRSINE
Inks by RYAN WINN

DIVINITY III: STALINVERSE #3, p. 22
Pencils by TREVOR HAIRSINE
Inks by RYAN WINN

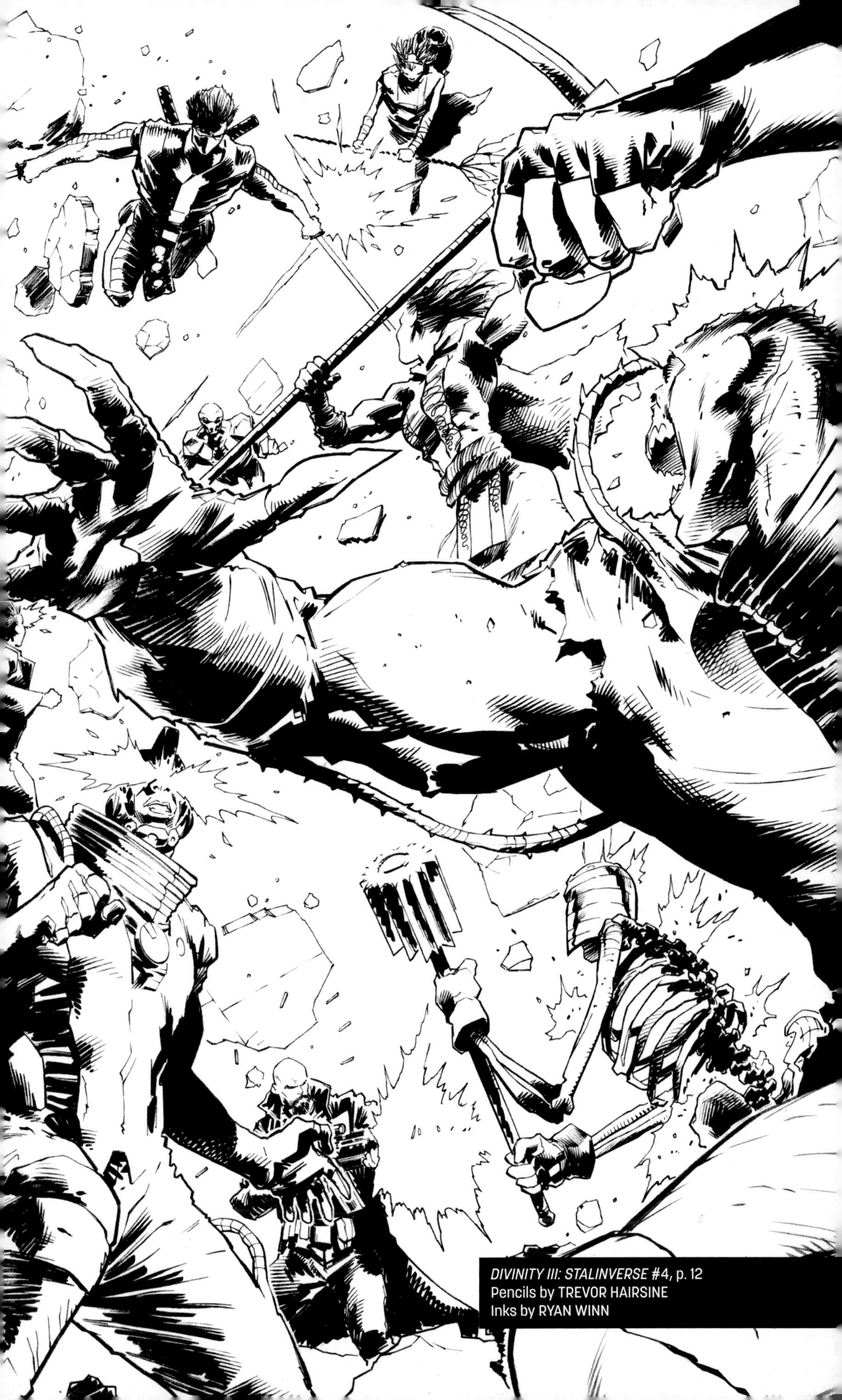

DIVINITY III: STALINVERSE #4, p. 12
Pencils by TREVOR HAIRSINE
Inks by RYAN WINN

EXPLORE THE VALIANT UNIVERSE

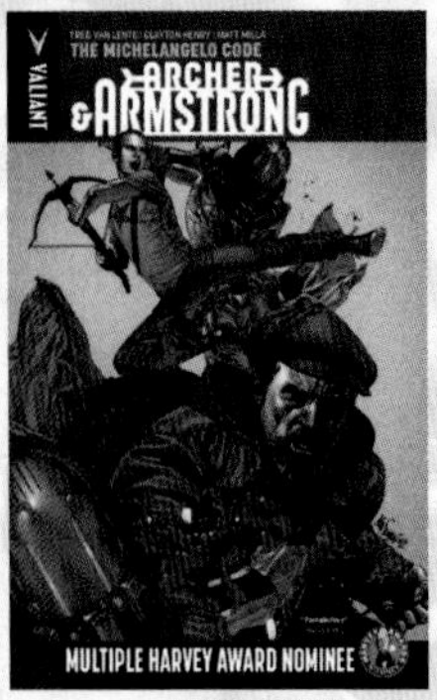
VALIANT
THE MICHELANGELO CODE
ARCHER & ARMSTRONG
MULTIPLE HARVEY AWARD NOMINEE

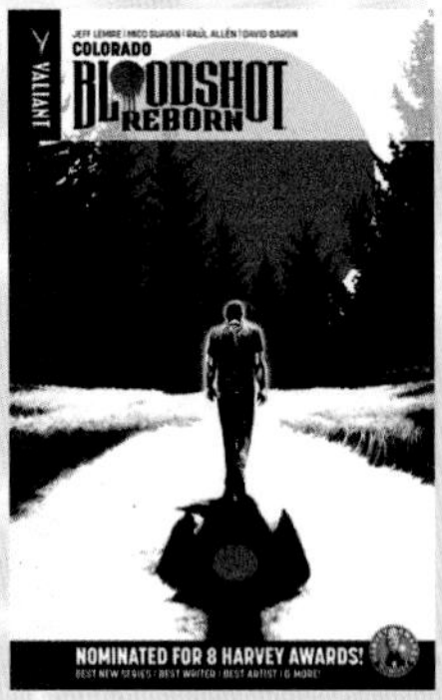
VALIANT
COLORADO
BLOODSHOT REBORN
NOMINATED FOR 8 HARVEY AWARDS!

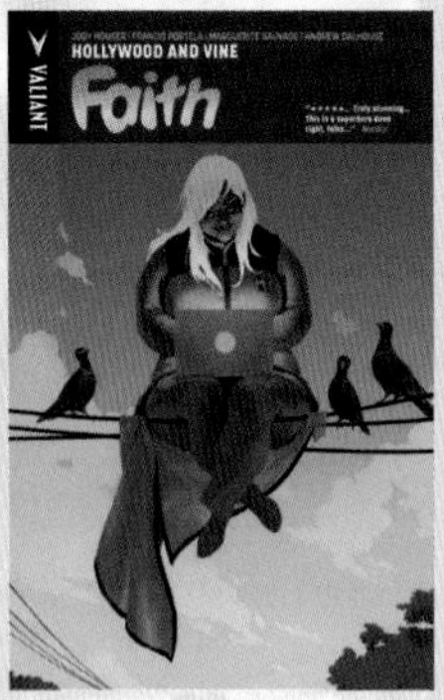
VALIANT
HOLLYWOOD AND VINE
Faith

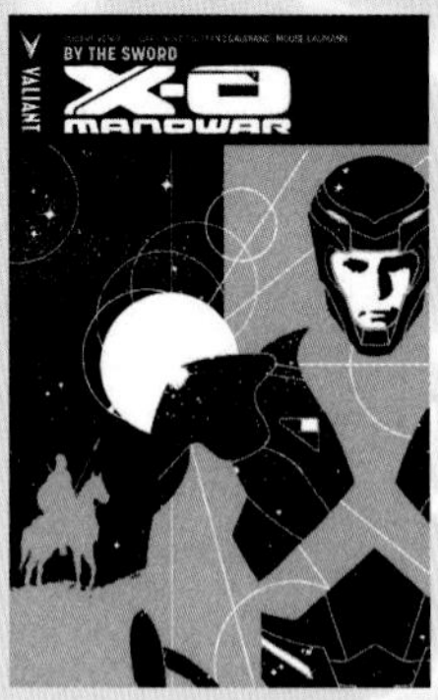
VALIANT
BY THE SWORD
X-O MANOWAR

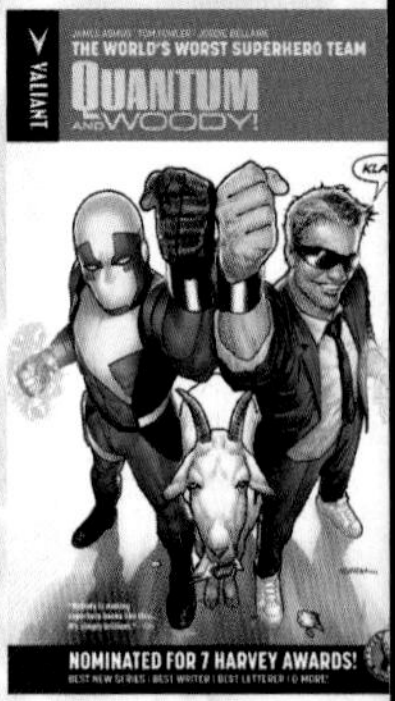
VALIANT
THE WORLD'S WORST SUPERHERO TEAM
QUANTUM AND WOODY!
NOMINATED FOR 7 HARVEY AWARDS!

4001 A.D.

4001 A.D.
ISBN: 9781682151433

4001 A.D.: Beyond New Japan
ISBN: 9781682151464

Rai Vol 4: 4001 A.D.
ISBN: 9781682151471

A&A: THE ADVENTURES OF ARCHER AND ARMSTRONG

Volume 1: In the Bag
ISBN: 9781682151495

Volume 2: Romance and Road Trips
ISBN: 9781682151716

ARCHER & ARMSTRONG

Volume 1: The Michelangelo Code
ISBN: 9780979640988

Volume 2: Wrath of the Eternal Warrior
ISBN: 9781939346049

Volume 3: Far Faraway
ISBN: 9781939346148

Volume 4: Sect Civil War
ISBN: 9781939346254

Volume 5: Mission: Improbable
ISBN: 9781939346353

Volume 6: American Wasteland
ISBN: 9781939346421

Volume 7: The One Percent and Other Tales
ISBN: 9781939346537

ARMOR HUNTERS

Armor Hunters
ISBN: 9781939346452

Armor Hunters: Bloodshot
ISBN: 9781939346469

Armor Hunters: Harbinger
ISBN: 9781939346506

Unity Vol. 3: Armor Hunters
ISBN: 9781939346445

X-O Manowar Vol. 7: Armor Hunters
ISBN: 9781939346476

BLOODSHOT

Volume 1: Setting the World on Fire
ISBN: 9780979640964

Volume 2: The Rise and the Fall
ISBN: 9781939346032

Volume 3: Harbinger Wars
ISBN: 9781939346124

Volume 4: H.A.R.D. Corps
ISBN: 9781939346193

Volume 5: Get Some!
ISBN: 9781939346315

Volume 6: The Glitch and Other Tales
ISBN: 9781939346711

BLOODSHOT REBORN

Volume 1: Colorado
ISBN: 9781939346674

Volume 2: The Hunt
ISBN: 9781939346827

Volume 3: The Analog Man
ISBN: 9781682151334

Volume 4: Bloodshot Island
ISBN: 9781682151952

BLOODSHOT U.S.A.

ISBN: 9781682151952

BOOK OF DEATH

Book of Death
ISBN: 9781939346971

Book of Death: The Fall of the Valiant Universe
ISBN: 9781939346988

BRITANNIA

Volume 1
ISBN: 9781682151853

DEAD DROP

ISBN: 9781939346858

THE DEATH-DEFYING DOCTOR MIRAGE

Volume 1
ISBN: 9781939346490

Volume 2: Second Lives
ISBN: 9781682151297

THE DELINQUENTS

ISBN: 9781939346513

DIVINITY

Volume 1
ISBN: 9781939346766

Volume 2
ISBN: 9781682151518

ETERNAL WARRIOR

Volume 1: Sword of the Wild
ISBN: 9781939346209

Volume 2: Eternal Emperor
ISBN: 9781939346292

Volume 3: Days of Steel
ISBN: 9781939346742

WRATH OF THE ETERNAL WARRIO

Volume 1: Risen
ISBN: 9781682151235

Volume 2: Labyrinth
ISBN: 9781682151594

Volume 3: Deal With a Devil
ISBN: 9781682151976

FAITH

Faith Vol 1: Hollywood and Vine
ISBN: 9781682151402

Faith Vol 2: California Scheming
ISBN: 9781682151631

GENERATION ZERO

Volume 1: We Are the Future
ISBN: 9781682151754

HARBINGER

Volume 1: Omega Rising
ISBN: 9780979640957

Volume 2: Renegades
ISBN: 9781939346025

Volume 3: Harbinger Wars
ISBN: 9781939346117

Volume 4: Perfect Day
ISBN: 9781939346155

Volume 5: Death of a Renegade
ISBN: 9781939346339

Volume 6: Omegas
ISBN: 9781939346384

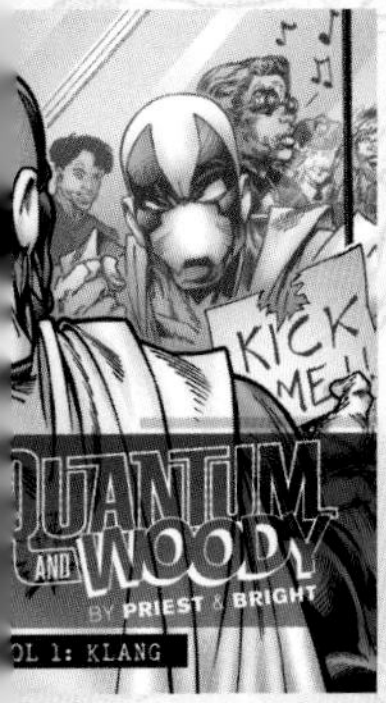
KICK ME
QUANTUM AND WOODY
BY PRIEST & BRIGHT
OL 1: KLANG
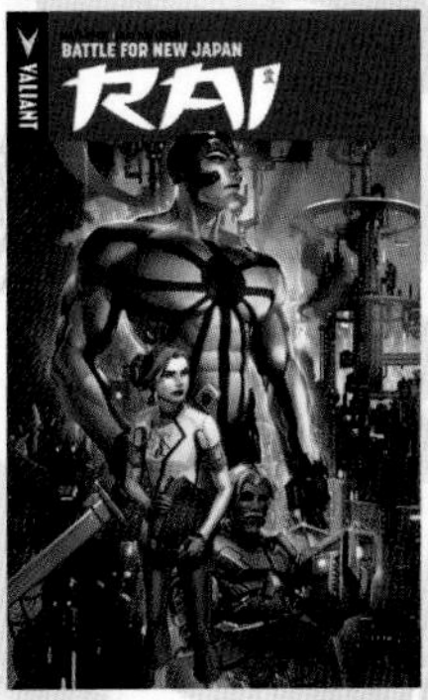
VALIANT
BATTLE FOR NEW JAPAN
RAI
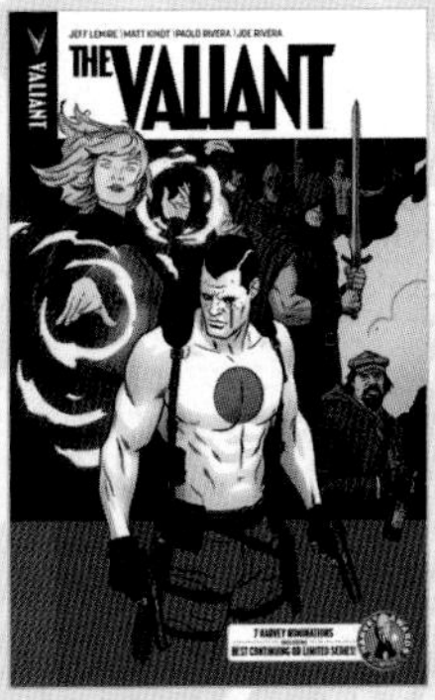
VALIANT
JEFF LEMIRE | MATT KINDT | PAOLO RIVERA | JOE RIVERA
THE VALIANT
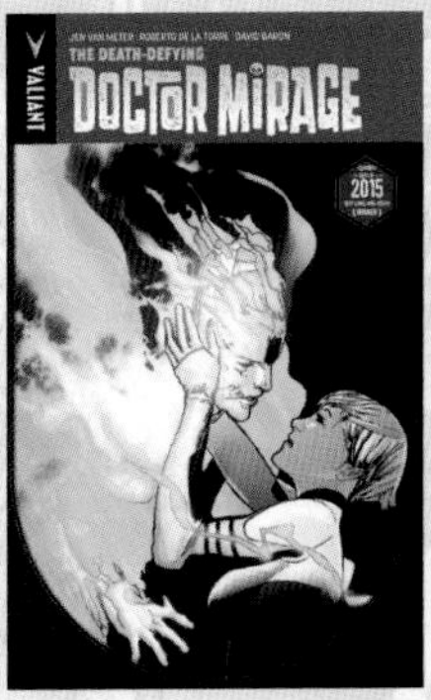
VALIANT
THE DEATH-DEFYING
DOCTOR MIRAGE
2015
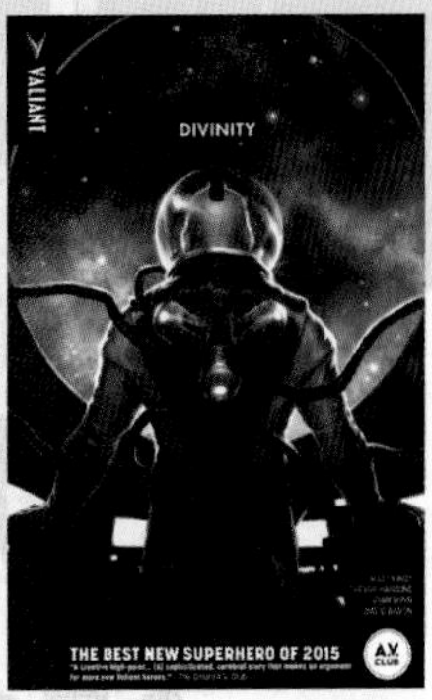
VALIANT
DIVINITY
THE BEST NEW SUPERHERO OF 2015

RBINGER RENEGADE

ume 1: The Judgment of Solomon
N: 9781682151693

RBINGER WARS

binger Wars
N: 9781939346094

odshot Vol. 3: Harbinger Wars
N: 9781939346124

binger Vol. 3: Harbinger Wars
N: 9781939346117

PERIUM

ume 1: Collecting Monsters
N: 9781939346759

ume 2: Broken Angels
N: 9781939346896

ume 3: The Vine Imperative
N: 9781682151112

ume 4: Stormbreak
N: 9781682151372

NJAK

ume 1: Weaponeer
N: 9781939346667

ume 2: The Shadow Wars
N: 9781939346940

ume 3: Operation: Deadside
N: 9781682151259

ume 4: The Siege of King's Castle
N: 9781682151617

ume 5: The Fist & The Steel
N: 9781682151792

ANTUM AND WOODY

ume 1: The World's Worst Superhero Team
N: 9781939346186

ume 2: In Security
N: 9781939346230

ume 3: Crooked Pasts, Present Tense
N: 9781939346391

ume 4: Quantum and Woody Must Die!
N: 9781939346629

ANTUM AND WOODY PRIEST & BRIGHT

ume 1: Klang
N: 9781939346780

Volume 2: Switch
ISBN: 9781939346803

Volume 3: And So...
ISBN: 9781939346865

Volume 4: Q2 - The Return
ISBN: 9781682151099

RAI

Volume 1: Welcome to New Japan
ISBN: 9781939346414

Volume 2: Battle for New Japan
ISBN: 9781939346612

Volume 3: The Orphan
ISBN: 9781939346841

Rai Vol 4: 4001 A.D.
ISBN: 9781682151471

SHADOWMAN

Volume 1: Birth Rites
ISBN: 9781939346001

Volume 2: Darque Reckoning
ISBN: 9781939346056

Volume 3: Deadside Blues
ISBN: 9781939346162

Volume 4: Fear, Blood, And Shadows
ISBN: 9781939346278

Volume 5: End Times
ISBN: 9781939346377

SHADOWMAN BY ENNIS & WOOD

ISBN: 9781682151358

IVAR, TIMEWALKER

Volume 1: Making History
ISBN: 9781939346636

Volume 2: Breaking History
ISBN: 9781939346834

Volume 3: Ending History
ISBN: 9781939346995

UNITY

Volume 1: To Kill a King
ISBN: 9781939346261

Volume 2: Trapped by Webnet
ISBN: 9781939346346

Volume 3: Armor Hunters
ISBN: 9781939346445

Volume 4: The United
ISBN: 9781939346544

Volume 5: Homefront
ISBN: 9781939346797

Volume 6: The War-Monger
ISBN: 9781939346902

Volume 7: Revenge of the Armor Hunters
ISBN: 9781682151136

THE VALIANT

ISBN: 9781939346605

VALIANT ZEROES AND ORIGINS

ISBN: 9781939346582

X-O MANOWAR

Volume 1: By the Sword
ISBN: 9780979640940

Volume 2: Enter Ninjak
ISBN: 9780979640995

Volume 3: Planet Death
ISBN: 9781939346087

Volume 4: Homecoming
ISBN: 9781939346179

Volume 5: At War With Unity
ISBN: 9781939346247

Volume 6: Prelude to Armor Hunters
ISBN: 9781939346407

Volume 7: Armor Hunters
ISBN: 9781939346476

Volume 8: Enter: Armorines
ISBN: 9781939346551

Volume 9: Dead Hand
ISBN: 9781939346650

Volume 10: Exodus
ISBN: 9781939346933

Volume 11: The Kill List
ISBN: 9781682151273

Volume 12: Long Live the King
ISBN: 9781682151655

Volume 13: Succession and Other Tales
ISBN: 9781682151754

EXPLORE THE VALIANT UNIVERSE

VALIANT
HARBINGER
DELUXE EDITION 2

VALIANT
ROBERT VENDITTI MATT KINDT JOSHUA DYSART JOE HARRIS ROBERT GILL
DOUG BRAITHWAITE DIEGO BERNARD TREVOR HAIRSINE STEPHEN SEGOVIA
ARMOR HUNTERS
DELUXE EDITION

VALIANT
JIM SHOOTER | DAVID LAPHAM
CHILDREN OF THE EIGHTH DAY
HARBINGER
VALIANT MASTERS

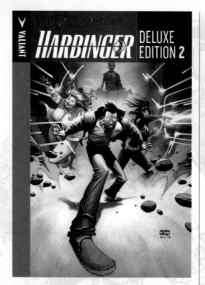

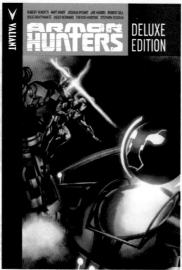

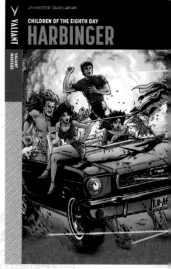

Omnibuses

Archer & Armstrong: The Complete Classic Omnibus
ISBN: 9781939346872
Collecting ARCHER & ARMSTRONG (1992) #0-26, ETERNAL WARRIOR (1992) #25 along with ARCHER & ARMSTRONG: THE FORMATION OF THE SECT.

Quantum and Woody: The Complete Classic Omnibus
ISBN: 9781939346360
Collecting QUANTUM AND WOODY (1997) #0, 1-21 and #32, THE GOAT: H.A.E.D.U.S. #1, and X-O MANOWAR (1996) #16

X-O Manowar Classic Omnibus Vol. 1
ISBN: 9781939346308
Collecting X-O MANOWAR (1992) #0-30, ARMORINES #0, X-O DATABASE #1, as well as material from SECRETS OF THE VALIANT UNIVERSE #1

Deluxe Editions

Archer & Armstrong Deluxe Edition Book 1
ISBN: 9781939346223
Collecting ARCHER & ARMSTRONG #0-13

Archer & Armstrong Deluxe Edition Book 2
ISBN: 9781939346957
Collecting ARCHER & ARMSTRONG #14-25, ARCHER & ARMSTRONG: ARCHER #0 and BLOODSHOT AND H.A.R.D. CORPS #20-21.

Armor Hunters Deluxe Edition
ISBN: 9781939346728
Collecting Armor Hunters #1-4, Armor Hunters: Aftermath #1, Armor Hunters: Bloodshot #1-3, Armor Hunters: Harbinger #1-3, Unity #8-11, and X-O MANOWAR #23-29

Bloodshot Deluxe Edition Book 1
ISBN: 9781939346216
Collecting BLOODSHOT #1-13

Bloodshot Deluxe Edition Book 2
ISBN: 9781939346810
Collecting BLOODSHOT AND H.A.R.D. CORPS #14-23, BLOODSHOT #24-25, BLOODSHOT #0, BLOODSHOT AND H.A.R.D. CORPS: H.A.R.D. CORPS #0, along with ARCHER & ARMSTRONG #18-19

Bloodshot Reborn Deluxe Edition Book 1
ISBN: 978-1-68215-155-6
Collecting BLOODSHOT REBORN #1-13

Book of Death Deluxe Edition
ISBN: 9781682151150
Collecting BOOK OF DEATH #1-4, BOOK OF DEATH: THE FALL OF BLOODSHOT #1, BOOK OF DEATH: THE FALL OF NINJAK #1, BOOK OF DEATH: THE FALL OF HARBINGER #1, and BOOK OF DEATH: THE FALL OF X-O MANOWAR #1.

The Death-Defying Doctor Mirage Deluxe Edition
ISBN: 978-1-68215-153-2
Collecting THE DEATH-DEFYING DR. MIRAGE #1-5 and THE DEATH-DEFYING DR. MIRAGE: SECOND LIVES #1-4

Divinity Deluxe Edition
ISBN: 97819393460993
Collecting DIVNITY #1-4

Faith: Hollywood & Vine Deluxe Edition
ISBN: 978-1-68215-201-0
Collecting FAITH #1-4 and HARBINGER: FAITH #0

Harbinger Deluxe Edition Book 1
ISBN: 9781939346131
Collecting HARBINGER #0-14

Harbinger Deluxe Edition Book 2
ISBN: 9781939346773
Collecting HARBINGER #15-25, HARBINGER: OMEGAS #1-3, and HARBINGER: BLEEDING MONK #0

Harbinger Wars Deluxe Edition
ISBN: 9781939346322
Collecting HARBINGER WARS #1-4, HARBINGER #11-14, and BLOODSHOT #10-13

Ivar, Timewalker Deluxe Edition Book 1
ISBN: 9781682151198
Collecting IVAR, TIMEWALKER #1-12

Ninjak Deluxe Edition Book 1
ISBN: 978-1-68215-157-0
Collecting NINJAK #1-13

Quantum and Woody Deluxe Edition Book 1
ISBN: 9781939346681
Collecting QUANTUM AND WOODY #1-12 and QUANTUM AND WOODY: THE GOAT #0

Q2: The Return of Quantum and Woody Deluxe Edition
ISBN: 9781939346568
Collecting Q2: THE RETURN OF QUANTUM AND WOODY #1-5

Rai Deluxe Edition Book 1
ISBN: 9781682151174
Collecting RAI #1-12, along with material from #1 PLUS EDITION and RAI #5 PLUS EDITION

Shadowman Deluxe Edition Book 1
ISBN: 9781939346438
Collecting SHADOWMAN #0-10

Shadowman Deluxe Edition Book 2
ISBN: 9781682151075
Collecting SHADOWMAN #11-16, SHADOWMAN #13X, SHADOWMAN: END TIMES #1-3 and PUNK MAMBO #0

Unity Deluxe Edition Book 1
ISBN: 9781939346575
Collecting UNITY #0-14

The Valiant Deluxe Edition
ISBN: 97819393460986
Collecting THE VALIANT #1-4

X-O Manowar Deluxe Edition Book 1
ISBN: 9781939346100
Collecting X-O MANOWAR #1-14

X-O Manowar Deluxe Edition Book 2
ISBN: 9781939346520
Collecting X-O MANOWAR #15-22, and UNITY #1

X-O Manowar Deluxe Edition Book 3
ISBN: 9781682151310
Collecting X-O MANOWAR #23-29 and ARMOR HUNTERS #1-4.

Valiant Masters

Bloodshot Vol. 1 - Blood of the Machine
ISBN: 9780979640933

H.A.R.D. Corps Vol. 1 - Search and Destroy
ISBN: 9781939346285

Harbinger Vol. 1 - Children of the Eighth Day
ISBN: 9781939346483

Ninjak Vol. 1 - Black Water
ISBN: 9780979640971

Rai Vol. 1 - From Honor to Strength
ISBN: 9781939346070

Shadowman Vol. 1 - Spirits Within
ISBN: 9781939346018

VALIANT
DIVINITY
MATT KINDT
TREVOR HAIRSINE
RYAN WINN
DAVID BARON
THE BEST NEW SUPERHERO OF 2015
"A creative high-point... [A] sophisticated, cerebral story that makes an argument for more new Valiant heroes." - The Onion/A.V. Club
A.V. CLUB

Divinity Vol. 1

VALIANT
BROKEN ANGELS
IMPERIUM

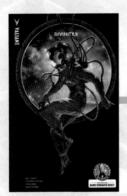

Imperium Vol. 2: Broken Angels
(OPTIONAL)

VALIANT
DIVINITY II

Divinity Vol. 2

VALIANT
DIVINITY III

Divinity III: Heroes of the Glorious Stalinverse
(OPTIONAL)

VALIANT
DIVINITY III
ONE OF THE BEST SERIES OF 2016

Divinity Vol. 3 : Stalinverse

Follow the entirety of the blockbuster superhero sci-fi saga that shook the world!

From New York Times best-selling writer

MATT KINDT

And blockbuster artist

TREVOR HAIRSINE!

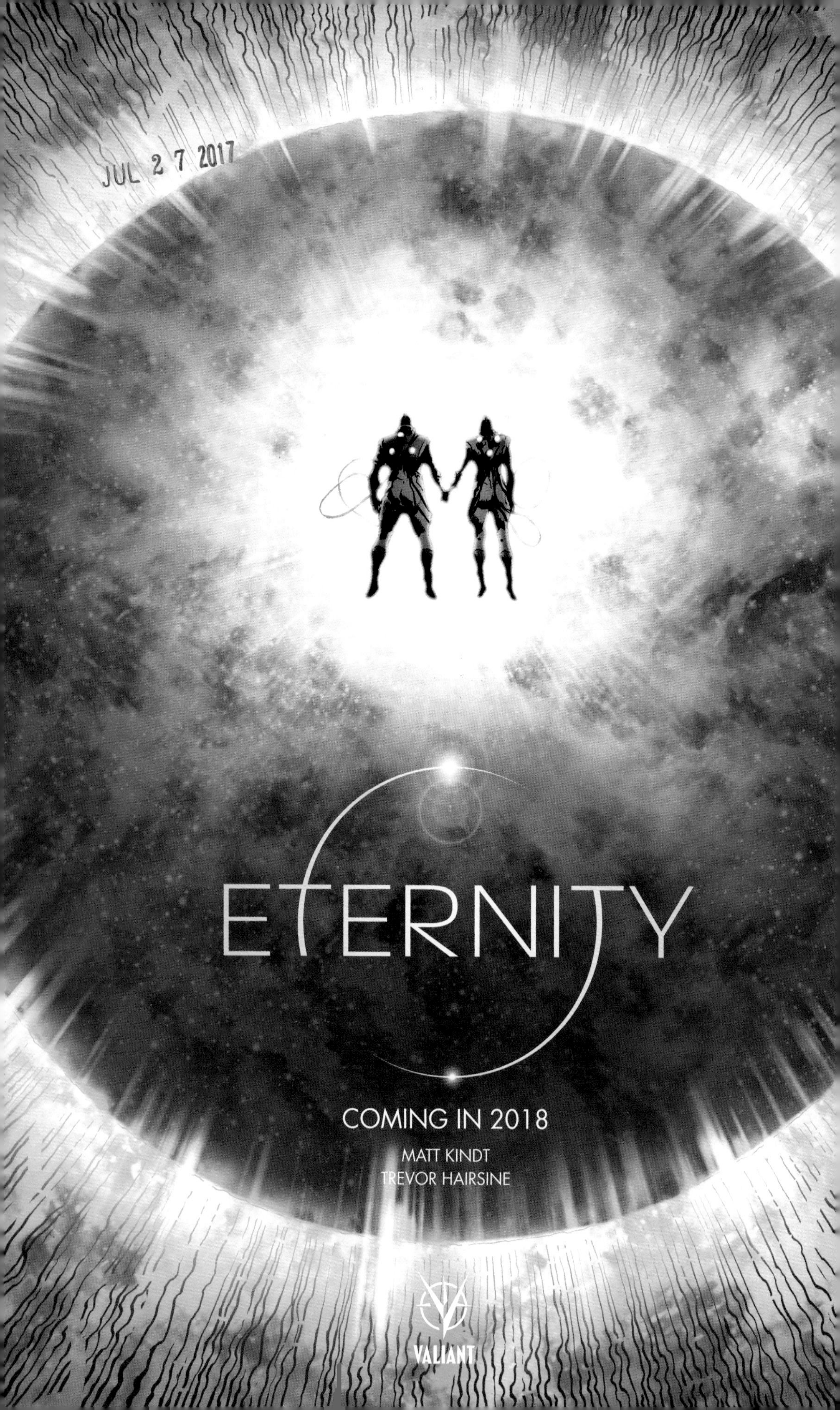
ETERNITY
COMING IN 2018
MATT KINDT
TREVOR HAIRSINE
VALIANT